New Casebooks

POETRY

WILLIAM BLAKE Edited by David Punter
CHAUCER Edited by Valerie Allen and Aries Axiotis
COLERIDGE, KEATS AND SHELLEY Edited by Peter J. Kitson
JOHN DONNE Edited by Andrew Mousley
SEAMUS HEANEY Edited by Michael Allen
PHILIP LARKIN Edited by Stephen Regan
DYLAN THOMAS Edited by John Goodby and Chris Wigginton
VICTORIAN WOMEN POETS Edited by Joseph Bristow
WORDSWORTH Edited by John Williams
PARADISE LOST Edited by William Zunder

NOVELS AND PROSE

AUSTEN: *Emma* Edited by David Monaghan
AUSTEN: *Mansfield Park* and *Persuasion* Edited by Judy Simons
AUSTEN: *Sense and Sensibility* and *Pride and Prejudice* Edited by Robert Clark
CHARLOTTE BRONTË: *Jane Eyre* Edited by Heather Glen
CHARLOTTE BRONTË: *Villette* Edited by Pauline Nestor
EMILY BRONTË: *Wuthering Heights* Edited by Patsy Stoneman
ANGELA CARTER Edited by Alison Easton
WILKIE COLLINS Edited by Lyn Pykett
JOSEPH CONRAD Edited by Elaine Jordan
DICKENS: *Bleak House* Edited by Jeremy Tambling
DICKENS: *David Copperfield* and *Hard Times* Edited by John Peck
DICKENS: *Great Expectations* Edited by Roger Sell
ELIOT: *The Mill on the Floss* and *Silas Marner* Edited by Nahem Yousaf and Andrew Maunder
ELIOT: *Middlemarch* Edited by John Peck
E.M. FORSTER Edited by Jeremy Tambling
HARDY: *Jude the Obscure* Edited by Penny Boumelha
HARDY: *The Mayor of Casterbridge* Edited by Julian Wolfreys
HARDY: *Tess of the D'Urbervilles* Edited by Peter Widdowson
JAMES: *Turn of the Screw* and *What Maisie Knew* Edited by Neil Cornwell and Maggie Malone
JOYCE: *Ulysses* Edited by Rainer Emig
LAWRENCE: *The Rainbow* and *Women in Love* Edited by Gary Day and Libby Di Niro
LAWRENCE: *Sons and Lovers* Edited by Rick Rylance
TONI MORRISON Edited by Linden Peach
GEORGE ORWELL Edited by Bryan Loughrey
SHELLEY: *Frankenstein* Edited by Fred Botting
STOKER: *Dracula* Edited by Glennis Byron
WOOLF: *Mrs Dalloway* and *To the Lighthouse* Edited by Su Reid

(continued overleaf)

DRAMA

BECKETT: *Waiting for Godot* and *Endgame* Edited by Steven Connor
APHRA BEHN Edited by Janet Todd
MARLOWE Edited by Avraham Oz
REVENGE TRAGEDY Edited by Stevie Simkin
SHAKESPEARE: *Antony and Cleopatra* Edited by John Drakakis
SHAKESPEARE: *Hamlet* Edited by Martin Coyle
SHAKESPEARE: *Julius Caesar* Edited by Richard Wilson
SHAKESPEARE: *King Lear* Edited by Kiernan Ryan
SHAKESPEARE: *Macbeth* Edited by Alan Sinfield
SHAKESPEARE: *The Merchant of Venice* Edited by Martin Coyle
SHAKESPEARE: *A Midsummer Night's Dream* Edited by Richard Dutton
SHAKESPEARE: *Much Ado About Nothing* and *The Taming of the Shrew* Edited by Marion Wynne-Davies
SHAKESPEARE: *Othello* Edited by Lena Cowen Orlin
SHAKESPEARE: *Romeo and Juliet* Edited by R. S. White
SHAKESPEARE: *The Tempest* Edited by R. S. White
SHAKESPEARE: *Twelfth Night* Edited by R. S. White
SHAKESPEARE ON FILM Edited by Robert Shaughnessy
SHAKESPEARE IN PERFORMANCE Edited by Robert Shaughnessy
SHAKESPEARE'S HISTORY PLAYS Edited by Graham Holderness
SHAKESPEARE'S ROMANCES Edited by Alison Thorne
SHAKESPEARE'S TRAGEDIES Edited by Susan Zimmerman
JOHN WEBSTER: *The Duchess of Malfi* Edited by Dympna Callaghan

GENERAL THEMES

FEMINIST THEATRE AND THEORY Edited by Helene Keyssar
POSTCOLONIAL LITERATURES Edited by Michael Parker and Roger Starkey

New Casebooks Series
Series Standing Order
ISBN 0-333-71702-3 hardcover
ISBN 0-333-69345-0 paperback
(outside North America only)

You can receive future titles in this series as they are published by placing a standing order. Please contact your bookseller or, in case of difficulty, write to us at the address below with your name and address, the title of the series and the ISBN quoted above.

Customer Services Department, Macmillan Distribution Ltd,
Houndmills, Basingstoke, Hampshire RG21 6XS, England

New Casebooks

ULYSSES

JAMES JOYCE

EDITED BY RAINER EMIG

palgrave
macmillan

First published 2004 by
PALGRAVE MACMILLAN
Houndmills, Basingstoke, Hampshire RG21 6XS and
175 Fifth Avenue, New York, N. Y. 10010
Companies and representatives throughout the world

PALGRAVE MACMILLAN is the global academic imprint of the Palgrave Macmillan division of St. Martin's Press, LLC and of Palgrave Macmillan Ltd. Macmillan® is a registered trademark in the United States, United Kingdom and other countries. Palgrave is a registered trademark in the European Union and other countries.

ISBN 0–333–54604–0 hardback
ISBN 0–333–54605–9 paperback

This book is printed on paper suitable for recycling and made from fully managed and sustained forest sources.

A catalogue record for this book is available from the British Library.

Library of Congress Cataloging-in-Publication Data
Ulysses: James Joyce/ edited by Rainer Emig.
p. cm. – (New casebooks)
Includes bibliographical references (p.) and index.
ISBN 0–333–54604–0 – ISBN 0–333–54605–9 (pbk.)
1. Joyce, James, 1882–1941. Ulysses. 2. Dublin (Ireland)–In literature. 3. Modernism (Literature)–Ireland. I. Emig, Rainer, 1964– II. New casebooks (Palgrave Macmillan (Firm))

PR6019.O9U7526 2004
823'.912–dc22 2003062240

10 9 8 7 6 5 4 3 2 1
13 12 11 10 09 08 07 06 05 04

Printed and bound in Great Britain by
Creative Print & Design (Wales), Ebbw Vale

Contents

Acknowledgements

The editor and publishers wish to thank the following for permission to use copyright material:

Andrew Enda Duffy, for 'Molly Alone: Questioning Community and Closure in the 'Nostos', in *The Subaltern Ulysses*, by Andrew Enda Duffy (1994), pp. 165–88, by permission of University of Minnesota Press; Richard Lehan, for 'James Joyce: The Limits of Modernism and the Realms of the Literary Text', *Arizona Quarterly*, 50:1 (1994), 87–108, by permission of the Regents of the University of Arizona; Michael Bruce McDonald, '"Circe" and the Uncanny, or Joyce from Freud to Marx', *James Joyce Quarterly*, 33:1 (1996), 49–68, by permission of *James Joyce Quarterly*, The University of Tulsa; Clara D. McLean, for 'Wasted Words: The Body Language of Joyce's Nausicaa', from *Joycean Cultures/Culturing Joyce*, ed. Vincent J. Cheng, Kimberley J. Devlin and Margot Norris, University of Delaware Press (1998), pp. 44–58, by permission of the author; Michael Murphy, for '"Proteus" and Prose: Paternity or Workmanship?', *James Joyce Quarterly*, 35:1 (1997), 71–81, by permission of *James Joyce Quarterly*, The University of Tulsa; Mark Osteen, for 'Cribs in the Countinghouse: Plagiarism, Proliferation and Labour in "Oxen of the Sun"', from *Joyce in the Hibernian Metropolis*, ed. Morris Beja and David Norris (1996), pp. 237–49, by permission of Ohio State University Press; Michael Stainer, for '"The void awaits surely all them that weave the wind": "Penelope" and "Sirens" in *Ulysses*', *Twentieth Century Literature*; 41:3 (1995), 319–31, by permission of *Twentieth Century Literature*; Jeffrey A. Weinstock, for 'The Disappointed Bridge: Textual Hauntings in *Ulysses*', *Journal of the Fantastic in the Arts*, 8:3 (1997), 347–69, by permission of M. E. Sharpe, Inc; Adam Woodruff, for 'Nobody at Home: Bloom's

Outlandish Retreat in the '"Cyclops" Episode of *Ulysses*', by permission of the author; Ewa Plonowska Ziarek, for '"Circe": Joyce's *Argumentum ad Feminam*', in *Gender in Joyce*, ed. Jolanta W. Wawrzycka and Marlena G. Corcoran (1997), pp. 150–69, by permission of the University Press of Florida.

The Estate of James Joyce, for extracts in contributors' essays from *Ulysses* by James Joyce. Copyright © the Estate of James Joyce, by permission of the Estate of James Joyce. The Estate is not in any way responsible for errors, omissions, etc. in the transcription/reproduction of James Joyce texts.

Every effort has been made to trace the copyright holders but if any have been inadvertently overlooked the publishers will be pleased to make the necessary arrangement at the first opportunity.

General Editors' Preface

The purpose of this series of New Casebooks is to reveal some of the ways in which contemporary criticism has changed our understanding of commonly studied texts and writers and, indeed, of the nature of criticism itself. Central to the series is a concern with modern critical theory and its effect on current approaches to the study of literature. Each New Casebook editor has been asked to select a sequence of essays which will introduce the reader to the new critical approaches to the text or texts being discussed in the volume and also illuminate the rich interchange between critical theory and critical practice that characterises so much current writing about literature.

In this focus on modern critical thinking and practice New Casebooks aim not only to inform but also to stimulate, with volumes seeking to reflect both the controversy and the excitement of current criticism. Because much of this criticism is difficult and often employs an unfamiliar critical language, editors have been asked to give the reader as much help as they feel is appropriate, but without simplifying the essays or the issues they raise. Again, editors have been asked to supply a list of further reading which will enable readers to follow up issues raised by the essays in the volume.

The project of New Casebooks, then, is to bring together in an illuminating way those critics who best illustrate the ways in which contemporary criticism has established new methods of analysing texts and who have reinvigorated the important debate about how we 'read ' literature. The hope is, of course, that New Casebooks will not only open up this debate to a wider audience, but will also encourage students to extend their own ideas, and think afresh about their responses to the texts they are studying.

John Peck and Martin Coyle
University of Wales, Cardiff

Introduction: *Ulysses*' Small Universes

RAINER EMIG

I

When Leopold Bloom returns home at the end of *Ulysses*, he thinks about the day he has spent wandering around Dublin. His thoughts, however, move well beyond the confines of the city to take in both existence in general and order in the smallest as well as largest sense. In particular, he muses on

> the universe of human serum constellated with red and white bodies, themselves universes of void space constellated with other bodies, each, in continuity, its universe of divisible component bodies of which each was again divisible in divisions of redivisible component bodies, dividends and divisors ever diminishing without actual division till, if the progress were carried far enough, nought nowhere was never reached.
>
> (p. 652)[1]

Despite the seeming conclusiveness of Bloom's musings, their convoluted form as well as their self-undermining ending ought to warn us against presuming that the novel has arrived at any unequivocal universal truths. As much as the text seems to define worlds of its own, their plurality as well as their ever-diminishing size and significance suggest that we in turn need to think carefully about *Ulysses*' universe.

The etymology of the word 'universe' informs us that its meaning has been 'the whole of created things' or 'the whole world' since the sixteenth and seventeenth centuries, but also that the noun originally derives from roots that signify 'all taken together', or literally 'turned into one'.[2] Universes in the plural are, therefore, a contradiction in terms, as are universes created through division as smaller constituents of a whole. But it is exactly these small universes that

Bloom talks about, universes that exist in relation to others, universes that are divided and divisive, often idiosyncratic, even hostile in their outlook, but at other times surprisingly amicable or even attracted to one another and productive in their interplay. By dividing wholes into smaller parts, but also by creating new universes, new macrocosms, out of microscopic episodes and a plurality of characters, Joyce's novel participates in a characteristically modernist endeavour. It acknowledges fragmentation in the reality it refers and relates to, but also wishes to perceive wholes, patterns, and meanings. Theodor W. Adorno characterises this ambivalence of modernist works of art in the following terms: 'they are fragments disclaiming to be wholes, even though wholes is what they really want to be.'[3]

A number of questions emerge from this: is Joyce's text an accomplice to the divisions and fragmentations that it depicts? Are the wholes that the text outlines (if generally in fleeting and often questionable shape) 'found' or created by it, and if the latter is the case, through which power and authority? Does the text really aim at shaping its own universe by 'taking it all together' and 'turning it into one', and if yes, does it reach its aim? And is Bloom, consequently, a prophet or merely a purveyor of paradoxes when he declares 'nought nowhere was never reached'?

These questions are not new. *Ulysses*' most prominent early critics, T. S. Eliot and Ezra Pound, interpreted the novel in diametrically opposed ways. Eliot calls it 'a way of controlling, of ordering, of giving a shape and significance to the immense panorama of futility and anarchy which is contemporary history.'[4] Pound, on the other hand, claims: 'It is the realistic novel par excellence, each character speaks in his own way, and corresponds to an external reality.'[5] John Coyle summarises their competing views as 'systematic symbolic epic' (Eliot) and 'the apotheosis of unflinching realism' (Pound).[6] The former verdict reads *Ulysses* as mythmaking, the latter as an acceptance of and perhaps even revelling in fragmentation and the absence of larger meanings.

One can trace this conflict to the character who lends his (Latinised) name to the very title of Joyce's novel. 'Odysseus' is itself a merger of the smallest and the largest, combining *outis* – nobody – and Zeus, the most powerful god in the Greek pantheon. However, in order to fill out this general impression, I want to use the rest of this introduction to outline the shape, significance, and potential problems of *Ulysses*' small universes in connection with ideas about space, time, objects, and the subject in the novel while introducing some of the contemporary positions regarding *Ulysses* in the essays that follow.

II

In the complexity and confusion of *Ulysses*, space is seemingly the least problematic element. The novel's plot is firmly played out on a map of Dublin that is so faithfully adhered to that tourists today can participate in guided tours following the steps of Stephen Dedalus and Leopold Bloom.[7] The technique culminates in 'Wandering Rocks', where two pillars of Dublin society, the representative of ecclesiastical authority Fr Conmee, and his civil counterpart the Earl of Dudley, move through Dublin with a precision that almost permits a tracing of their positions with a stop-watch.

In keeping with the insistence on realistic movements of characters, locations in *Ulysses* are generally mundane and believable: private rooms, shops, streets, offices, pubs and bars, cemeteries, brothels, cab shelters, etc. Yet among them are some that Michael Foucault would call 'heterotopias', literally 'other spaces'.[8] The most obvious ones are the cemetery and the brothel, both places of loss and abandonment, but with diametrically opposed significance in relation to existence and cultural values. The cemetery is of course a reminder of mortality, a *vanitas* motif in the manner of the skull in painting. Yet it is also the space where personality is debated and thereby constituted in an act of belatedness. Dignam's funeral in the 'Hades' episode becomes the occasion for an assessment of the deceased's life and personality, but also for the narration (and suppression) of other life stories, including that of Bloom's father's suicide. The space opened up by death becomes the space for *creation* in the sense that *Ulysses* constantly shows how identities, stories, lives and history are produced through narrative, if usually from a questionable, because biased perspective. Michael Murphy discusses this ambivalence of creation in relation to Stephen Dedalus and the 'Proteus' section in his essay (2) below. The smallest details become the means through which larger meanings, the divided universes of Bloom's speculations, are established by 'taking them all together'. Richard Lehan's essay (1) outlines how these universes are merged into one by analysing Joyce's narrative strategies in the context of realist and modernist literary models.

In contrast to this, identities and stories are dissected, taken apart and sacrificed in the brothel of the 'Circe' episode. There concepts of subjective and objective reality are suspended. Visions and nightmares take over, and individual identities are lost when characters mutate into others or reappear from earlier sections of the novel. Bloom himself pretends to be someone else when he is arrested in the vision, and his subsequent trial revolves around confused identities. Among the most startling of these blurred identities are those of gender and sexuality. Ghosts also appear in 'Circe', among them a raging Shakespeare, Edward VII, Tennyson, the late Lord Mayor Harrington, diverse Archbishops of Armagh, Bloom's mother Ellen, father Leopold and grandfather Lipoti Virag (the name change between generations adds another layer to the debates on identity), an unnamed 'Croppy Boy' as well as anonymous 'Irish Evicted Tenants'. The sequence, significantly, concludes with the silent apparition of Bloom's son Rudy, who died at the tender age of one 10 years before. The brothel thus forms a bracket with the cemetery of the 'Hades' section as spaces in which identities (personal, cultural, racial, and national) are enacted, suspended, lost, but ultimately also produced. Since it is a crucial conceptual episode in the novel, two essays in this collection debate its significance. Ewa Plonowska Ziarek (essay 8) analyses its gender implications, while Michael Bruce McDonald (essay 9) emphasises the significance of the Freudian 'uncanny' in it.

The inclusion of these borderline areas reminds us that *Ulysses* has more dimensions than its setting on a street plan of Dublin suggests. Its spaces are not safe and stable; some of them are profoundly unsettling, and all of them are contested. This becomes evident at the novel's very beginning. It is set outside Dublin, in the suburb of Sandycove near Dun Laoghaire, where Stephen finds himself evicted from his temporary accommodation in a Martello tower (a British military structure raised against a possible French invasion in the early nineteenth century). The Homerian parallel is Telemachus, Odysseus' son, who is pushed around in his own house by his mother's suitors. The contest over space in *Ulysses* is triggered by personality clashes, but also involves money and cultural and national identity.

The parallel trails of the dispossessed Stephen and the seemingly merely rambling Bloom add a further complication to the mapping of *Ulysses*. While the latter returns home safely at the novel's conclusion – just like his Homerian parallel Odysseus – Stephen, more in keeping with his namesake Daedalus (another accident-prone high-flyer), is left, at least metaphorically, at sea and homeless. But the seeming epitome of safety, the security of domesticity, is problematised in *Ulysses* when it emerges that even Bloom's marital bed is not exclusively his. Molly's affairs undermine the stability of intimate spaces and turn Bloom's into the equivalent of what emerges in the heated debate between Stephen and John Eglinton in 'Scylla and Charybdis' (with reference to Shakespeare's will) as a 'second-best Bed' (p. 195).

Space is further contested in Stephen's position as a teacher in the 'Nestor' section, in Bloom's feelings of rejection when he is repeatedly ignored in the newspaper offices in the 'Aeolus' episode, and in Mr Deasy's anti-Semitic declarations in 'Nestor' that culminate in the rhetorical question why Ireland never persecuted Jews, to which his answer is: 'Because she never let them in' (p. 36). Intellectual space is heavily contested in 'Scylla and Charybdis' where Stephen pitches his wit against a number of scholars in the National Library. The most drastic struggle over space occurs, however, in the 'Cyclops' section, where a narrow-minded 'citizen' turns on Bloom. Bloom is first ridiculed for his definition of a nation as 'the same people living in the same place' (p. 317), an echo of 'taking it all together', and then attacked for being Jewish, which is seen as coterminous with 'having no place', thus no allegiances.

The argument in 'Cyclops' once again emphasises the continuing theme of cultural and national belonging in *Ulysses*. Stephen's quarrel, at the novel's outset, with the Englishman Haines prepares the tone for the Anglo-Irish debates and disputes that are to follow. They are not restricted to characters and plot in a text that is, on the one hand, so firmly anchored in the capital of Ireland, yet is also an exploration of English language and culture and, in fact, ridicules Celtic revivalism at various points. The issues of space and belonging are debated in Adam Woodruff's essay on nationalism and its problematic foundations (essay 4) and Enda Duffy's chapter on *Ulysses*' questioning of community (essay 10).

The contests over space in *Ulysses* leave it in a productive suspense whether mundane places, such as Bloom's marriage bed, matter less or more than the grandiose spaces of imaginary Irishness or equally imaginary English cultural greatness as embodied by Shakespeare. The big and the small refuse to enter simple hierarchies, and neither do the small and banal spaces merely add up to form the larger symbolic ones. At the same time, the small does not deny the existence – and much less the importance – of the larger symbolic arenas, whose power, most drastically in the debates about cultural, national, and racial belonging, continues to come to the fore. Indeed, having no space, as polemically attributed to Bloom by the narrow-minded citizen, might provide the biggest space of all, the space of possibility or utopia – which translates simultaneously as 'the good place' and 'no place'. This impossible good place might offer greater opportunities for at least envisaging a good life than the commodified utopia of 'Agendath Netaim' (Hebrew for 'Plantations Association') that Bloom encounters in an advertisement for investment schemes in citrus groves in Palestine in the 'Calypso' section, and which repeatedly conjures up dreams of escape intermingled with sensual fantasies.

III

Time shapes Joyce's novel in a similarly deceptive way. Ostensibly set on one particular day, the now celebrated 'Bloomsday' of 16 June 1904, the novel appears to adhere to a very traditional artistic convention, Aristotle's unities of space, time, and action, originally developed for drama.[9] Yet in the same way as Aristotle's rules were no guarantee for dramatic realism, *Ulysses*' allegiance to a time scheme in which the reading of the book – if it was possible to read it sensibly in 24 hours – would roughly correspond to the time it depicts by no means signals that the time portrayed in it is either linear or mimetic of 'real time'. While the novel's initial episode still clings to this possibility and indeed appears dramatic in the sense of employing descriptions that could act as stage instructions and dialogue by several speakers, this linearity and unity is immediately disrupted when the action jumps to the school in which Dedalus works as a part-time teacher. It is significant that the two subjects he tries to squeeze into his lesson are history and poetry. His history lesson centres on Pyrrhus, a Greek king who became famous for a victory against the Romans in 279 BC which severely depleted his reserves. The winner as loser forms a telling paradox in connection with history, both personal and national, in *Ulysses*, and adds to the debates about big and small, universal and specific. Stephen's attempt to teach his pupils Milton's elegiac poem 'Lycidas', another triumph (here of poetry) generated out of loss, this time a personal one, is similarly ambivalent.

History and poetry merge in the epic, the very form that *Ulysses* is modelled on. Yet historiography and poetics also exist in a traditional enmity, each claiming universal authority and truth for itself. When Stephen makes his famous pronouncement that: 'History ... is a nightmare from which I am trying to awake' (p. 34), he uneasily fuses history (which is supposedly based on facts) and the visionary fictions of the dream.[10] He also once again connects the great and small by making all of history (another universalism) his own particular and, therefore, rather banal problem.

Dreams, memories, and fantasies make up a large part of *Ulysses* and further disrupt a possible linearity of narrative time, since all of them are characterised by what Freud describes as condensation and displacement.[11] In the same way as dreams lack 'real' time for Freud, the time of Joyce's novel is both linear and 'realist' as well as a multiple, surreal or hyper-real time in which an imaginary and a factual past, the diverging presents of different characters' views, possible futures and impossible realities coexist.

A further challenge to linearity in *Ulysses* is the discussions of paternity that are, with fetishistic constancy, reiterated by both Bloom and Stephen. Bloom's traumatic loss of his father through suicide forms a bracket with the premature death of his only son Rudy in childhood. Both are taboos for Bloom, but they also form the linchpins around which his life story revolves. Stephen, who has lost his mother and not his father, but whose father considers him a lost cause[12] (once again classical Greek myth, that of Daedalus, the engineer of a successful flying machine, and Icarus, his disobedient son, is employed as a parallel), insists on a debate about the meaning of fatherhood in 'Scylla and Charybdis'. His arguments do not revolve around responsibility or emotions, but around mere temporality and presence, the ingredients of traditional historiography. The questions for him are: what needs to be there and what has to come first in order to establish the identities of fathers and sons? What could be a banal splitting of hairs when applied to Shakespeare and Bloom once more achieves much larger dimensions when linked with Catholic dogma concerning the three persons of God in the Trinity and the heresy of Sabellius, who upheld that the Father was 'Himself His Own Son' (p. 199). Temporality and its disruptions once again connect the banality of facts and the evasiveness of ultimate truths, neither of which are completely disqualified in *Ulysses*, but neither of which is granted unchallenged precedence either.

The textual equivalent of paternity is literary tradition, something which today's literary theorists call intertextuality. *Ulysses* displays an impressive awareness of the issue in employing and exploiting literary modes and models extensively. The most extreme of these modes are the already named epic one of classical poetry and the commercial one of journalism. In connection with temporality they pursue related but also diametrically opposed purposes. Epic poetry aims at conveying great deeds by great characters at least supposedly for all eternity, while journalism thrives on turning events and personalities into easily digestible news items – to be forgotten after a day. *Ulysses* often describes its small events in either of these forms, again refusing to privilege one over the other. Bloom makes his livelihood by selling advertisements, thus bridging the gap between the ephemeral, the easily discarded paper, and the durable, the advertising slogan that hopes to be memorised in the same way as traditional epic poetry in the manner of *Beowulf* or indeed the *Odyssey*.

Stylistically, *Ulysses* not only follows established literary modes, it also incorporates them into its own universe as quotations and pastiches, most notably in 'Oxen of the Sun'. Ostensibly set in a maternity hospital in Holles Street, it deals with sacrilege in the same way as Homer describes the slaughter of the sacred cattle of the sun god Helios. Yet if the section is about fertility, it also uses procreation in connection with language. Its language shifts from an un-English prose style based on Latin via Anglo-Saxon alliterative patterns, Middle English, the fourteenth-century style of Mandeville, echoes of the Renaissance plays of Beaumont and Fletcher (who feature as 'Beau Mount' and 'Lecher'; p. 375), the English of the Authorised Version of the Bible, Samuel Pepys' robust seventeenth-century style, the eighteenth-century prose of Joseph Addison and Richard Steele, late eighteenth-century political oratory and the sombre tones of the historian Edward Gibbon, snippets of the Gothic novel, the Romantic styles of Charles Lamb and Thomas de Quincey to imitations of the nineteenth-century writings of Landor, Macaulay, Dickens, Newman, Pater, Ruskin, Meredith and Carlyle.[13] Joyce's novel incorporates in its universe the styles of its cultural and literary inheritance. It rearranges and parodies them in the same way as the conclusion of the section pokes fun at the dominant figure of Anglo-Irish literature at the time, William Butler Yeats. It refers to artistically produced volumes from the 'Druiddrum press by two designing females'

(p. 403) – Yeats published with the Dun Emer Press in Dundrum, which was run by his two sisters[14] – before disintegrating into corrupted colloquialisms and the cacophony of multiple voices. Mark Osteen analyses this episode in terms of literary and cultural value in his essay (7) below.

Does Joyce's text accept its status as a mere part in the universe of (here English) literature, or does it turn itself into an even larger structure that strives to dominate the forms and modes it employs? This is more than a question of style. It is a question of mastery and therefore related to the issues of power and authority and, ultimately, linked with the attempts of some critics to declare *Ulysses* the 'master text' of modernism, if not the whole of literature.[15]

Another compression of time happens in 'Sirens'. The episode is structured like a musical composition. This is another example of the way in which *Ulysses* not merely alludes to universes to be found in an external reality, but constantly insists on creating its own universes in strategies that can be labelled metatextual: a term for describing a text that is fully aware of, and makes an artistic point of, its textuality. Music is the least referential of the arts in that it gains its significance through the arrangement of its material, sounds, in temporal patterns of differing durations, pauses, and repetitions. Its use in the novel supports the assertion that the text models its own universe without a need for an attachment to an exterior reality. However, once again this autonomy claim is undermined when music reappears in the penultimate 'Ithaca' section in the shape of the anti-Semitic ditty of 'Little Harry Hughes' who is killed by the Jew's daughter (dressed in the green of Ireland) for breaking her father's windows (pp. 643–4). All of a sudden, music is as little exempt from the debates in *Ulysses* as was the theme of 'Love's Old Sweet Song', a tune in Molly Bloom's repertoire, that accompanies her husband's musings on love and sex throughout the text. Michael Stainer's essay (5) below indeed argues that in the form of 'Sirens' the most radical onslaught on coherence (of identity, gender, and meaning) in *Ulysses* takes place.

In terms of the novel's plot, playing with and perhaps controlling temporality therefore fails to elevate the text onto a higher plane where it would miraculously leave behind its subjection to time (as is attempted in Yeats's poems when they try to create 'timeless moments') and become superhistorical, in the sense that Friedrich Nietzsche has outlined.[16] Nor does it make the novel all-inclusive in the sense of swallowing history altogether (an attempt most drastically undertaken in Ezra Pound's *Cantos* with their aim of becoming 'a long poem including history'[17]). *Ulysses* is conclusive in the sense of reaching an affirmative ending at a particular time and a particular place, the 'Yes' uttered by Molly Bloom in bed at the end of a long day. Yet it reaches this end in a temporal form that is both exceedingly traditional and modernist: the cycle. The cycle is a temporal structure characteristic of myths, traditional forms of imposing sense on reality. The mythical time is both a vague past and an equally imprecise 'forever', since the messages of myth assume universal significance. In the modern period, however, circularity tends to be associated with stagnation, repetition and, often, with the mechanical structuring of life in an alienated reality (the intrusive clocks in Eliot's early poems are evidence of this). Circularity is thus both a consequence and a contradiction of Enlightenment beliefs in the progress and perfectibility of culture and human beings. *Ulysses* employs both the positive and negative meanings of circularity, most notably in Bloom's homecoming.

IV

While the colourful characters and lively events in *Ulysses* have gained as much critical attention as its stylistic experiments and ostensible display of literary and cultural learning, the objects that are scattered all over the text and perform important functions in it have scarcely been featured in readings of the novel. This may be explained by their carefully crafted surface-banality. There are no precious, special or dramatically crucial objects in Joyce's novel. Yet a second glance shows that these objects are further small universes hovering between forming part of larger, perhaps symbolic, macrocosms and questioning exactly the viability of such universal patterns.

Milk is the first of the potentially symbolic objects that litter the surface of *Ulysses*. Brought into the tense atmosphere of the Martello tower in the introductory 'Telemachus' section by an old Irishwoman, it triggers a string of mythical visions in Stephen that turn the woman into a possible 'messenger' entering twentieth-century reality from a 'morning world' of Irish myths (p. 14). However, the possible linking of myth and reality via a symbol – milk representing fertility, nourishment, purity and ultimately life itself – is already undercut when Stephen's associations separate the milk from its purveyor: 'rich white milk, not hers' (pp. 13–14). When it adds 'Old Shrunken paps', we are in a similar reality to that of Eliot's *The Waste Land* (published in the same year as *Ulysses*, 1922), in which the central figure of the blind seer Tiresias also possesses shrivelled female breasts. Modernism's use of milk signals that the lifelines of nature, myth, and culture run separate courses in modernity, that the mystical unity of reality, history, and legend no longer convinces the modern observer, although there lingers a nostalgic yearning for it.

It is telling that the medical student Buck Mulligan quickly embarks on a more mundane and 'modern' speculation on milk: 'If we could only live on good food like that ... we wouldn't have the country full of rotten teeth and rotten guts' (p. 14). Myth is replaced by science; one explanatory universe paves the way for another.[18] Yet ultimately the milk ends up neither restoring Irish legends nor protecting the health of the Irish; it ends up in three cups of tea. More importantly, it remains unpaid for. Although Mulligan manages to produce a florin (the only event that merits the label 'A miracle!' in the episode), two pence of the balance remain outstanding until the end of the novel. The woman's repeated stoic pronouncement, 'Time enough, sir', thus achieves a negative symbolic significance: time is a time of debts rather than a time of fullness. At the same time, the issue of debt that is introduced at the beginning of *Ulysses* (and that is eventually summed up in Bloom's budget for 16 June 1904 in the penultimate 'Ithaca' section) colours the entire novel. Far from giving it a pessimistic outlook, though, it permits an ethical perspective of responsibility concerning the interaction of characters – as becomes evident when at the end of the novel Leopold and Molly Bloom are reunited exactly by a mutual awareness of the lack (physical and mental) in their relationship. Connection need not rest on presence or indeed similarity, but may also (and perhaps more challengingly and responsibly) be achieved by separateness and difference. This principle determines more than merely the relationships between characters in Joyce's novel; it influences its entire setup of patterns and allusions.

Connection via dismemberment also characterises the theme of innards in *Ulysses*. After Mulligan's speculations on the rotten guts of the deprived Irish, Bloom's penchant for offal, that makes him decide to have mutton kidneys for breakfast, appears macabre at first glance (p. 53). Yet this preference ties in neatly with his later speculations on parts, wholes, divided and divisive universes which started this introduction. Food in *Ulysses* forever approaches symbolic significance as parts related to wholes, and nowhere is this more evident than in the so-called 'Lestrygonians' section. In Homer, the Lestrygonians are cannibals who decimate Odysseus' crew drastically. In Joyce's novel they become the crowd in Burton's restaurant that is suddenly perceived by Bloom as crude animals devouring other animals. Yet again the text layers and partly undermines its symbolic gestures: at the beginning of the section it makes Bloom note a publishing howler which places a newspaper advertisement for potted meat among the obituaries. Beyond the cruelty of the analogy, the novel once again depicts the connections of existence and textuality as complex: both feed on each other in a cannibalistic way, and this undermines any attempt at a hierarchy of reality and fiction. While neither is the other's universe, both try to become each other's parasite whenever possible.

We have already seen how literary and cultural traditions feed on themselves in the pastiches of 'Oxen of the Sun'. Consequently, when Bloom reads the newspaper on the toilet in 'Calypso', he blends writing and digestion with a theme that will be discussed below, money: 'He glanced back through what he had read and, while feeling his water flow quietly, he envied kindly Mr Beaufoy who had written it and received payment of three pounds thirteen and six' (pp. 66–7). Another vivid link of the highest with the lowest via ideas of ingestion and digestion is Bloom's pubescent fantasy of checking whether the statues of goddesses have anuses, again in 'Lestrygonians' (p. 168). Wholes and holes are thus drastically linked in the same way as the paradox of universal powers relying on parts and divisions is prepared.

Just as unpaid for as Stephen's milk is the bar of lemon-scented soap that Bloom acquires in 'The Lotus Eaters'. It provokes both sensual dreams and those of transgression when it is linked with his clandestine correspondence with Martha Clifford and her attempt to learn the name of the perfume used by his wife. It also furthers the escapist fantasies of plantations that were triggered by the 'Agendath Nethaim' advertisement. Simultaneously, however, it works in a diametrically opposed way when it reminds Bloom of his rejected Jewishness through the related name of a former Jewish friend called 'Citron' (p. 58), and the soap's later reappearance as 'Citronlemon' (p. 118). Its physicality intrudes into Bloom's gloomy speculations on the way to Dignam's funeral in the 'Hades' section, where he has to remove it from his hip pocket, almost as if the soap's associations refuse to be integrated into sombre speculations on mortality. At the same time – and perhaps as an extension of this contrast – the soap forms an unlikely pair with the potato that Bloom carries as a talisman (it is first mentioned when he leaves the house to fetch his breakfast kidney in 'Calypso'). In the unlikely universe of Bloom's trouser pockets congregate two universes rolled into balls in the manner of Marvell's poem 'To His Coy Mistress'. The first one signals possibilities, future opportunities as well as those abandoned in the past, but also mere fantasies, all embodied in the ephemerality of lemon scent. The second is tied to the ground, Ireland's ground to be precise, even though the potato also, and perhaps more realistically, holds a promise of renewal.

One of the features of *Ulysses* that supports Pound's characterisation of the novel as unflinching realism is the fact that almost without exception the objects of the text carry price tags. We have already seen how Bloom instantly prices the story that provides him with entertainment during his bowel movements. Milk and soap, although not paid for, are nonetheless entered into the novel's meticulous bookkeeping. Hardly an episode occurs in the text without money changing hands. Mulligan borrows money from Stephen in 'Telemachus' (Stephen again lends money, this time to the drunkard Corley, in the 'Eumaeus' section); the already mentioned part-payment of the milk takes place; and in 'Nestor' Mr Deasy pays Stephen his wages of three pounds twelve, but not without supplementing the transaction with a lecture on the proper attitude towards money: '*I paid my way. I never borrowed a shilling in my life.* Can you feel that? *I owe nothing.* Can you?' (p. 31; emphases in the original). In connection with what was claimed above, that debts ensure interaction, make responsibility possible, and in fact create relationships in the first place, Mr Deasy's comments disqualify him as much in the universe of *Ulysses* as do his inaccurate summaries of Irish history. The most significant of these exchanges is Bloom's loan of one pound and seven shillings to Stephen – a loan that is actually repaid (p. 664).

In Joyce's novel characters always and never 'pay their way'. Everything they do is at least also regarded in materialistic and often straightforwardly monetary terms (see the dealings in the newspaper offices, the acquisition of food and drink, down to the somewhat unsatisfactory transactions in the brothel in 'Circe'). But at the same time material values are not considered the only or, indeed, the dominant ones. Although Stephen is near-penniless, his main characteristic (and that employed by most people surrounding him) is his intellectual potential. Bloom in fact turns him into 'professor and author' when describing him to Molly in the 'Ithaca' section. Crawford, in the newspaper office in 'Aeolus', asks him to write for him on the basis of mere impressions. Bloom, too, is the very opposite of a financial success story, yet neither this nor his wife's declining singing career ever really assume centre stage.

While money can indeed be regarded as a universal system in a culture based on material and symbolic values and their exchange, money is at the same time nothing in itself. As Karl Marx cunningly suggests, money as such has no value, since this would have to be determined against itself.[19] Once again, the seemingly most mundane as well as the apparently least wordly concepts – money and death – help the novel to set big and small against each other without coming out in favour of either of the two sides. When Dignam's funeral understandably provokes debates on death, they lead, via the question 'Was he insured?' (p. 98), to an aside on horse racing ('Same old six and eightpence') and the idea of a whip-round for Dignam's children ('A few bob a skull'; p. 99). Bloom even manages to divert Mr Kernan's solemn admission that the promise of resurrection and eternal life 'touches a man's inmost heart' into an earlier and brusquer version of his speculations on universes and organisms, when he declares in a pointedly materialistic way that once again reiterates his interest in inner organs: 'Your heart perhaps but what price the fellow in the six feet by two with his toes to the daisies? No touching that. Seat of the affections. Broken heart. A pump after all, pumping thousands of gallons of blood every day' (p. 102).

Letters form the other side of the equation in the ingenious linking of material and abstract values in *Ulysses*. They are the material manifestation of thoughts, ideas, and fiction, but inside a novel letters also refer to the text's engagement with textuality, its own as well as that of the many texts informing it. Letters in *Ulysses* are never straightforward messages. They fail to reach their addressee, are hidden, contain innuendos and teases, carry false names, and sometimes arrive too late and become mere ghostly traces. The first letter in Joyce's novel is already double and a failure. It is Garrett Deasy's epistle about foot-and-mouth disease, written in duplicate to two Dublin newspapers and pressed into the hesitant hands of Stephen Dedalus in the 'Nestor' section. It consists of platitudes and clichés, despite his deluded assertion 'I don't mince words, do I?' (p. 33). Naturally, Deasy wants his words 'to be printed and read', yet although Stephen delivers the letters to the newspapers in 'Aeolus', nothing more is heard of them. Paradoxically, however, by being part of the fictional world of a novel, Deasy's wish indeed comes true: his letters gain manifestation and a readership. Once again, the smallest (here, meaningless drivel) and the largest (the largest entity that the novel can safely know, namely itself) form an interesting allegiance in which the smaller part relativises the larger while being simultaneously elevated into the latter's fictional universe.

The second letter in *Ulysses* is delivered by Bloom to his wife in 'Calypso', although it is written by his rival Boylan and Bloom knows this. Molly quickly hides it under her pillow. The contents of this letter are never revealed, but just as in Edgar Allan Poe's story 'The Purloined Letter' and Jacques Lacan's now equally famous analysis of the same, this does not diminish the potential of the inaccessible communication.[20] What is hidden gains significance through the desire of the disempowered onlooker, and showing and hiding enter a relationship that is intense and erotic, as can be seen in Bloom's simultaneously arousing and nightmarish vision of Molly having intercourse with Boylan in the 'Circe' episode, where he expresses his contradictory desires in the ejaculation 'Show! Hide! Show!' (p. 528). Boylan's hidden letter mirrors the reader's desire to come to terms with the complex negotiations of meaning in *Ulysses* itself. Another letter that reaches the Bloom household the same day, one addressed to Bloom by his daughter Milly, has a similar effect. The feelings of anxiety and sexual jealousy it provokes bear no relation to the actual facts that Milly's rambling communication relates.

Joyce's novel actively plays with this desire when it continually sets up patterns and traces of potential meaning and locates them in places, temporal structures, mundane objects, and words. The most provocative of these riddles is the 'word known to all men' that is repeatedly alluded to, the first time by Stephen in the early 'Proteus' episode.[21] The success of *Ulysses*' game with the desire of readers and critics can be gauged from the plethora of criticism that the novel has engendered. The awareness with which the text uses fiction as a generator of desire but also anxiety can be seen in the remaining correspondences in *Ulysses*, Bloom's clandestine exchange of letters with Martha Clifford and Rudolph Virag's suicide note that his son Leopold wishes to forget but cannot. In both cases, control is exerted over communication, and its symbolic power is meant to be banned from the realm of everyday existence.

In terms of establishing meaning, Joyce's novel thus once again refuses as much as it desires. It withholds and uncovers, suppresses and gives away, and it does so in a self-conscious way that sometimes even finds expression in symbolic objects. Both protagonists of the novel embark on their adventures without keys. Yet while Bloom consciously decides to leave his at home, Stephen's lack of the means to return home is accidental. We are again faced with a self-conscious and metatextual play on expectations. The keys to *Ulysses* are there, but they have been left behind, exactly in the place that Bloom wishes to return to, though Stephen is not so sure about his desire to reach home. Even returns might not be unproblematic, as has been pointed out in the section on space. In Homer's *Odyssey* the key to Odysseus' return is indeed not a physical object, but a riddle. By convincing his wife that he knows that their marriage bed cannot be moved, since it has been built around a living tree, Odysseus finally achieves recognition. The riddle is also another favourite modernist strategy, copiously employed in Eliot's *The Waste Land*. But as in *The Waste Land* so in the *Odyssey* and also in *Ulysses*, simply solving one riddle by no means solves all.

V

Characters in *Ulysses* are parts of the novel's textual universe rather than its centre. As became evident in the emphasis on form in 'Sirens', relations of distance and proximity are as important as seemingly obvious features – of persons, objects, places and events. In terms of characters it is indeed the superabundance of features of its central protagonists that erases meaning as much as it generates it. If unproblematic realist subjectivity in the shape of 'round' characters is difficult to find in *Ulysses*,[22] how then is subjectivity displayed and generated in the novel? The 'Nausicaa' episode is instructive in this respect. It presents Gerty MacDowell, who becomes the object of both the gaze and the sexual fantasies of an onlooker when she is sitting with her friends Cissy and Edy on the rocks on Sandymount shore. Only when the episode has reached its climax with the onlooker masturbating into his shirt do we learn that he is no other than Bloom. Yet the episode is not simply evidence of Bloom's active erotic imagination or lack of inhibitions. The fantasies of the episode are shared between him and Gerty, and he is as much a voyeur as she carefully exhibits herself. The style of the episode, a parody of sentimental prose, permits Gerty self-characterisations that hover between worldly-wise young woman and pure romantic heroine with traces of the Virgin Mary. Yet it fails to repress a realist awareness of her situation, her menstrual problems, unlikely hopes for marriage to Reggy Wylie, and her drunkard of a father – although she tellingly represses the fact that, despite her beauty, she is handicapped by a limp. Bloom, too, becomes the clichéd object of her daydreams: 'The very heart of the girlwoman went out to him, her dreamhusband, because she knew on the instant it was him' (p. 342).

Both Bloom and Gerty are exercises in subject-creation through narrative. Gerty is created through her own ideas as well as by the observations and judgements of her friends and the onlooker: 'She was pronounced beautiful by all who knew her ...' (p. 333). But the former as well as the latter are also simultaneously constructions of Gerty's lively imagination. Only when Bloom has been identified does he actively participate in Gerty's creation. In stark contrast to Gerty's romantic ideas, his observations are crude and materialistic:

> Poor girl! That's why she's left on the shelf and the others did a sprint. Thought something was wrong by the cut of her jib. Jilted beauty. A defect is ten times worse in a woman. But makes them polite. Glad I didn't know it when she was on show. Hot little devil all the same. Wouldn't mind. Curiosity like a nun or a negress or a girl with glasses.
>
> (p. 351)

Nonetheless, this list of sexist pronouncements is by no means evidence of a hierarchy of gazes and positions. The crudity of masculine judgements makes them as questionable as the clichés transported in prose traditionally aimed at women. Both Gerty and Bloom are exposed in the episode, physically and mentally. Yet it remains debatable who is more in control, since Gerty knows very well what she is doing when she shows Bloom her underwear, and Bloom's masturbating only ironically gives him a hold on himself.

Subjectivities are not stable or given in *Ulysses*, but result from relations and perceptions, from clichés and judgements that are ultimately tied to language, the narratives that structure culture and its 'knowledge'. This 'knowledge' is never immediate, 'pure' and untainted by personal and ideological bias. Yet subjectivities are also not up for grabs. The inherited and repeated narratives of culturally conditioned 'truths' place them in hierarchies that forbid, for example, that Gerty approach Bloom to find out more about him. Clara D. McLean's essay (6) below provides a detailed investigation on the link between bodies, their boundaries and excretions, and subjectivity in 'Nausicaa'. Rather than opting for one of E. M. Forster's alternatives, 'flat' or 'round' characters, Joyce's novel seems to insist on a multilayered flatness for its protagonists, neither organically given nor two-dimensionally constructed. *Ulysses* thus mirrors some modernist paintings, most notably Pablo Picasso's *Les Demoiselles d'Avignon* (1906–7), a cubist picture that refrains from a simulated three-dimensionality while maintaining a multiplicity of planes.

The situation is further complicated by the omniscient narrator in the episode who provides insights into Gerty's, her friends' as well as Bloom's minds. Is this narrator the ultimate guarantor of 'truth' in the text? This remains doubtful, since the episode reaches no satisfactory conclusion (with the notable exception of Bloom's isolated climax that merely leaves him with a wet shirt). On the contrary, it seems as if the narrator once again plays with the reader in a similar way as Gerty plays with Bloom, by teasing and partially unveiling the desired detail, but ultimately evading, withdrawing and escaping from meaning. Bloom is as much in control as he is ridiculed. Gerty is as much a 'damaged good' ('left on the shelf') as she is almost a damaged god, the Virgin Mary, and idealised Irish beauty. If she is a model of subject-creation in *Ulysses*, she might also be an ironic Oedipus, since Oedipus as a model of tragic self-knowledge shares with her his limp. Hence knowledge of the self merges with deception about the self, and the desire for characterisation is equated to the only form of sexuality in which total control is possible, yet only at the price of complete solipsism: masturbation.

Circular and, if not masturbatory, then certainly fetishistic are the ghosts that appear throughout *Ulysses*. Dead mothers (Stephen's) and fathers (Bloom's as well as Dignam) abound, but there are also ghosts that function on a more universal plane than the Freudian 'family romance'. Shakespeare is the ghost of cultural greatness that haunts many debates about cultural identities and values in the novel. If selves are created through the judgements of others and characters also ceaselessly create themselves, then Stephen's self is at the mercy of several spectral forces indeed. He becomes a doppelganger of Eliot's Prufrock, forever measuring himself or being measured by others. Similarly Bloom's identity is suspended between two constitutive taboos, the deaths of his father and son. It is no coincidence that they share a name: Rudolph/Rudy. Rather than on presences, his self therefore rests on absences, yet they are absences that refuse to remain blanks and emerge as examples of Freud's repressed to structure (or undermine) the present.[23] Jeffrey A. Weinstock's essay (3) below reads the ghosts as *Ulysses*' constitutive principle of undermining meaning that is created through hierarchical binary oppositions.

The most obvious 'release' (or at least theatrical enactment) of these ghosts occurs in the 'Circe' episode. Already in the 'Hades' section, when Bloom reads the list of the deceased in the newspaper, he encounters the ghost of himself when he notices that Martha Clifford's flower has made the paper disintegrate: 'Inked characters fast fading on the frayed breaking paper. Thanks to the Little Flower. Sadly missed' (p. 88). The pun on the fading characters on the unstable medium of printed language and the evasive and often ghostly characters in Joyce's unstable novel is evident. Perhaps not so evident is the play on Bloom himself (the name behind 'Flower') who, through the capitalised 'Little', first merges with his son, little Rudy Bloom, only to be 'missed' with him in the novel's attempts to establish characters. When Bloom is ultimately denied manifestation in the newspaper report on Dignam's funeral in the 'Eumaeus' section, where his name is corrupted to 'Boom' (p. 602), the novel achieves its *coup de grâce* concerning organic characters. Identity is reduced to a fleeting effect, yet it is an artistic, a musical effect, the hollow sound of a drum beat, that once again links it with the temporal and spatial structures that form the small universes in *Ulysses*.

Names are the signs that link identity to textuality most evidently, yet, they, too, are not so much guarantors of identity as troubling areas of uncertainty, repetition and contest. Leopold Bloom features, among other things, as 'Poldy' for his wife Molly (p. 59). She has been transformed herself from the more upmarket 'Marion' into a synonym of the loose woman. Her removal of the 'lion' ('Leo') from Bloom's first name emasculates her husband as much as their daughter's affectionate 'Papli' (p. 63) turns him into something babyish and edible. Bloom himself enjoys turning his name into anagrams (p. 631).[24] Milly in turn becomes a miniature version of Molly through a simple act of naming, and the repetition of Rudolph in Rudy connected with the similarity of their untimely and traumatic deaths has already been mentioned. Stephen also carries the name of the first Christian martyr. While the plays on Bloom's first name signal contests within intimate relations, his various surnames have social significance. When Leopold's father Rudolph changed his name from the Hungarian 'Virag' to the English 'Bloom', social acceptance was the obvious motivation. A similar move can be observed in the newspaper manager Nannetti, whose Italian descent has been so successfully eclipsed by his assumed Irishness that Bloom mentally addresses him as 'Nannan' (p. 115). In contrast, Bloom's 'true' identity continues to shine through his disguises, when he chooses exactly the English equivalent of his father's abandoned name as a pseudonym in his letters to Martha. The ultimate ironic gesture concerning the power of naming in *Ulysses* is of course the process by which an unknown man in a mackintosh at Dignam's funeral is transformed into the M'Intosh that features in the newspaper report on the event. Yet in a more conscious way Bloom also asks the reporter Hynes to add the name of the absent M'Coy to the list of mourners (p. 107). Texts manipulate, but also bring into being identities; this is what *Ulysses* signals with an ironic nod towards journalism, but also with some humorous winks in its own direction when Bloom muses 'If we were all suddenly somebody else' (p. 106).

Inventing and substituting names, getting facts and identities wrong as the only way of establishing them at all is far more than a measure of irony in *Ulysses*. It hints once again at the literary model underlying its structures, the epic. The epic tells stories as histories, by listing names and genealogies and the deeds related to these identities who consequently achieve a larger-than-life status. Yet simultaneously Joyce's novel refuses to recognise anything that is larger than life. Its universes are relational and relative, of reduced size and plural rather than monolithic. This robs them of explanatory power, as is most evident in the continually unanswered questions concerning the reasons behind the two most significant absences for Bloom, the deaths of his father and son. In the traditional genealogy of the epic, this severs the family ties required for a firm placing of the epic hero. It makes Bloom a hero *manqué*, the dislocated self populating so many modernist texts, trying to attach itself to other fleeting and floating selves, objects, scenarios, plots and stories. Because he is simultaneously too much and too little, exactly because he is no man and everyman, Zeus, Sinbad, the Wandering Jew *and* none of them, he becomes an epitome of the modernist self as textual process.

Yet even there *Ulysses* refuses to establish a monolithic model of Bloom as the only form in which subjectivity manifests itself in a modernist work. He is counterpointed with Stephen throughout, but most effectively the novel's narrative is eventually supplanted by another voice, other in terms of style and gender. Molly's monologue in 'Penelope' adds a complication to what has hitherto been observed. Her stream-of-consciousness musings are both affirmative and monologic – unlike anything else in the novel. Her unpunctuated monologue begins and ends with an affirming 'Yes'. Still, nothing could be less convincing than seeing it as the complement of the masculine odysseys in the novel. When Harry Blamires claims enthusiastically 'To enter the mind of Molly Bloom after so much time spent in the minds of Stephen and Leopold is to plunge into a flowing river. If we have hitherto been exploring the waste land, here are the refreshing, life-giving waters that alone can renew it',[25] he overlooks that there is water in Eliot's *The Waste Land*, too, in the shape of the river Thames. Unfortunately it is polluted by the same junk and debris that make up so much of *Ulysses*' narrative, the relics of an alienated materialist culture and its commodified personal relations. Enda Duffy's essay (10) concludes with an outline of the ambivalence of assertion and subjection in 'Penelope'. Molly's monologue is not so much an alternative universe as another example of a small one, not so much competing with as exemplifying the inextricable relations between the multiple universes in Joyce's novel.

VI

In the universes of *Ulysses*, language and meaning form opposite poles. *Ulysses* engages and plays with both. Letters as well as newspapers hold together the narrative of Joyce's novel, and the text proudly demonstrates the power of the typesetter in 'Aeolus', whose mechanical imperative of setting language backwards makes him turn even the most venerated terms and expressions into something resembling the satanic formulas of a black mass. Indeed, textuality can be the very undoing of significance and meaning, as is shown when Bloom's very real and present self is completely ignored when Nannetti checks proofs in his office. *Ulysses* again plays a paradoxical game by seemingly privileging the transient newspaper print over the assumed 'real presence' of a character. Of course, though,

Bloom is as real or as unreal as the 'limp galleypage' (p. 116). Once again *Ulysses* is not so much suspended between an emphasis on the mere material (Stephen's Aristotelian objectivism or Pound's 'unflinching realism') and the idealist claims of universalism as stretching itself to encompass both positions, but also to ridicule their one-sided claims of total authority and truth. Language itself can be corrupt and impotent, as is demonstrated when Bloom laments that his wife has forgotten the little Spanish she had as a girl (p. 54) or conjectures that her Italian pronunciation might be faulty (p. 61). His own grasp of languages is quite impressive, but far from perfect. A telling mistake occurs when he describes his ideal home in grammatically incorrect Latin as '*Alma Mater, vita beni*' (p. 599) – rather than the correct '*bene*'. Since realities and utopias are always textual in *Ulysses*, this is more than a lapse, but an indication that fictional universes are threatened by the unreliability of their material.

This is embodied in an allegorical nutshell when a drunken Bloom presents his vision of a realised (rather than an impossible) utopia to Stephen in 'Eumaeus'. His ideal society is an all-inclusive one ('taking it all together' again), with 'all creeds and classes pro rata having a comfortable tidysized income, in no niggard fashion either, something in the neighbourhood of £300'. When he continues that this would also produce friendlier relations between the sexes and a patriotism based on living well, Stephen declares brusquely 'Count me out' (p. 599). Stephen is unwilling to be part of a society in which, as Bloom puts it, 'You belong to Ireland, the brain and the brawn'. But more than negating universalism by dissenting, he reverses it by claiming that 'Ireland must be important because it belongs to me' (p. 599). He unsettles universalist claims by reversing hierarchies. His exaggeration of his own importance is ridiculous, but so is Bloom's homogenising utopia. Which is the universe of which, the text asks, the self or its environment, personal identity or nationality? The answer is that there is no firm answer, but that universality claims are to be regarded with suspicion.

The same ultimately applies to the universe of the text and its form. The novel is itself an often harmonising and homogenising structure capable of swallowing dissent, diverse characters and plotlines. Stephen, cynical as usual, envisages national styles in literature as English water closets and Irish running streams. Yet it would be far too simple to follow his acerbic remark and declare (in a similar fashion as for Molly's monologue) that stream-of-consciousness is more essentially Irish, modernist or simply superior than the anal retentive modes of English writing. For a start, *Ulysses* stands alone (very much like Stephen, its allegory of dissent) and can therefore hardly claim to be part of a tradition. It is dubious if the text would even like this, since its attitude towards literary legacies is generally distanced, disrespectful, and perhaps ultimately pessimistic (the cacophony at the end of 'Oxen of the Sun' does not bode well for a future literature). The text is also too clearly indebted to bottled-up English styles and simultanously enjoys swallowing, digesting and excreting far too much to make water closets a term of abuse. Streams, as we have seen with reference to Molly's monologue and *The Waste Land*, need not be pure, and 'running' in the sense of escaping can be less desirable than stability. In a similar fashion, the apparent competition between the corruptible printed word and the voice (Molly's as a singer, that of the barmaids in 'Sirens', and the gramophone in 'Hades') lacks a clearly predictable outcome. In 'Hades' Bloom comes up with the odd idea of preserving the memory of the deceased by placing a gramophone in each tomb (p. 109). Yet this would not safeguard a presence, but merely the mechanical repetition of absence – in a similar way as Roland Barthes sees photography establish a sense of 'having been there' rather than a presence.[26]

Repetition is indeed the dominant mode of creating characters, events and significance in *Ulysses*, as can be seen in the compulsive return to key events, objects, characters and ultimately slogans and phrases. *Love's Old Sweet Song* (p. 61) is a popular song that forms part of Molly's repertoire, and it stands for the continuing, but also circular appeal of love and sexuality, the force that pulls Bloom back to his starting point at the end of the novel. Yet again, this idyllic circularity and repetition does not remain uncontested. It has to compete, for instance, with *Sweets of Sin*, the title of a pornographic novel that Bloom purchases for Molly in 'The Wandering Rocks' (p. 226). Apart from throwing a sordid light on what might or might not be 'the word known to all men', it slyly calls up death again, the reward of sin according to the teachings of St Augustine.

The text cannot and indeed refuses to hold its universes together, or rather it thrives on their dissent which ultimately guarantees their plurality and interaction. Stephen's cynical pastiche of Wilde at the novel's outset that 'a symbol of Irish art' is the 'cracked lookingglass of a servant' (p. 7) already sums up the themes of fragmentation within wholes and the power struggles (here: the Irish one again) of which they always form part.[27] While *Ulysses* tries to be a self-sufficient textual universe in which everything happens inside loops of repetition and gaps of meaning, it also retains an awareness that it is forever tied to an outside that it yearns for, fantasises about, but fails to reach. Death as the text's constitutive taboo but also as that which it ultimately cannot contain makes this most evident. This productive and tragic split between word (the material of the novel) and world (a world that is simultaneously only that of the text and always more than the text) is allegorised in the letter 'L' that forms the link and the barrier between the two universes in the fictional 'wor(l)ds' of *Ulysses*. Martha accidentally adds it in her letter to Bloom: 'I called you naughty boy because I do not like that other world' (p. 74), and turns the textual realm of his erotic musings into a 'real' world. A typesetting accident removes the 'L' from Bloom's name in the newspaper and turns 'reality' into its textual travesty. Just as with the unholy trinity of potato, soap and absent key in Bloom's pocket, here again a reality principle (that of orderly signification) meets a pleasure principle (the messy simultaneity of experiences, visions and dreams).[28] What could hold them together in a meaningful way is significantly absent. Yet the missing keys in *Ulysses*, the keys to interpretation, hermeneutics in short, do not create despair or nothingness. They permit the recurring play of patterns, their meaningful and meaningless interaction, the desire of the reader and its frustration, and again more desire. As Stephen states prophetically (and even more pertinently when seen in relation to the voids, the nothings and nowheres in *Ulysses*): 'I am getting on nicely in the dark' (p. 37).

VII

It is the accepted role of criticism to elucidate obscurity. In the case of *Ulysses*, however, it would be foolish to assume that a text that controls meaning on so many levels would passively offer itself as a neutral object of investigation. Traditional criticism of Joyce's novel has indeed tended to latch on to its own play with idealist, Platonic, mythical positions and their realist, Aristotelian, materialist counterparts. The question was, in a simplified form: is *Ulysses* ultimately a realist or a symbolist text? Following Pound's lead, critics such as

Hugh Kenner have advocated the realist reading, while Eliot's mythical interpretation was taken up by the likes of Richard Ellmann.[29] The predictable outcomes of the debate were a reading of the novel as fragmented, open, and often pessimistic (especially from a Marxist perspective) by the 'realist' camp, and as ultimately unified, reconciliatory, and closed by the symbolist one. None of these positions is wrong, since *Ulysses* gestures in both directions. Yet upholding one as exclusively true contradicted the novel's own plurality. It also required strategic blindness: the realist camp had to overlook hints at symbolic systems (religion, myth, nationalism) or declare them to be ironic. The symbolist critics needed to play down crudeness and materialism or elevate them to a 'higher' level of significance.

The deadlock seemed to be overcome when poststructuralist positions attempted to open up the closure that *Ulysses* had suffered. By refusing to see the text as a whole (either mimetic or symbolic),[30] critics like Colin MacCabe, Maud Ellmann, and David Lodge took the materiality of Joyce's language seriously while turning exactly *Ulysses*' refusal to establish meaning into its significance.[31] Often influenced by psychoanalysis, especially in its 'post-Freudian' Lacanian variety, and by Bakhtin's ideas of the carnivalesque and dialogism, they described the text as the creator of realities rather than a response to reality.

Deconstructive readings of Joyce's novel, developed by French scholars such as Philippe Sollers and radicalised by the likes of Jacques Derrida, then shifted the emphasis away from questions of meaning altogether. The style of the novel and, if meaning at all, then its ruptures, were declared to be what *Ulysses* was all about.[32] Since its style is uniquely multiple and the novel offers gaps and obscurities in abundance, almost any emphasis seemed possible, so that deconstruction with its distrust of the unified art work not only opened it up, but often appeared to dissolve it altogether. Against its own intentions it could sometimes be seen to generate a new universalism, summed up in the claim that 'the text is about text'. In an obvious way, this is blatantly true for *Ulysses* with its interest in signification, textuality, and the materiality of communication. Yet as a monolithic universal truth claim it is also evidently reductive. *Ulysses* is concerned with itself as a text, but also with a large number of other issues.

Rather than opposing deconstruction, a new generation of critics, some of whom are assembled in this collection, have tried to steer readings of *Ulysses* back from a interpretive free-for-all into areas where ruptures, contradictions, and plurality need neither be overcome or ignored nor elevated to substitute truths. They often return to the old questions, for example that of realism, but do so via the deconstructive emphasis on form and style. Their overall aim might be summarised as reading *Ulysses* as a complex (and generally open-ended) debate on subjectivity, creativity, signification, power, gender, nationality, and politics. Particularly prominent positions in the 1990s are reassessments of Marxist and feminist positions as well as postcolonial readings. The essays that follow fall into this pattern, reassessing *Ulysses* both on a large and a small scale. While the essays for the most part focus on a particular episode, they also move across the whole text and the critical debates it has inspired and provoked. Brief descriptions of each essay are to be found in the headnotes. The essays themselves are both challenging and demanding in the way they often draw upon contemporary critical theory, particularly psychoanalytic ideas concerning subjectivity and cultural theories encompassing the body, gender and sexuality as well as economics, class, nationalism, and politics. Like *Ulysses* itself, the essays ask both narrow and wide questions about the human subject and its place within the universes of language, meaning, and power.

NOTES

1. All page references to *Ulysses* in this book refer to the Oxford World's Classics edition, ed. Jeri Johnson (Oxford and New York, 1993).
2. C. T. Onions (ed.), *The Oxford Dictionary of Etymology* (Oxford et al., 1983), p. 961.
3. Theodor W. Adorno, *Aesthetic Theory*, trans. C. Lenhardt, ed. G. Adorno and R. Tiedemann, The International Library of Phenomenology and Moral Sciences (London, 1984), p. 184.
4. T. S. Eliot, '*Ulysses*, Order and Myth', *Selected Prose*, ed. Frank Kermode (London and Boston, 1975), pp. 175–8 (p. 177) [first published in *The Dial* (November 1923), 480–3].
5. Ezra Pound, 'James Joyce et Pecuchét', in Robert H. Deming (ed.), *James Joyce: The Critical Heritage*, 2 vols, vol. 1 (London, 1970), pp. 263–7 (p. 266) [first published in *Mercure de France*, CLVI (June 1922), 307–20].
6. John Coyle (ed.), *James Joyce*, Icon Critical Guides (Cambridge, 1997), p. 33.

7. See Victor Luftig, 'Literary Tourism and Dublin's Joyce', in Mark A. Wollaeger, Victor Luftig and Robert Spoo (eds), *Joyce and the Subject of History* (Ann Arbor, MI, 1996), pp. 141–54.

8. Michel Foucault, 'Space, Knowledge and Power', in *The Foucault Reader: An Introduction to Foucault's Thought*, ed. Raul Rabinow (London, 1984), pp. 239–56 (p. 252). The essay was first published in *Skyline* (March 1982).

9. *The Poetics of Aristotle*, trans. and ed. Stephen Halliwell (London, 1987), esp. chs 7 and 23.

10. Stephen's declaration echoes a poem by the French Symbolist Jules Laforge: 'L'histoire est un vieux cauchemar bariolé', *Mélanges posthumes* (Paris, 1903), p. 279; see Johnson (ed.), *Ulysses*, p. 780.

11. Sigmund Freud, *The Interpretation of Dreams* [1900], trans. James Strachey, ed. Angela Richards, Pelican Freud Library, 4 (London, 1976), pp. 383–419.

12. 'He's in with a lowdown crowd' is Dedalus Senior's verdict on his son (p. 85), a criticism, however, that also ironically reflects back on the entire set-up of *Ulysses* and includes its readers.

13. Harry Blamires, *The New Bloomsday Book: A Guide through Ulysses*, 3rd edn (London, 1997), p. 155.

14. The joke is the repetition of an earlier one in 'Telemachus' where the allusion is clearer and the sisters become the witches in *Macbeth*: 'Five lines of text and ten pages of notes about the folk and the fishgods of Dundrum. Printed by the weird sisters in the year of the big wind' (p. 13); see Johnson (ed.), *Ulysses*, p. 771.

15. Even the otherwise subtle Hugh Kenner falls into this trap when he equates *Ulysses* with the biblical story of God's creation of the world in his conclusive remarks: 'The final text of *Ulysses*, before it was released for our collaboration, was a three-way collaboration: between Ithacan omniscience, and Molly Bloom, and the author inspecting what he had been writing for seven years, and seeing that it was good'; *Ulysses*, Unwin Critical Library (London, 1980), p. 157.

16. Friedrich Nietzsche, *On the Advantage and Disadvantage of History for Life* [1877], trans. Peter Preuss (Indianapolis and Cambridge, 1980).

17. Pound tellingly borrows this idea from the characterisation of Homer's *Odyssey* by its translator into Latin, Andreas Divus; see Hugh Kenner, *The Pound Era* (London, 1972), pp. 360–1.

18. The seminal discussion of the relation of myth and Enlightenment is Max Horkheimer and Theodor W. Adorno, *Dialectic of Enlightenment*, trans. John Cummings (London and New York, 1979). They write: 'Just as the

myths already realise enlightenment, so enlightenment with every step becomes more deeply engulfed in mythology. It receives all its matter from myths in order to destroy them; and even as a judge it comes under the mythic curse' (pp. 11–12).

19. As against this [commodities], money has no price. In order to form a part of this uniform relative form of value of the other commodities, it would have to be brought into relation with itself as its own equivalent; Karl Marx, *Capital: A Critique of Political Economy* [1867–94], trans. B. Fowkes, 3 vols, vol. 1 (London, 1982), p. 189.

20. Jacques Lacan, 'Seminar on The Purloined Letter', in *The Poetics of Murder*, ed. Glenn W. Most and William W. Stowe (London, 1983), pp. 21–54.

21. Jeri Johnson informs us that in the *Rosenbach Manuscript* holograph of 'Scylla and Charybdis', Stephen knew the answer: 'Love, yes. Word known to all men' (p. 791), but seems to overlook that even in this rejected version an ambivalence remains, for 'Love' and 'yes' are two words – and very significant ones throughout *Ulysses.*

22. The terms 'round' and 'flat' for the description of fictional characters derive from E. M. Forster, *Aspects of the Novel and Related Writings* [1927] (London, 1974), pp. 44–54 and 132–3.

23. Sigmund Freud, 'Repression' [1915], in *On Metapsychology: The Theory of Psychoanalysis*, trans. James Strachey, ed. Angela Richards, Pelican Freud Library, 11 (London, 1984), pp. 139–58.

24. Daniel P. Gunn lists 'Leopold, Siopold, Stoom, blue Bloom, on the rye, Bloohoom, Him, even Him, ben Bloom Elijah, greasabloom, Poldy, Poldycock, Henry Flower, so lonely, blooming, Senhor Enrique Flor, of Flowerville, of Bloom Cottage, of the new Bloomusalem' as Bloom's synonyms in the novel; 'The Name of Bloom', in *Joycean Occasions: Essays from the Milwaukee James Joyce Conference*, ed. Janet E. Dunleavy, Melvin J. Friedman and Michael Patrick Gillespie (Newark, 1991), pp. 33–45 (p. 34).

25. Blamires, *New Bloomsday Book*, p. 233.

26. Roland Barthes, 'The Photographic Message', in *Selected Writings*, ed. Susan Sontag (London, 1982), pp. 194–210 (p. 209).

27. The allusion is to Oscar Wilde, 'The Decay of Lying' (1889); see Johnson (ed.), *Ulysses*, p. 770.

28. Sigmund Freud, 'Beyond The Pleasure Principle' [1919–20], in *On Metapsychology*, pp. 269–338.

29. Kenner, *Ulysses*. Richard Ellmann, *James Joyce*, revd edn (New York, 1982).

30. An attitude that still finds an echo, for example, in Marilyn French, *The Book as World: James Joyce's 'Ulysses'* (New York, 1976).

31. Colin MacCabe, *James Joyce and the Revolution of the Word* (London, 1979) and Maud Ellmann, 'To Sing or to Sign', in *The Centennial Symposium*, ed. Morris Beja et al. (Chicago, 1986), pp. 66–9, are representative of poststructuralist readings.

32. Some of these positions are assembled in Derek Attridge and Daniel Ferrer (eds), *Post-Structuralist Joyce: Essays from the French* (New York, 1984).

1

James Joyce: The Limits of Modernism and the Realms of the Literary Text

RICHARD LEHAN

I

James Joyce oversaw the modern novel through its evolution of various narrative modes. Such movement takes us from realistic fiction (the kind of slice-of-life portraits that we have in *Dubliners*) to the literature of self-consciousness and the indeterminate that we find in *Finnegans Wake*. Joyce's development as a novelist thus recapitulates – indeed replicates – the evolution of the modern novel. Joyce's work is a microcosm of the macrocosm – proof that ontogeny recapitulates phylogeny – and Joyce is the paradigmatic modern.[1]

This argument presupposes that there was a radical shift in narrative conception between the novels of Dickens and the naturalistic novels of Zola. This shift came about because the new commercial/urban process no longer accommodated the sentimental hero/heroine with his/her capacity to convince us that what was good in the human heart could overcome the evil embodied in the new megalopolis. Dickens himself no longer felt confident in his sentimental endings, as his rewriting of *Great Expectations* would indicate. Dickens always tried to conclude his novels with a new sense of life and energy, inseparable from the idea of sentiment and the nuclear family, but by the time he got to *Our Mutual Friend* such plots were wearing thin, and the sense of death that emerges from that novel is stronger than the sense of new life. No longer could the novel be recuperated in terms of comic realism – that is, in terms of a moral centre embodied by a Squire Allworthy, a Mr Knightley, an Esther Summerson, or a John Harmon. And where comic realism left off, literary naturalism began. Zola's world turns on force – biological and environmental – and not on moral order. The centre of the *Rougon-Macquart* novels is Paris, and Zola took us from the world of the new proletariat in *L'Assommoir* to the decadent salons of *Nana*, from the source of money in *L'Argent* to its effects in the northern coalfields in *Germinal*, from the way the new commercialism had transformed the peasantry in *La Terre* to the way it led up to the gigantic military defeat in *La Débâcle*.

Joyce's connection to Zola was remote and indirect, but the connection was nevertheless real. It was most directly mediated by George Moore, whose early novels were written under the influence of Zola, and whose works like *The Lake, The Untilled Fields*, and *Vain Fortune* Joyce knew well. Joyce often disparaged some aspects of this work, especially novels like *The Lake* in which Father Oliver Gogarty's (Moore and Joyce saw different things in the original of Buck Mulligan) sexual awakening came coincidental with his nude swim across a lake in County Mayo. Joyce thought all this was a bit too much. But like Moore, Joyce believed that Ireland was in the grip of a morally overbearing church, that the moral timidity of the nation undercut the drive for home rule and independence, and that the parochialism of the country would keep it locked into a peasant mentality. The Irish were obsessed with sex and death, suppressing one and celebrating the other in a ritual that became grotesque. Caught in the tension of such self-destructive play, young men and women in Ireland were destined to express their energies neurotically, to desire escape while succumbing to the invisible walls that held them. Joyce did not have to look far to find in Moore analogues to such stories of his own in *Dubliners* as 'Eveline', 'A Little Cloud', 'Counterparts' and 'The Boarding House'. Moreover, Moore had moved away from the omniscient point of view of Zola's novels toward more psychologically narrated stories – stories which unfold through a central consciousness.

Joyce realised that the unfolding of such consciousness could be the basis for a new kind of novel – a novel with an aesthetic hero for whom sensibility was more important than sentiment, and who was more interested in being defined in the context of the beautiful than in the naturalistic context of biological necessity and a determining commercial/industrial environment. In *The Sentimental Education*, Flaubert had shown Frédéric Moreau playing sentiment out to its final absurdity. Flaubert had also shown in *Salammbô* and *The Temptation of Saint Anthony* how an aesthetic consciousness could transform the novel. But the greatest catalyst here was Walter Pater. In *The Renaissance*, Pater had said, 'What is important ... is not that the critic should possess a correct abstract definition of beauty for the intellect, but a certain kind of temperament, the power of being deeply moved by the presence of beautiful objects.'[2] Henry James had given us such a novel – one that turned on a character who could be moved by beautiful objects, a character like Hyacinth Robinson in *The Princess Casamassima* who, in the presence of St Mark's Square in Venice, abandons his anarchistic plans because he has come to believe that it is more important to create, especially the beautiful, than to destroy. This kind of commitment to aestheticism became one of the controlling ideas behind literary modernism. Virginia Woolf, Marcel Proust (whose early imagination was deeply influenced by Pater's contemporary, John Ruskin), and Thomas Mann would turn this impulse into a literary movement.

Joyce saw such an aestheticism as the basis for rewriting his *bildungsroman, A Portrait of the Artist as a Young Man*, where the novel turns in the famous beach scene of Stephen Dedalus' commitment to the beautiful at the exclusion of other values. As Stephen walks through Dublin, he begins to see through aesthetic eyes, and objects take on impressionistic meaning:

> His morning walk across the city had begun, and he foreknew that as he passed the sloblands of Fairview he would think of the cloistral silverveined prose of Newman, that as he walked along the North Strand Road ... he would recall the dark humour of Guido Cavalcanti and smile, that as he went by Baird's stone-cutting works in Talbot Place the spirit of Ibsen would blow through him like a keen wind.[3]

As comparisons between *A Portrait* and *Stephen Hero* clearly show, Joyce moved us away from modern realism toward modern aestheticism – two different modes of narrative reality. There was some carryover in this transition. Behind naturalism was the romantic belief that nature was a mirror of truth, that symbols reveal the evolutionary nature of reality hieroglyphically. And even as he abandoned neorealism, Joyce clung to the belief that objects in nature unfold their meaning. Such a process of unfolding was inseparable from the idea of the epiphany – and such unfolding was inseparable from a theory of symbolism. But Joyce went beyond both literary naturalism and symbolism when he began to control such symbols in the context of myth. The beautiful birdlike girl who supplies the epiphany in chapter four of *A Portrait* takes on symbolic meaning because the novel is controlled by the Daedalus–Icarus myth – that is, by the myth of birdlike flight. Joyce had begun to develop this method in the story 'Grace', where the major details of the narrative are controlled by a Dantean vision of hell, and he brought the method to near perfection in 'The Dead' where the feast of the Epiphany itself controls the meaning of the story, from the names given the key characters to the date (January 6th) on which the story takes place. There is little doubt that he was influenced in developing such a symbolic-mythic method by Gabriele D'Annunzio, whose assumed name becomes a commentary in itself on Joyce's story.

In moving from aestheticism to mythic symbolism, Joyce moved us from the early stages of modernism to what today we think of as high modernism. In fact, it is the works of Joyce, Yeats, Pound, Eliot, Mann, among others, who embody our very definition of the modern, and the novel that best reflects this process is, of course, *Ulysses*, where Joyce brings all of these narrative elements into play, where a realistic plane of reference is symbolically held in place once a mythic structure has been superimposed upon it. What we have here is the literary complement to what was going on in archaeology – the discovery of layered cities, the realisation that different historical realms were superimposed upon each other. Jackson Cope and others have convincingly argued that Heinrich Schliemann's discovery of Troy and Arthur Evans' discoveries in Crete (Knossos) had a tremendous influence on such works as D'Annunzio's *El Fuoco* and *La Città Morta* – works which in turn influenced Joyce as early as when he was completing the *Dubliners* stories. In fact, in George Moore's *The Lake*, the character of Nora Glynn participates in such an archaeological dig. After Schliemann, we knew that there were as many as nine cities superimposed on each other in Troy: Cities 7A and B were the city of Homer. The archaeological structures here found their equivalent in *The Cantos*, *The Waste Land*, and especially *Ulysses*.

Joyce's interest in the Mediterranean world may have been motivated by another source. As early as 1907 we know that he believed that there was a connection between Mediterranean and Irish culture. In a lecture he gave in Italian at the Universita Popolare in Trieste in April of 1907, he argued not only for a connection between Iberia and Ireland (long speculated) but also for a direct connection between Ireland and the early Phoenicians and later Egyptians based on a theory of sea trade and common elements of language. Speaking of the special nature of the Irish language, he began:

> The language is oriental in origin, and has been identified by many philologists with the ancient language of the Phoenicians,[4] the originators of trade and navigation, according to historians. This adventurous people, who had a monopoly of the sea, established in Ireland a civilization that had decayed and almost disappeared before the first Greek historian took his pen in hand. It jealously preserved the secrets of its knowledge, and the first mention of the island of Ireland in foreign literature is found in a Greek poem of the fifth century before Christ, where the historian repeats the Phoenician tradition. The language that the Latin writer of comedy, Plautus, put in the mouth of Phoenicians in his comedy *Poenulus* is almost the same language that the Irish peasant speaks today, according to the critic Vallancey. The religion and civilization of this ancient people, later known by the name of Druidism, were Egyptian. The Druid priests had their temples in the open, and worshipped the sun and moon in groves of oak trees. In the crude state of knowledge of those times, the Irish priests were considered very learned, and when Plutarch mentions Ireland, he says that it was the dwelling place of holy men. Festus Avienus in the fourth century was the first to give Ireland the title of Insula Sacra; and later, after having undergone the invasions of the Spanish and Gaelic tribes, it was converted to Christianity by St. Patrick and his followers, and again earned the title of 'Holy Isle'.[5]

From this passage one can see why Joyce would eventually have been attracted to Victor Berard's theory that the Ulysses story was deeply influenced by Phoenician culture, hence making it a Jewish poem. Joyce's belief in the symmetry among ancient Phoenicia, Greece, Crete, Egypt, and Ireland played into his eventual acceptance of the Viconian theory of history.

While Joyce's interest in Vico has been generally connected with *Finnegans Wake*, we know from Richard Ellmann that Joyce was interested in Vico while he was working on *Ulysses*.[6] This is not surprising given Joyce's interest in Flaubert – especially novels like *Bouvard et Pecuchét* which indict the supremacy of the rationalistic, enlightenment mind with its trust in factual accumulation and, more to the point, *Salammbô*, the novel that reveals Flaubert's own use of Vico, and where one order of space and time (Carthage at the time of the Punic Wars) reflects another order of space and time (Paris in the Second Empire). Vico believed that there are three cycles of time and then a ricorso – the age of the gods, of heroes, and of men; or the primitive, semi-history, and the historic; the first characterised by rites of religion, the second by marriage, and the third by burial. The first turn in the cycle took place before the Trojan War, the second during the Trojan War, and the third at the time Athens and Rome became republics. The reflux or the ricorso occurred with the fall of Rome, whereby civilization gave way to a new barbarianism, which gave way to a new age of feudal or medieval heroes, which in turn gave way to the Enlightenment democracies that Vico thought he was observing in his own day. The reflux, however, began with the end of the Enlightenment and with the commercial paralysis and moral decadence from which modernism seemed unable to extricate itself.

The Viconian cycles lead inevitably to the parallax view, to use a term which, like 'metempsychosis', comes to us from *Ulysses* itself. 'Parallax, as explained by Sir Robert Ball (whose work "The Story of the Heavens" Bloom thinks of as he looks up at the Ballast Office Clock), is the visual sensation received when one holds up a finger in front of one's eyes and observes a far object. The finger appears to be doubled. Conversely, if one looks at the finger, the far object appears to be doubled. In the astronomical sense of parallax, distant heavenly bodies observed from different points on the planet appear to be in different positions even though their positions remain the same.'[7] This notion is clearly significant to Joyce's new way of thinking about narrative. The parallax view creates two realms of activity – a foreground and a background, one of which blurs when the other is focused upon, which is to say that the positioning between the two is subjective, held together by historical consciousness. As I have suggested, Joyce was already using something similar to this method in 'Grace' and 'The Dead' and *A Portrait*; but in *Ulysses* the method dominates by calling attention to itself.

We know that Joyce was thinking of adding a story entitled 'Ulysses' to *Dubliners* – a story based on his own experience of being knocked unconscious in a fight and assisted by a Dublin Jew named Albert Hunter, who took him home. But if the Ulysses myth was early in Joyce's mind, it compared with another myth that also obsessed him at this time – the myth of the Wandering Jew. The origins of this tale are complex, but the legend seems to involve a 'man in Jerusalem who, when Christ was carrying his Cross to Calvary and paused to rest for a moment on this man's doorstep, drove him away (with or without physical contact, depending on the variants), crying aloud, "Walk faster!" and Christ replied, "I go, but you will walk until I come again!" '[8] The Wandering Jew is fated to walk the world and neither to die nor to find rest until the Second Coming. Earlier forms of the legend involved Enoch in the Old Testament who 'walked with God'. 'Better known is the case of Elijah, who not only was carried up to heaven in a fiery chariot as a reward for his courageous and untiring efforts on behalf of Jehovah, but also became identified in Semitic mythology with Al-Khadir ... who was a vegetation god and a healer of the sick.'[9] The legend has many analogues, including the Sinbad the Sailor legend, which Joyce clearly had in mind while writing *Ulysses*.

One can see why Joyce would have been interested in the Wandering Jew legend. If one begins with Al-Khadir and moves through Enoch to Elijah to Leopold Bloom, one completes the Viconian cycle of time. Moreover, the Wandering Jew legend was very close to Joyce's own sense of exile, a subject that he had just treated in a play by that title. There is no question that much of this legend gets into *Ulysses*, not only the idea of Bloom as Jewish wanderer, but the idea of Bloom, in contrast to Alexander J. Dowie, as the new Elijah, searching for a new Jerusalem (Bloomusalem). In the 'Circe' section, a gramophone blares out that the Holy City is the new Jerusalem, and a newspaper boy shouts the safe arrival of Reuben J. Dodd, the new Elijah and wandering Jew. Stephen then sees Bloom as Reuben J. Anti-Christ, bearing on a boatpile his son recently taken from the Liffey – an episode which ties together the theme of the Wandering Jew, father and son, and Eternal City.[10]

Why Joyce abandoned the Wandering Jew legend for the Ulysses story is perhaps obvious: first, the Ulysses legend was better known to a general public; second, it existed in more coherent form and was thus more easily foregroundable; third, the Ulysses legend allowed him to carry the theme of the family and the idea of return (*nostes*) in a way the Wandering Jew legend did not; and fourth, once Joyce had become aware of Victor Berard's theory of the

Phoenician – that is, the semitic – influence on the Ulysses legend, he had, in effect, collapsed the Wandering Jew story into the story of Ulysses. So it was proper that his modern Ulysses be Jewish, just as he had come to believe that the Mediterranean connection with Ireland justified making Dedalus into an Irishman.

The argument over the importance of the Ulysses legend to Joyce's novel has gone on since its publication with key critics like T. S. Eliot and Richard Ellmann emphasising the mythic parallels, and Ezra Pound and Hugh Kenner minimising them. But if Joyce was interested in Vico as early as *Ulysses*, and if he was trying to establish a parallax view, I think we can see that the argument, as stated, is a needless one. Joyce did not believe that the two planes of the novel, the foreground and the background, could be held firmly in focus at once, but he did believe that Bloom had reified both the story of Ulysses and the Wandering Jew. And while the Viconian connection seems there, one does not have to insist upon it, because what Joyce was doing here was simply adapting the elements of romantic realism to the modern. Romantic realism involves the use of romantic themes and myths in an urban context. Hawthorne had used the method in *The Marble Faun*, Melville in *Pierre*, Hugo in *Les Miserables*, Eugène Sue in *The Wandering Jew* and *The Mysteries of Paris*, and Flaubert in *Salammbô* and *The Temptation of Saint Anthony*, where Flaubert reveals an awareness both of the legend of the Wandering Jew and of Vico's theory of history. In repositioning romantic realism, Joyce had in effect created what we mean by modernism. Many critics have seen this in different terms: Edmund Wilson and Harry Levin, for example, by talking of Joyce's superimposition of symbolism onto naturalism, and Wyndham Lewis in his attack on Joyce for spatialising time – that is, for allowing the simultaneous to overpower the sequential.

What Joyce was doing in *Ulysses* was creating a great archetypal structure. And, as in every archetypal pattern, the emphasis was upon the repeat in history, to use Pound's phrase. What is essential to see in *Ulysses* is that Joyce's archetypes are organically positioned – that is, they reflect natural occurrences built into time. The emphasis in *Ulysses* is on flow – life flows through the novel the way the river flows through the city. Bloom in the jakes, Stephen and Bloom on the beach, Stephen and Bloom urinating in the garden, Molly and Gerty MacDowell at the start of their periods – Joyce does not spare us from the fact that life involves flow. We live in a world of physical processes and change – and flow at this level leads to what we mean by history. As physical matter is transformed, so is historical matter; Al-Khadir gives way to Elijah, and Elijah to the Wandering Jew, all replicated in the person of Ulysses/Bloom, just as the embodiment of Molly's life flows through her memory, and just as the English language in the 'Oxen of the Sun' is as much a part of the gestative process as that of a newly born child. Of the four great paradigms of the western world – nature, history, consciousness, and language – Joyce used all of them, sometimes all at once. But in *Ulysses* he never thought of life as inseparable from natural and historical process, from the organic processes that control flow. What he was doing was in harmony with what Virginia Woolf, William Butler Yeats, Ezra Pound, Thomas Mann, and William Faulkner were doing – and what we mean by the term modern.

Postmodernism as a movement involves a radical shift in the paradigm. The assumptions of the postmodern take their being from a belief that reality is bracketed – that is, that language or some other semiotic or conceptual system mediates between man and nature and, by extension, history. We thus do not know nature or history but know only the systems by which we explain nature and history to ourselves. We move, to repeat, from the realm of substance to sign, from reality to relation, from metaphysics to semiotics. The physical reality of nature is no longer a mirror of meaning, and historical time is no longer cyclically encoded. All elements within such a system become self-referential, endowed with manmade meaning that comes from the system itself. Such a system, in fact, becomes a commentary on itself. Modernism puts the emphasis upon archetypal characters, symbolically located in a myth, functioning organically in cyclical time; postmodernism puts the emphasis upon the relation of one archetypal character to another within a totalising system such as Vico's. No longer do we have change in nature and history; instead we have transformations within the system itself.

[...]

II

Modernism as an ideology and system of literary technique preexisted its textuality. Joyce more than any other novelist helped bring literary modernism into being. The turn toward symbolic myth, cyclical history, primitive awareness, organic reality, and an aesthetic sensibility resulted in a shared belief of what a literary text should include. Inseparable from modernism were the twin beliefs in the power of human consciousness (often defined in Bergsonian terms) to illuminate reality and to find in nature and natural process the meaning, symbolic and literal, that explains the nature of human existence. Postmodernism as a cultural movement transformed such beliefs by collapsing consciousness into forms of language and by mediating the processes of nature through paradigms of thought, which undid nature as a symbolic presence and put the emphasis upon the *way* we interpret rather than what we interpret – upon the paradigms we bring to an understanding of nature rather than nature as an unmediated reality. While Joyce in *Finnegans Wake* may have been moving away from some of the elements of modernism, he never moved completely away from his belief in the power of nature to speak directly to a receiving consciousness. Nature was always there in the process of flow and life force – always acting upon our minds. Language gave us insight into such processes rather than substituting its own reality for such meaning. Thus any attempt to read Joyce beyond the limits of modernism creates a literary reality separate from its own special mode of textuality.

As I have already indicated, modernism ended where postmodernism began – and the two ideas are not mutually compatible. To oversimplify for a moment, modernism begins where Nietzsche left off – with man's consciousness confronting an unmade universe, a universe without a creator. This sense of consciousness took many forms – Henry James' privileged narrators, the Bergsonian consciousness that informs the novels of Virginia Woolf and William Faulkner, to the *amor fati* kind of neo-stoicism one finds in Hemingway. As diverse as these writers are, they did employ forms of consciousness that distanced us from the universe – and that often took on mythic or symbolic embodiment. Postmodernism takes us one step beyond this and asks what would happen if we simply postulate a universe without such subjectivity – a universe that is intelligible only in terms of the way we choose to talk about it – and the way we talk about it is inseparable from a notion of structure, discourse, episteme, or systems theory, depending on which version of the postmodern we might want to enlist. Consciousness becomes part of the system we bring into play, rather than something out front, all-directing, like a traffic cop. In this new context, drastic things happen to literary texts. We no longer have the romantic sense of art versus life with the author exercising his or her genius; we no longer have a sense of history filtered through a centred and all-powerful subjectivity. Art is life and life is art; myths are inseparable from history rather than, as T. S. Eliot had told us, the way of ordering history; symbolism gives way to metonymy, reality becomes relational in a system that creates and sets it own meanings. Postmodernism moves us to self-reflexive language, which delimits by substituting itself for physical reality.

Almost all of the readings of Joyce that we have had in the past thirty or forty years come off one or the other of these assumptions about the natural of realism – and lead to an idea of the literary text. The modernist text, as we have seen, concentrated on the mythic/symbolic, emphasised the cyclical, pursued the archaeological and the primitive in *Ulysses* and *Finnegans Wake*, and most important created forms of consciousness that informed *A Portrait* or *Ulysses*, leading to the distinct thought of Stephen, Bloom, and Molly, as well as that of the narrator, whether it be David Hayman's Arranger or Hugh Kenner's Uncle Charles principle. In the last twenty years the modernist text has given way to the postmodern text in which consciousness has been collapsed into discourse, giving us readings totally based on Joyce's language. As a result, there has been a tendency to collapse Joyce's novels into each other and to read them as a piece – to read postmodern assumptions back into *Ulysses* and to create two radically different texts of the novel and two radically different Joyces. The works of Karen Lawrence, John Paul Riquelme, Fritz Senn, Brian McHale, Patrick McGee, and many others have followed this pattern. The unstated argument seems to be that Joyce is large enough to contain such differences. But a closer look at such an argument reveals a number of hitherto unaddressed problems. The philosophical implications of such diverse textuality can be seen by looking at two representative readings of *Ulysses* – one modernist, the other postmodernist.

A good modernist reading is S. L. Goldberg's *The Classical Tempter: A Study of Ulysses* (1961). Goldberg's reading emphasises moral-aesthetic principles embodied in characters. Stephen, for example, reveals 'that his aesthetic objectives depend upon the artist fulfilling himself as a moral being, that aesthetic *stasis* and *kinesis* originate in, and reflect, states of soul'.[11] Goldberg emphasises character meaning and development and de-emphasises style and language. Goldberg, in fact, seems unsympathetic to all those elements in the novel which diverge from a notion of the mimetic, especially the stylistic extravagances of the middle sections. The 'real achievement of *Ulysses*', according to Goldberg, does not lie in its parodic irony but 'in its underlying and overarching vision of human life, a vision both more humane and more complex than is always perceived'.[12]

A very different reading of *Ulysses* is Karen Lawrence's *The Odyssey of Style in 'Ulysses'* (1981). Lawrence points out that Joyce abandons third-person narrative halfway through *Ulysses* and argues that Joyce uses a series of rhetorical masks to conceal himself and to undo the authenticity of any style. She concludes that the unreliability of narrator gives way to the unreliability of narrative.[13] While Goldberg concentrates on the 'Telemachus', 'Nestor', 'Calypso', 'Hades' chapters, Lawrence's *Ulysses* is abstracted from the 'Aeolus', 'Sirens', 'Cyclops', 'Nausicaa', 'Oxen of the Sun', 'Circe', and 'Eumaeus' chapters. For Lawrence, *Ulysses* is ultimately about itself. The writing of a story becomes the story of a writing. Both the Goldberg and Lawrence books are useful, intelligent readings that arrive at very different conclusions. Both readings depend on taking the text as a construct, although Lawrence constantly calls our attention to this fact, while Goldberg attempts to conceal it. Since Lawrence's reading today is the dominant or prevailing one, a closer look at some of the theoretical assumptions behind her work may be justified.

The first question involves a theory of language itself. Language is a construct among constructs: there are a number of divergent constructs of language and not simply one structural theory stemming from Saussure. Moreover, postmodern theories of language are representational rather than referential, or to put this differently, postmodern language is self-referential: the language system is taken for our only reality. The notion of such discourse begs a serious question. If we turn to perhaps the most influential theoretician on discourse, Michel Foucault, we discover that he never really tells us where discourse comes from. Supposedly it comes fully formed, belying, of course, the subjectivity of the critic who brings it into being and then uses it for his own ideological purposes. As a result, studies like Lawrence's tend to exclude the authorial/historical text: we move, that is, from a text based upon the creative process to a text based upon the reading process. We have been overpowered by Roland Barthes' and Foucault's assumptions that the author is dead – that language is 'always already' and that the function of the author is simply to pull discourse up from the well of language. (Stanley Fish, for example, tells us that we can read 'Lycidas' as a pastoral poem while denying that Milton could have written it as a pastoral poem.)

Since there is a subjectivity at work in postmodern language that gets repressed, a key question here involves whether Joyce's language in *Ulysses* is a self-enclosed as Lawrence insists when she claims that after the 'Aeolus' chapter we are no longer reading a novel – that is, a narrative – but sequences of experimental prose. But what Lawrence takes as non-referential language, in contrast to the earlier chapters, takes on a totally different meaning once we see it as a kind of urban consciousness at work in the novel – a consciousness of the city as much at work expressing a state of mind as 'Proteus' reveals the consciousness of Stephen, 'Hades' of Bloom, and 'Penelope' of Molly. Bloom walks through Dublin speaking to the city. In 'Aeolus', 'Sirens', and 'Eumaeus', the city speaks back in the stylistic modes of journalism, the musical hall, and the gossip of the coffee shop (the cab shelter). Walter Benjamin has described the kind of consciousness that Baudelaire brought to the city. What Joyce gave us in *Ulysses* was a language to go with that consciousness – a language which became a literary legacy for writers like Dos Passos, Döblin, and others.

There is thus an essential difference in this context between what is happening in *Ulysses* and *Finnegans Wake*. In *Ulysses* myth is superimposed upon the physical city of Dublin; in *Finnegans Wake* myth is superimposed upon a dream. What becomes 'unrepresentational' is thus as much a matter of content as of language. So what we have in *Ulysses* may not be the pure psychological/character narrative that Goldberg gives us, but we are not cut off from a singularity of consciousness as Lawrence would have it. Once we come to terms with the way consciousness positions itself in language – that is, once we begin to inquire whether or not language can escape the forms of subjectivity that bring it into being (a phenomenon, by the way, to which Lawrence is often quite sensitive, albeit contradictorily so) – we will get a third text that can mediate between the extremes of a Goldberg and a Lawrence, leading to readings that, while thematically divergent, are far more philosophically consistent than anyone today might believe.

The main difference, then, between a modern and postmodern text involves the loss of the subject. But more often than not we get a return of the repressed subject. This happens in *Ulysses*, just as it happens in the works of Foucault. As experimental as *Ulysses* might be, Joyce never lost his sense of the subject in the telling as a critic like Goldberg constantly shows us. We can see this in even clearer terms if we look at another reading of *Ulysses* – Patrick McGee's *Paperspace: Style as Ideology in Joyce's* Ulysses (1988) – that begins more or less where Karen Lawrence's reading leaves off. McGee begins with actual reference to the Lawrence book, as well as to Derek Attridge and Daniel Ferrer's *Post-Structuralist Joyce* (1985). Attridge and Ferrer tell us that they have collected these 'new' readings of *Ulysses* 'to confront its unreadability ... to look at the mechanisms of its infinite productivity ... to record the perpetual flight of the Subject ... to follow up within it the strategies that attempt a deconstruction of representation'.[14]

Claiming familiarity with such an agenda, McGee tells us that we need to go one step further and show how the philosophical subject has been negated by language, absorbed in the act of writing. Such a subject becomes 'papered over': 'another surface, a page, that can be folded over the surface of the other. ... In paperspace, self and other' write without recognition.[15] Once McGee negates the subject, a character like Gerty MacDowell becomes a 'style' – and not a character. She is 'an imaginary style, a purely ideological way of looking at the world'.[16] It is the language in the 'Nausicaa' section that takes on life for McGee – not Gerty.

But we can ignore representation only so far. If we have to go through language to get to life, language cannot be substituted for life. Style is an *attitude* an author takes toward his subject and toward his audience – not a sustained system of belief. In 'Nausicaa', Joyce is clearly calling parodic attention to a way of looking at romantic reality – but such a reality looks outside of its language toward the performative, toward a life style and not a writing style. Thus it is not surprising that as McGee continues to talk about Gerty, her sexuality becomes something distinct from language. Gerty begins to take on distinct, individuating human motives. As McGee moves from language to ideology, Gerty begins to *embody* cultural values, the values of a nineteenth-century patriarchal society in which women are subsumed to the courtship and childbearing rituals of overbearing males.[17] As a result, the contact between Gerty and Bloom comes to life, even for McGee, when he tells us that Gerty desires to be desired:[18] McGee's argument thus comes full circle, with Gerty as a compliant object of sexual desire, and we end on exactly the note of sexual representation that McGee had been trying to suppress. McGee's attempt to bleed *Ulysses* of its physicality finally fails.

The same kind of slippage occurs in McGee's discussion of Molly Bloom. Critics have seen Molly on a spectrum that has taken her from the mythic or archetypal 'other' to whore or commonplace woman. Almost every traditional reading of the novel has seen Molly as inseparable from her own sexuality and thus inseparable from the forces of nature. But here McGee demurs. What Joyce shares with Molly is 'not nature but "like" nature. Something in the nature of writing'.[19] Molly also, we are told, functions as a signifier that opens to question the patriarchal code of the novel. In perhaps his most desperate attempt to turn natural process into cultural construct, McGee insists that even Molly's menstruation can 'function as a kind of writing – a remaking of some originary ... mark that is absent'.[20] Despite his claim to a deconstructionist reading of *Ulysses*, at some point McGee is reading like an old-new critic. While he may not believe a text has organic unity, he nevertheless organises his critique around all-controlling assumptions (such as, *Ulysses* involves writing about writing), and he ends up looking for the elements in the text that he can use to support that belief.

McGee's critique is an extension of what Geert Lernout has termed *The French Joyce* (1990). In this valuable study, Lernout meticulously maps the interest of French literary criticism in Joyce. Lernout tells us, 'when I read French and American poststructuralists, I found it increasingly difficult to link their texts to Joyce's; when I could, Joyce very often came out saying something that however much I tried I could not find in the original'.[21] Lernout sees the shift in the balance of power between traditional and poststructuralist readings of Joyce taking place at the 1984 International Joyce Conference at Frankfurt. The way had been prepared by critics like Philippe Sollers who, in his influential journal *Tel Quel*, kept Joyce in the critical foreground. Sollers helped move Joyce through a variety of critical prisms – such as, structuralism and poststructuralism – to his own belief that Joyce's later works reconciled (a mystic) Catholicism and Judaism, just as Soller's marriage to Julia Kristeva had united his early Catholicism with her Jewishness. Such interest obviously puts the emphasis more upon the personal connections that might exist between Sollers and Joyce. And indeed French criticism, as a whole, tended to use Joyce as a springboard for peripheral concerns. Initially, Lacan's ideas were run through Joyce's texts by critics like Hélène Cixous and Julia Kristeva who, once their own literary reputations were established, encouraged disciples like Jean-Michel Rabaté and Stephen Heath.

Lernout's emphasis upon the 1984 Frankfurt Joyce Conference is astute for other reasons: there, Jacques Derrida gave one of the principal papers, 'ULYSSES GRAMOPHONE: Hear say yes in Joyce', a three-hour reading involving the 'yes' words in *Ulysses*. What is interesting about Derrida's paper is that it puts as much emphasis upon his own thought processes as he was working on this paper as it does upon any residual meaning in Joyce: the paper involves Derrida reading Derrida reading Joyce. He tells us of a trip he took to Tokyo a month before the conference, at which time he discovered in a basement news-stand of the Hotel Okura a book entitled, *16 ways to avoid saying no*, next to another book entitled, *Never take yes for an answer*. Such books become part of the 'text' of *Ulysses* for Derrida, as do his jottings as he comes close to an accident while driving out of the Paris airport. Even if one might argue that Derrida's associative thoughts are not unrelated to the narrative method of *Ulysses*, it still remains true that whoever reads Derrida's essay will learn as much about Derrida as Joyce. The text now has come to embody whatever the critic decides to bring to it.

This is not to deny that Derrida's reading contains a hidden agenda. Like Lacan and Foucault, Derrida's work has challenged the humanistic assumptions of philosophers like Jean-Paul Sartre. Derrida's early attacks on Saussure and Lévi-Strauss stemmed from his belief that Saussure had created a metaphysical centre with his theory of *langue*. Derrida wanted to undo not only the idea of human nature by negating any principle of transcendental metaphysics but also any principle that would give writing a logocentric basis. Thus meaning in a text becomes free-floating, totally ungrounded. The critic does this by undermining one meaning in a text with another – and by ignoring any controlling context. Bloom talks into a telephone, which involves a system of communication, just as Derrida talks to the Joyce Society, a system of scholars in the pursuit of literary meaning. But such systems break down: how do we ground a 'yes' when there is no 'presence' to give authority to meaning? Derrida's catalogue of 'yes' words points to tenuous relationships between *subject* and *other*. If 'yes' is tenuous in meaning, what equally can 'no' mean? Supposedly the meaning of human relationships slides between 'yes' and 'no'. But surely there is more stability in *Ulysses* than this: we know where Bloom stands in his concern for Paddy Dignam's family, Mina Purefoy in labour, Stephen's welfare, and the intolerance of the Citizen; we know where Stephen stands in his attitude toward Buck Mulligan; we even know where Molly and Bloom stand despite the volatility of their love, altered perhaps once more now that Molly has experienced the sexual coarseness of Blazes Boylan. Change rather than indeterminacy seems to be the linchpin of *Ulysses*: from Ulysses to Bloom a changing cast has been subject to the same processes of time and nature. Strangely, in his elaborate discussion of the 'yes' words in *Ulysses*, Derrida ignores the suggestion that Molly's 'yes' could refer to her own sexuality (her consenting to Bloom on the Hill of Howth) or to some kind of life force – the power of the female to bring forth new and ongoing life. Once again, the discussion is kept free of both referentiality and of natural process. Derrida closes his essay with words from *Ulysses* that he has jotted down while leaving the Paris airport on his return from Tokyo: everything is text; where one text stops another begins; all we have is intertextuality.

Critics like Derrida turned literary modernism on its head by co-opting Joyce, the premier modernist. Writing is once again substituted for narrative unfolding, and Joyce – the paradigmatic modern – is subsumed to a postmodernist vision of constructed reality. To be sure, there is no *Ur Ulysses*, no essentialised text to which we can return for stabilised meaning. But there are limits beyond which a reading of *Ulysses* can go, limits to critic-generated discussions that replicate textual meaning. A middle ground between these two extremes, as I have suggested, is a theory of narrative modes – a system of pre-textualised meaning that allows us to see a novel like *Ulysses* as part of the movement of literary modernism which Joyce helped bring into being. Such a context would also allow us to see *Ulysses* as part of a larger cultural and aesthetic process, at the same time as it would give limits to textual meaning. And finally, it would return us to literary modernism as a realm of referentiality and representation, removing the artificial blockage that now dams the circular flow in novels where one day creates its own cycle of meaning, where a character is part of a cycle of history, and where rivers that run to the sea are part of the cyclical flow of physical nature.

From *Arizona Quarterly*, 50: 1 (Spring 1994), 87–108.

Notes

[Richard Lehan's essay places *Ulysses* at a crucial stage between the stylistic echoes of nineteenth-century naturalism, symbolism and aestheticism in *Dubliners*, the neo-realism of *A Portrait*, and the experiments with self-conscious open-ended structures in *Finnegans Wake*. It describes how *Ulysses* projects an archetypal story onto very real settings and thus achieves a modernist 'repositioning' of 'romantic realism'. While prefiguring postmodernism with its radical challenge to the possibility and legitimacy of systems of explanation, such as nature and history, *Ulysses* simultaneously remains attached to a very modernist emphasis on archetypal heroes and cyclical systems that include, most tellingly, the possibility of return. Lehan's essay concludes by outlining recent theoretical positions that claim Joyce as a modernist and postmodernist respectively. He argues in favour of a modernist reading of *Ulysses* – against what he regards as opting for a position in which everything is merely text, a stance that Lehan sees embodied in some poststructuralist readings of Joyce, notably Derrida's. All page references to *Ulysses* are to the Oxford World's Classics edition, ed. Jeri Johnson (1993). Ed.]

1. ['Ontogeny' and 'phylogeny' are Greek terms for the biological origin of an individual and the evolution of an animal or plant type respectively – Ed.]
2. Walter Pater, *The Renaissance*, 'Preface' and 'Conclusion', *Criticism: The Major Texts*, ed. W. J. Bate (New York, 1952), p. 509.
3. James Joyce, *A Portrait of the Artist as a Young Man* (London, 1977), pp. 159–60.
4. While linguists today do not support Joyce here, the point is that Joyce believed in a connection between the Gaelic and Phoenician languages at the time he was preparing to write *Ulysses*.
5. James Joyce, *The Critical Writings*, ed. Ellsworth Mason and Richard Ellmann (Ithaca, NY, 1989), p. 156.
6. Richard Ellmann, *James Joyce*, revd edn (New York, 1982), p. 340.
7. Zack R. Bowen and James F. Carens (eds), *A Companion to Joyce Studies* (Westport, CT, 1984), p. 469.
8. Chester G. Anderson, *James Joyce and his World* (New York, 1968), p. 11.
9. Ibid., p. 11.
10. Bowen, *Companion*, p. 524.
11. S. L. Goldberg, *The Classical Tempter: A Study of 'Ulysses'* (New York, 1961), p. 115.

12. Goldberg, *Classical Tempter*, p. 116.

13. Karen Lawrence, *The Odyssey of Style in 'Ulysses'* (Princeton, NJ, 1981), p. 24.

14. Quoted in Patrick McGee, *Paperspace: Style as Ideology in Joyce's 'Ulysses'* (Lincoln, NE, 1988), pp. 6–7.

15. Ibid., p. 78.

16. Ibid., pp. 86–7.

17. Ibid.

18. Ibid., p. 90.

19. Ibid., p. 178.

20. Ibid., p. 180.

21. Geert Lernout, *The French Joyce* (Ann Arbor, MI, 1990), p. 15.

2

'Proteus' and Prose: Paternity or Workmanship?

MICHAEL MURPHY

Unlike Menelaus in the *Odyssey*, Stephen Dedalus, in the 'Proteus' episode of *Ulysses*, does not ask why he has been held up for so long on his island. He knows the banal financial answer to that. Rather, he is seeking the answer to another question from a Proteus of his own who takes on the form of the 'Old Men' of his island, most of them dead – Columbanus, Jonathan Swift, George Berkeley, Oscar Wilde – one figure after another, '*nacheinander*', his literary fathers, and of some elders still very much alive, '*nebeneinander*' (p. 37)[1] – AE, W. B. Yeats, Douglas Hyde, even Bram Stoker. Each of these men has made a name for himself, and Stephen is wrestling with them to obtain an answer to his question: what must *I* do to be memorable like you, my fellow Dubliners? Or, as the catechism question might have been put at Clongowes: what must I do to gain eternal life? – on earth, of course, not in heaven.

What must Stephen, an Irishman, do to memorialise his mother with something as good as what the Englishman John Milton wrote for a friend – and is he really grieving or is he using her as Milton used Edward King? In 'Lycidas', that poem recently much in Stephen's mind, Milton says, 'Fame is the spur'.[2] In his 'Verses on the Death of Dr Swift', Stephen's Dublin precursor – a man also much on Stephen's mind here – had suggested that it might be envy.[3] Is there a difference? Does it matter provided either gives the necessary impetus?

Some of the Irishmen that Stephen thinks about here were 'Wild Geese' who had made it out of Ireland with widely different motives,[4] and some had returned and become famous. Others had become famous abroad. The least successful of those who flew was Kevin Egan, the forgotten nationalist, who did not return and was not famous. There is no future, and certainly no immortality, in imitating Egan. Immortality lies with Swift and Berkeley and Wilde and Yeats, the writing men, all unionists and Protestants, unlike Stephen and Egan. But Stephen is like them in one way: they are all men of the Pale, that small area of Ireland that included Dublin, where the English language and English culture prevailed. Their books are Protestant and protean,[5] in many places at the same time, like the Catholic Eucharist in which these writers did not believe and about which they did not write. But all copies of Berkeley's philosophical discussions are eucharistic at least in the sense that they are the same wherever seen or read: Occident and immortal and ubiquitous. By contrast, poor Kevin Egan's name will die with the few who remember him, for he only sets in type what others write. His legacy is not protean, eucharistic, immortal. Even his son Patrice does not believe in his father's country, his father's faith, or his father's politics, any more than Stephen does in his father's politics, his mother's faith, or his own country.

The scene switches, in protean fashion, from Dublin to Paris and back, and the part played by the failed Egan is unexpectedly prominent, though oddly ignored in most of the commentaries on this episode. Egan's foregrounded presence suggests Stephen's fear that even escape to Paris might be the end of his literary ambitions as it was of Egan's political hopes. At this point, Stephen is no more than a conglomerate of other people's thoughts, just as Egan is a printer of other people's words. Still, Egan, as a printer, *is* a man of letters, and Stephen may well turn out to be little more successful, even if he escapes again to Paris. The Dublin men of letters, whom he rather arrogantly despises as belletristic, are better off than that. And Egan showed daring and courage and risked prison or a death sentence in a selfless cause as none of these literary men had or would, including Stephen, as he acknowledges. And what is Egan's reward? He is '[l]oveless, landless, wifeless' (p. 43), an unromantic exiled rebel who did serve all those things that Stephen in *A Portrait* said he would not serve. Yet Egan is not mocked. He has been, not a Byronic or Luciferian failure, but just a common one who still has, however, one thing in common with Byron and

Lucifer, whom Stephen admires: Egan has put everything on the line. Men who serve a cause, political or literary, and men and angels who serve nothing and no one, who say '[n]on serviam' (p. 541), may all end up with silence, exile, and nothing.

'Where are my comrades?' is the other question asked of Proteus by Menelaus. What Telemachus asks Menelaus is 'where is my father?' but that is not Stephen's question. A twenty-one-year-old youth who thinks himself in a league with Byron or Lucifer is not generally in search of a father, especially if he has left his father's house '[t]o seek misfortune' (p. 575). Contrary to the opinion of some critics, Stephen is looking here not for a father, in Simon Dedalus or Leopold Bloom, but for father*hood*, in effect, his own.[6] And it is not biological but artistic fatherhood that he seeks. He is wrestling, as I have said, with his literary forebears, Berkeley, Swift, and the rest, to get the answer to the following question: how or when am *I* to father a work of art?

By the time that this metaphor has been explored in the episode, an unavoidable conclusion has been reached: the artist does not *father* a work of art nor create it *ex nihilo*. Unlike the body, which is begotten not made by the father, and unlike the Word, which is begotten not made by the Father, the word is made rather than begotten by the author. It is fabricated by artifice, by the force of the artist's mind and hand working on the protean flux of experience with the language left him by his predecessors and his elder contemporaries; it is forged, as the younger Stephen might have put it, in a smithy with material and tools. Adam, our first father, was not begotten; he was formed from the dust of the earth by his Maker, and Eve was formed from Adam's rib. Hence, Eve 'had no navel. ... buckler of taut vellum' (p. 38). An artist, a poet, a writer on vellum, is also a *maker*, to use the apt medieval English word. Hence, he is like God making man and woman, not like God begetting the Word.

Stephen is wrong about his own conception and birth: 'Wombed in sin darkness I was too, made not begotten' (p. 38). His own father Dedalus, old father Daedalus, and even father Egan begat sons just by the natural act of lust. But Daedalus the artificer had to *shape* the cow with artifice, to *make* it so that it was good enough to deceive the bull from the sea – a trick of sorts, perhaps somewhat like Bishop Berkeley pulling the veil of the temple out of his shovel hat (p. 48), but certainly not the kind of genetic fact of birth over which men and bulls have no control after the momentary act of sexual union. And the artistic work must be done alone, with cunning not coupling. One can possibly make one's self immortal by fathering children, an idea that Shakespeare explores in his sonnets, as Stephen well knows, but children too within time's sickle's compass come. An author can, however, write eternal lines in books that cannot *all* be destroyed: 'So long as men can breathe or eyes can see, / So long lives this, and this gives life to thee.'[7]

This is not entirely true, of course. The name of the beloved 'thee' is not in our minds today nor on our lips; we do not know who 'thee' was, and we were never meant to know, any more than we know the identity of 'the onlie *begetter* of these insving sonnets Mr W. H.' to whom the dedication wished 'all happinesse and that eternitie promised by ovr ever-living poet' (1749, my emphasis). It is the poet-artist who lives eternally: 'So long lives this, and this gives life to *me*.'[8] The pen is mightier than the penis or the womb. In the fourteenth episode of *Ulysses*, where the idea of fatherhood and creativity is taken up again, Stephen will say, 'In woman's womb word is made flesh but in the spirit of the *maker* all flesh that passes becomes the word that shall not pass away' (p. 373, my emphasis).

Given a maker, what about the method and matter of the literature that the maker is to fashion? Well, first are the things and people and thoughts that come *nacheinander* or *nebeneinander*, to be ordered into words printed on a page. This process is rather like good composing in the printing house: 'Proper Words in proper Places', in the phrasing of that other reluctant Dubliner,[9] Swift, not to mention proper letters. This is, of course, easier said than done. Later, in 'Aeolus', Bloom admires the artifice of a printer: 'He stayed in his walk to watch a typesetter neatly distributing type. Reads it backwards first. Quickly he does it. Must require some practice that mangiD.kcirtaP. ... How quickly he does that job. Practice makes perfect. Seems to see with his fingers' (p. 118). But if 'mangiD.kcirtaP' is typeset, it will not come out as 'Patrick Dignam' or 'Dignam Patrick'. One needs a dayfather, a printing house artificer, a Nannetti or Egan, not an ad seller or a midwife, for the midwife may have to handle a miscarriage of something begotten, not made, something that came out mangiD.kcirtaP, though she is not responsible for it. And it is a printer who errs in producing Bloom's name because of Bloom's interruption (see p. 602), though he does not err as badly as Bloom would have in botching Patrick Dignam's name. Bloom thinks of the printer, 'Queer lot of stuff he must have put through his hands in his time: obituary notices, pubs' ads, speeches, divorce suits, found drowned' (p. 118), all of it ephemera and much of it the substance and the accidents of *Ulysses*.

In 'Proteus', the mind of Stephen, the would-be poet, is still an incoherent sea of words, phrases, and ideas in no printable order: back to front, upside down, in 'Proteese', with bits of nearly every major European language, alive and dead, and very minor ones like gypsy cant and Gaelic; hence, most of them are other people's words and phrases, and some are those that have been set in eternal type: the Bible, Catholic ritual, Shakespeare, Milton – better quality stuff than the clichés of Mr Deasy's letter but still not Stephen's original thoughts. To put it (as he does) melodramatically and in mixed metaphors, he remains a dog 'vulturing the dead' (p. 46); in a more quotidian way, he is a dog sniffing and partly digging up old dogsbodies, an intellectual cocklepicker or a ragman dealing in scraps of texts of poets and philosophers: 'Tatters! Out of that, you mongrel' (p. 46). He is a composite of bits of major and minor authors from Aristotle to Taxil, from Matthew Arnold and Berkeley to Lucien Millevoye and Louis Veuillot.[10]

If we attribute most of the original language of the episode to Stephen, rather than to Joyce, whose schema informs us that the 'art' of the episode is philology, we see that Stephen already has considerable mastery of the protean English language in linguistic skills with which he handles the tools left to him by his predecessors and in tools that he has fashioned for himself from what they have bequeathed to him. He has the ability, for example, to switch frequently from scene to scene, from time period to time period, to change from first to second to third person the grammar of the apparent narrator.[11] Protean pronoun changes all refer to the same person: 'Stephen closed *his* eyes to hear his boots crush crackling wrack and shells. *You* are walking through it howsomever. *I* am, a stride at a time. ... Open *your* eyes. No. Jesus! If *I* fell over a cliff that beetles o'er his base' (p. 37, my emphases).

Stephen can mint neologisms such as 'moondrawn', 'myriadislanded', 'ghostcandled', 'unbeheld', 'shamewounded', and 'longlashed' (pp. 47, 48), all self-explanatory past participles made from items in an inherited vocabulary. The present participles are nearly as plentiful, inventive, and colourfully pellucid: 'lowskimming', 'redpanting', 'vulturing', and 'almosting' (p. 46). And this merely a selection of the coins that he can forge at will.

He can also draw directly on his inherited treasury, selecting with the care of a skald or a scop archaic words with the flavour of the Spenserean Pale rather than the peat smoke of John Millington Synge's Aran Islands: 'a *buckler of taut vellum*', '*moiety*', 'her *matin* incense', '*jerkined* dwarfs', '*nans* and *sutlers*', 'a *scullion* crowned', '[o]n a field *tenney a buck, trippant, proper, unattired*', '*seamorse*', 'the dead dog's bedraggled *fell*', and 'a *pard*, a panther, *got in spousebreach*' (pp. 38, 39, 42, 45, 46, my emphases).

What else might a literary artist need in addition to manipulated grammar and an endlessly renewable vocabulary? He might require verbal sound effects perhaps: onomatopoeia and assonance, alliteration and internal rhyme, all together or separate, such as 'crush crackling wrack and shells', already quoted, or '[d]ead breaths I living breathe, tread dead dust, devour a urinous offal from all dead. Hauled stark over the gunwale he breathes upward the stench of his green grave, his leprous nosehole snoring to the sun' (p. 49).

But all these verbal resources are apparently not enough to enable Stephen to produce an elegy for his mother. Milton wrote 'Lycidas' for 'the drowned man', and Wilde wrote 'Requiescat' for his sister, just as Alfred, Lord Tennyson, gentleman poet, wrote 'In Memoriam', for Arthur Hallam, Thomas Gray an elegy for the nameless villagers of Stoke Poges, and Yeats two elegies for Lady Gregory's son.[12] Within the fiction of *Ulysses*, even Mr Deasy has written a kind of elegy for dead or dying cattle, a bullock-befriender, if no bard. With all his rhetorical skills, why cannot Stephen drive out his demon by writing an effective exorcism, a lament for his mother, instead of always letting Yeat's poetry or the Catholic ritual do it for him? If he must turn aside and brood, let him come out with something other than the poet's 'Fergus'[13] or the Church's '*Liliata rutilantium*' (p. 10). Let him stop caressing his own single phrase, 'odour of rosewood and wetted ashes' (p. 28); and fit it into some coherent poem that will '[p]ut a pin in' (p. 47) to hold it down and give rest to his mother's perturbéd spirit and his own.

Wait. 'Oomb, allwombing tomb. ... roar of cataractic planets, globed, blazing' (p. 47). The mountain, no, the universe, is in labour. 'Paper!' (p. 47). To deliver a baby on? To deliver a thought on? Quickly. Out it comes from a 'parent' alternately solemn or sceptical. What is it? Perhaps a poetic prosy version of the menstruation just referred to? If so, then he is not pregnant with a great thought. Perhaps it is a miscarriage of a gothic-erotic elegy begotten by the very *thought* of the kiss of the vampire of Bram Stoker, fellow Dubliner, creator of Dracula: 'Mouth to her mouth's kiss' (p. 47), 'her mouth' his mother's, the vampire's kiss her death sentence?[14] Or perhaps his body has just 'emitted' something.[15]

Whatever Stephen has 'produced', the effort exhausts him, and he lies down on the rocks to take his well-earned postproduction rest, like and unlike an earlier Creator, because he looked and saw, or thought he saw, that what he had made was exceedingly good: '*Et vidit De[dal]us. Et erant valde bona*' (p. 48). With a contented sigh (?) comes Yeats's line once more (for the last time, we hope), since Stephen should not need it again: '*And no more turn aside and brood*' (p. 49). We should hear no more of '*liliata rutilantium*' or of the dead man or disconnected phrases about Stephen's mother: exorcism by verse or worse, finally. Stephen should be able to set out '[t]omorrow to fresh woods and pastures new', to coin a phrase.[16]

The episode should end about here with a triumphant display of the new production, but it does not. We do not get to see the '*valde bona*'. Instead, we get another page of prose that tries in every way to cover up the fact that we are not hearing the verse that Stephen produced in that moment of creation or excretion. We later learn (in 'Aeolus,') that he has fashioned four lines of four words each, all but two of them monosyllables, many from Hyde and others.[17] The lines are largely the waste product of what Stephen has ingested mentally, a natural emission, a child's 'making', perhaps, but not a mature poet's. Stephen seems to realise this by the time of the 'Aeolus' episode, for there he has enough self-critical taste not to recite the 'romantic' verse to the audience but instead produces a sardonic prose story incorporating the solid reality of the two older women on the beach, the ones carrying the 'misbirth' (p. 38).

'Cousin Stephen, you will never be a saint' (p. 40), but 'poet', not 'saint', is the word that Stephen is avoiding, the word John Dryden used to Swift, writer of great prose, fellow-countryman, fellow-Dubliner of Stephen, and fellow-hater of his neighbour as himself.[18] What Stephen seems to learn from the beach experience is that he cannot become Yeats's rival, but he can make Swift his master.

Here on the strand, looking at the same scene that Swift and Yeats had known before him, Stephen's organs of artistic generation, male and female, imagination and experience, have not managed to unite like the sexual organs of his own father and mother who 'clasped and sundered, did the coupler's will' (p. 38). Nothing worth much artistically is either begotten or made. And his physical organs have simply spilled water, seed, faeces, if any of these *is*, indeed, what has happened. Artistic *making* would need an artificer's imaginative Act of Union between hand and mind, between imagination and protean raw material. To beget, one does not try to control the forces of nature. There is an act of physical union, and some months later, without any further effort, there one is, Daedalus or Dedalus, father of a perfect human specimen, a repeatable miracle. This is creation or procreation; it is not art. God the Father spoke the Word, which was 'begotten not made', according to the Creed, and from both Father and Son together 'proceeded' the Holy Ghost, who brooded upon the void to produce the world – the mystery of Creation – and who brooded upon a Virgin to produce the Word made flesh – the Incarnation that began the Redemption, Love's bitter mystery.[19] This is Divine consubstantiality, more neologistically, more irreverently, and indeed more blasphemously, it is 'contransmagnificandjewbangtantiality' (p. 38). It is not art either. But that newly-minted word *is*.[20]

Stephen Dedalus, would-be artificer, will not go with Fergus and will not embrace Ireland, his own country, for he finds her repellent, and such a union would be barren of any artistic issue, he thinks. So he will turn his back on her; he will take with him the assorted legacies left him by his literary 'forefathers', mentioned earlier in this essay, together with memories of his own family, city, faith, companions, acquaintances, pissing dogs, seagulls, old women, porter bottles, crucified shirts – and, with the tools at his disposal, he will turn *them* into a work of art that will do honour to him but not to her. The problems to be solved are: how is he to organise this foul rag-and-bone shop – how control the language of neologism and archaism so they will be something more than circus animals' tricks and the ocean of separate, yet conjoined, experiences so that he rules the waves – how weld *disjecta membra* into a cow good enough to attract a bull or into a horse impressive enough to subvert a city?

The answer of *Ulysses* seems to be that the task cannot be done in *one* way but, like the metamorphoses of Proteus, only in a variety of ways, by the changing rhetorics of the episodes. The artist must devise artifices to make his work the protean polytropic device of Dedalus, rather than the static construct of Daedalus. But for now, some of the prose that he produces is still Wildean or Swinburnian matter that he can mass-produce or excrete on demand. It is easy to make and easy to leave, pleasantly exhausting perhaps, like a good bowel movement, but not a Purefoy product – Beaufoy, maybe.

Stephen, the would-be maker of original things from commonplace things – from the dust of the earth, from bodily emissions – does not pare his fingernails coolly; he picks his nose, placing a piece of snot on a rock. '*Super hanc petram.* ... Upon this rock I will put my snot.' We are, perhaps, present at the founding of a new church of one, with Stephen not a protomartyr who dies for a cause but an absurd 'heresiarch', his Latin quarter hat doing duty for the beaded Greek mitre of Arius (p. 38), his crozier the ashplant, a branch of Yggdrasil, the giant tree of his Lochlann predecessors whose longships beached here (p. 45) and who showed as little reverence for Christian episcopacy as Stephen. Indeed, this rebel aspires to be like the Lucifer '*qui nescit occasum*' (p. 50), but he may end up like the Lucifer who said '*non serviam*' and who thereafter and therefore knew a spectacular fall. Or he may end up like Ibsen's Brand (p. 49), who would not compromise and who lost everything, or like Icarus who was 'found drowned' (p. 118) or like Odysseus who was promised 'Seadeath, mildest of all deaths' (p. 49) by Tiresias and who was seen on his way 'beyond the utmost bounds of human thought', by Lawn Tennyson. He may end like Wilde, who brought himself down, or like Christ on the crosstree, who had dared to say something very different from everyone else and who died for it.

Ambitious heights and depths. But Stephen is still shown at the end of the episode wearing another man's suit, another man's shoes, quoting other men's words. He is not, however, going back to the tower, and so he just may be about to shed the intellectual and literary castoffs that he has been wearing. His mind may be 'homing, upstream, silently moving, a silent ship' (p. 50) where he is the one master. When we next meet him in 'Aeolus', the literary work that he produces *seemingly* spontaneously is ready, he knows, for immediate, albeit oral, publication and is of an entirely different order from the thing that he produced on the beach. It is not something he has emitted; it is something that he has *made*.

From *James Joyce Quarterly*, 35:1 (Autumn 1997), 71–81.

Notes

[Michael Murphy's challenging essay outlines Stephen Dedalus' struggle with creation in *Ulysses*. In the same way as he struggles with (and against) the cultural greats that surround him, figures such as Swift, Berkeley and Wilde, Joyce's novel is not so much looking for origins (a father in the case of Stephen, its literary roots in the case of the novel) as investigating father*hood*, i.e. the very possibility of creation, artistic creation to be precise. In typical modernist fashion *Ulysses* must advocate a creation *sui generis* and privilege the potency of textuality over other forms of creativity, biological or theological. It delivers its baby, i.e. itself, on the medium of paper, but in doing so it also embraces and transcends other forms of creativity. It attempts to overcome the limitations of gender and the traditional separation of body and mind, nature and culture, through its insistence that creation is multiple and a process – rather than ever fixed and completed. All page references to *Ulysses* are to the Oxford World's Classics edition, ed. Jeri Johnson (1993). Ed.]

1. In German, *nacheinander* means 'one after another in time', and *nebeneinander* means 'next to each other in space'.
2. John Milton, 'Lycidas', *The Poetical Works of John Milton*, ed. Helen Darbishire (Oxford, 1955), 2: 167, line 70.
3. Jonathan Swift, 'Verses on the Death of Dr Swift', *The Complete Poems*, ed. Pat Rogers (New Haven, CT, 1983), pp. 485–98.
4. 'Wild Geese' was an expression in Ireland for those fighting men who left Ireland after the surrender of Limerick to William of Orange in 1691. The term was later applied sometimes to anyone who left Ireland. See Frank Gifford, with Robert J. Seidman, *'Ulysses' Annotated: Notes for James Joyce's 'Ulysses'*, revd edn (Berkeley, CA, 1988).
5. These works take widely differing forms such as 'F' (folio?), 'Q' (quarto?), and 'W' (whatever?) (p. 41).
6. Two critics who have questioned the notion of a son in search of a father are Morris Beja, in his introduction to 'The Mystical Estate or the Legal Fiction: Paternity in *Ulysses*', in *James Joyce – The Augmented Ninth: Proceedings of the Ninth International James Joyce Symposium, Frankfurt, 1984*, ed. Bernard Benstock (Syracuse, NY, 1988), pp. 215–18, and Jean-Michel Rabaté, in 'Paternity, Thy Name is Joy', ibid., pp. 219–25. In addition, Rabaté touches upon the idea of paternity as metaphor for artistic creation, which I examine here in some detail.
7. William Shakespeare, 'Sonnet 18', *Sonnets, The Riverside Shakespeare*, ed. G. Blakemore Evans (Boston, 1974), p. 1752, lines 13–14. Further references to the sonnets will be cited parenthetically in the text.
8. See Donald W. Foster, 'Master W. H., R. I. P.', *PMLA*, 102 (January 1987), 42–54, for the argument that 'Mr. W. H.' is a typographical error for 'Mr. W. Sh.'
9. See Swift, 'A Letter to a Young Gentleman, Lately Entered into Holy Orders', *Selected Prose Works of Jonathan Swift*, ed. John Hayward (London, 1949), p. 463.

10. These bits comprise, in all, about one quarter of the whole episode, according to Murray McArthur in 'Signs on a White Field: Semiotics and Forgery in the "Proteus" Chapter of *Ulysses*', *ELH*, 53 (Autumn 1986), 633–52 (649). The extended list of authors included can be found in Erwin Steinberg, *The Stream of Consciousness and Beyond in 'Ulysses'* (Pittsburgh, PA, 1973), p. 71.

11. '[A] conscious virtuosity in the handling of language as an end in itself and an exploitation of the affective resonance of words' is how Stuart Gilbert defines the 'art' of this episode, philology, but he does little to illustrate the truth of this definition. See Gilbert, *James Joyce's 'Ulysses': A Study* (New York, 1958), p. 116. Others cite Joyce's words to Frank Budgen: 'Everything changes – sea, sky, man, animals. The words change, too' and ' "Almosting!" I said. "Yes", said Joyce. "That's all in the Protean character of the thing. Everything changes: land, water, dog, time of day. Parts of speech change, too. Adverb becomes verb"'; Budgen, *James Joyce and the Making of 'Ulysses'* (Bloomington, IN, 1960), pp. 48, 54. Budgen's commentary on this episode, which is one of the best, does not do as much to display Joyce's verbal creativity as I try to here. J. Mitchell Morse, in his chapter 'Proteus', in Clive Hart and David Hayman (eds), *James Joyce's 'Ulysses': Critical Essays* (Berkeley, CA, 1974), pp. 29–49, does a good job on the other transformations in the episode.

12. Oscar Wilde, 'Requiescat', *The Works of Oscar Wilde*, ed. G. F. Maine (London, 1957), p. 709; Alfred, Lord Tennyson, 'In Memoriam', *The Poems of Tennyson*, ed. Christopher Ricks (London, 1969), pp. 861–88; Thomas Gray, 'Elegy Written in a Country Churchyard', *The Complete Poems of Thomas Gray*, ed. H. W. Starr and J. R. Hendrickson (Oxford, 1966), pp. 37–43; and W. B. Yeats, 'In Memory of Major Robert Gregory' and 'An Irish Airman Foresees his Death', *Collected Poems* (London and Basingstoke, 1982), pp. 148–52, 152.

13. Yeats, 'Who Goes with Fergus?', *Collected Poems*, pp. 48–9.

14. The phrase is referred to again in 'Oxen of the Sun', where the implication is that the vampire impregnates with a kiss (p. 372).

15. 'Was he short taken?' asks Miles Crawford later when he sees the torn letter (p. 127). Mr Deasy was not, but Stephen was, perhaps. In 1977, David Hayman suggested that the major emission in the episode comes from Stephen's masturbation in the course of an erotic fantasy: Stephen's Masterstroke. See Hayman, 'Stephen on the Rocks', *James Joyce Quarterly*, 15 (Autumn 1977), 5–17. Perhaps. But, as I suggest here, one could match Hayman by bringing together phrases to indicate (inconclusively) a number of emissions, real or metaphorical, including the possibility that Stephen is squatting at stool and wiping himself with part of Deasy's letter, as Bloom does with another piece

of journalism. We are told that Stephen has stuffed the scribbled note back in his pocket with the pencil (p. 48), but did he wipe himself on the blank part and write his poem over or on the back of the typed part? Stephen does not pull it out of his pocket with Deasy's letter in 'Aeolus'. In 'Nausicaa' later, Bloom writes his ephemeral inscription on the sand in much the same spot as Stephen composed his poem. Bloom comes across something there: 'Mr Bloom stooped and turned over a piece of paper on the strand. He brought it near his eyes and peered. Letter? No. Can't read. Better Go. Better. I'm tired to move. Page of an old copybook. ... All these rocks with lines and scars and letters' (pp. 363–4). Did Stephen drop the poem from his pocket when he rummaged for his handkerchief? [. . .] In his Paris notebooks, Joyce posed the question 'Why are not excrements, children, and lice works of art?' His negative answer is: 'Excrements, children, and lice are human products – human dispositions of sensible matter. The process by which they are produced is natural and non-artistic; their end is not an aesthetic end: therefore they are not works of art'; James Joyce, *The Critical Writings*, ed. Ellsworth Mason and Richard Ellmann (Ithaca, NY, 1989), p. 146. He discussed the question again in James Joyce, *A Portrait of the Artist as a Young Man* (London, 1977), p. 211. Whatever his opinion about lice, Stephen's answer there to the question about the other two 'products' seems to be the same as Joyce's.

16. Milton, 'Lycidas', p. 170, line 193.

17. See Robert Adams Day, 'How Stephen Wrote His Vampire Poems', *James Joyce Quarterly*, 17 (Winter 1980), 183–97.

18. John Dryden's words to Swift, 'Cousin Swift, you will never be a poet', are quoted in Sir Walter Scott, *Life of John Dryden*, ed. Bernard Kreissman (Lincoln, NE, 1963), p. 318.

19. The Nicene Creed was regularly recited at Mass in Joyce's day. The phrases alluded to here are 'one lord Jesus Christ, the only-begotten Son of God, born of the Father before all Ages ... begotten, not made, being of one substance with the Father by whom all things were made' and 'I believe in the Holy Ghost ... who proceedeth from the Father and the Son.' See Gifford and Seidman, *'Ulysses' Annotated*, 1: 612, 1: 651, 3: 45, and 9: 838–9.

20. For a very full discussion of the credal and heretical ideas on the Trinity that go through Stephen's mind, see Frederick Lang, *'Ulysses' and the Irish God* (Lewisburg, 1993).

3

The Disappointed Bridge: Textual Hauntings in Joyce's *Ulysses*

JEFFREY A. WEINSTOCK

Shari Benstock, in '*Ulysses* as Ghoststory', considers some of the more obvious ways in which Joyce's text incorporates ghosts, primarily dwelling on Stephen's Shakespeare theory and the figure of Stephen's mother. However, she fails to offer her own definition of what constitutes a ghost, perhaps relying on the reader's recollection of Stephen's definition of a ghost as 'One who has faded into impalpability through death, through absence, through change of manners' (p. 180). Yet, Stephen's definition is more complicated than it may first appear; to begin with, it subverts the commonplace notion that a ghost is the soul of a dead person. The ghost, for Stephen, has metaphorical connotations having to do more with 'fading' and 'impalpability' than with actual, physical death. The ghost is that which is ambiguous, that which cannot be touched, that which cannot be immediately experienced. In its 'fading', the ghost joins the many metaphors of incompleteness that suffuse *Ulysses* and Joyce's other writings: the Pisgah sight of Palestine, the gnomon, the disappointed bridge, the condition of 'almosting'.[1]

However, the ghost is that which, paradoxically, is evident in its fading. Marjorie Garber, in *Shakespeare's Ghost Writers*, provides another definition of the ghost: 'It is a memory trace. It is the sign of something missing, something omitted, something undone.'[2] In its role as a 'trace', as a presence pointing toward an absence, as an empty presence, the ghost functions as the paradigmatic deconstructive gesture, as that which reverses and ultimately displaces the hierarchical binary oppositions of presence/absence, life/death, speech/writing, voice/silence, and as that which unseats the linear progression of time. In the algebraic formula Mulligan suggests whereby Stephen supposedly demonstrates that 'Hamlet's grandson is Shakespeare's grandfather and that he himself is the ghost of his own father' (p. 18), the ghost is the mathematical empty set, the set of brackets containing an absence. And in this role of empty set, as the problematic entity destabilising oppositional categories, the ghost becomes a powerful overarching metaphor for Joyce's text as a whole. Far beyond the appearance of 'actual' ghosts, Joyce's text is 'haunted' by ghosts on every level; from the microscopic level of the individual word to the macroscopic level of the text as singular object, Joyce's text is a story about and filled with ghosts.

DA

Eliot's thunder rings out across the wasteland, promising renewal and regeneration for arid plains and thirsting lives. The coming rain, like tears, will begin the gradual healing process. Not a drowning, not a drifting, not a forgetting, but the melancholy acceptance of the past, of pain, of suffering – an experience to remember and from which to learn. The memory of death will inspire life, the recollection of dearth will foster fecundity. Fragments of splintered lives will recoalesce as the thunder instructs how to restore meaning to existence and how to re-establish connections with others: *Datta, Dayadhvam, Damyata.* Give. Sympathise. Control.[3]

The thunder speaks and yet, as Jewel Brooker and Joseph Bentley remind us, the thunder actually says nothing; not until the event of the thunder is perceived and interpreted is meaning imposed. Even the 'empty' representation 'DA' is not the real, the thing-in-itself, but an onomatopoeia, a linguistic formulation which both displaces and recalls the unrepresentable real of the event itself. DA is a ghost, a mark of absence that gestures toward but always falls short of the thing itself, the event which it can never contain.

If we now summon forth the ghost of Freud, as well as that of Lacan (as if we could summon the latter without the former), we realise that the thunder speaks DA because it can say nothing else.

In Lacan's interpretation of Freud's famous story in *Beyond the Pleasure Principle* of the young child and the reel, the utterance of 'da' is truly thunderous.[4] Kaja Silverman details that, as the binary counterpart to the unary '*fort*', 'da' initiates the creation of meaning, the exclusion of the drives, the formation of the unconscious, the emergence of the subject into the symbolic order, and the inauguration of desire.[5] The fullness of the thunder can be represented only by a linguistic sign, a representation pointing to the lack of the thing itself. All words are ghosts, empty shells pointing toward the mythical fullness of the experience of the thing-in-itself.[6]

The voice of the thunder, the realisation of lack, the entrance into the symbolic order of language, effects the 'ghosting' of the subject; in Lacanian terminology (or is it Stephen's?), the subject *fades* under the weight of the signifying chain[7] and 'is subordinated to a symbolic order that will henceforth entirely determine its identity and desires'.[8] Born into and positioned by language, the subject's entrance into the symbolic order is a traumatic break with the fullness of the imaginary register.

The emergence of the subject into the symbolic order is concurrent with the inauguration of desire. The subject, partitioned from its own drives, subordinated to a symbolic order that will henceforth entirely determine its identity and desires, discovers itself to be 'castrated',[9] lacking, incomplete. According to Lacan, the inexpressible desire to be affirmed as whole, recognised as complete, underlies every demand. Beneath language exists this inarticulatable desire – the desire of the ghost to be resurrected, reaffirmed, fulfilled.

A.D.

It seems we have entered an underworld, a world where both words and subjects are, in certain respects, ghosts, and where the use of the former effects the 'ghosting' of the latter. Does the speaking subject then constitute a double negative, a negation of a negation thereby constituting an affirmation? Can the 'faded' subject employ signifiers detached from their signifieds to get back to an essential fullness, to 'write' oneself into being? If Hamlet (or Stephen) walks about 'reading the book of himself', is the book fixed and finished or can he, in fact, write the book of himself he himself reads? *Ulysses* puts to the reader the question of the possibility of autobiography, of writing one's own life. In this manner, the question of the ghost is also the question of the artist: is true creation possible? If one is born into and defined (ghosted) by (ghostly) language, if there is no position outside of language, no distanced objective stance, is innovation possible? Can language, which effects a rupture of the self from the drives and instills the sense of lack also be used to overcome this lack? Can fullness be created out of lack?

[...]

'Dear Henry', writes Martha, 'I do not like that other world' (p. 74). Her slip of the pen foregrounds the logocentric conjunction of writing and death. Writing, states Derrida in 'Signature, Event, Context', rather than an extension of presence, is really a rupture in presence – for writing to be writing, it must continue to be readable in the absence of the writer. Writing thus always carries the mark of absence, the taint of death. Yet, the ghost of the dead author, in spite of Barthes's famous pronouncement of the liberation of the reader, returns again and again, lingering in the gaps of the text, hovering over the reader's construction of the text.

Barthes, in 'The Death of the Author', famously attempts to kill off the author, joyously proclaiming the liberation of the reader from the domineering father-figure of authorial intent. Michel Foucault, however, points out that Barthes's last rites have been premature, or rather that the author may be dead, but he is by no means gone. The author returns as a 'ghost', as a spectre haunting the margins of the text. The text will always gesture toward its creation, toward a producer. Yet the author who emerges from the text, who haunts its margins, is not the 'real' person, the existing historical figure in her entirety, but a fiction, an 'author function', a creation produced by the text and the reader.

Reading constitutes a resurrection of sorts, conjuring up an image of the author from across time. And yet it is a resurrection of one that never lived – a new author is created each time the text is interrogated. Stephen's Shakespeare, 'an assessment based on lies, factual distortions, intentional misreadings of the literature and critical notions plagiarised from earlier scholars',[10] certainly differs from the Shakespeare each reader discovers in the individual texts. The ghost of Shakespeare is an 'everchanging form', a fiction recomposed by each reader and theorist.

The figure of Shakespeare however offers the ideal vehicle for raising questions about the authority of the author and the artistic process; as Marjorie Garber details:

> [Shakespeare's] plays can be seen to dramatise questions raised in the authorship controversy: who wrote this? did someone else have a hand in it? is the apparent author the real author? is the official version to be trusted? or are there suppressed stories, hidden messages, other signatures?[11]

Garber explores what she dubs the 'Shakespeare function', the ways in which the figure of Shakespeare has come to 'haunt the culture'.[12] Her conclusion is that the name Shakespeare (like any author function), refers to a concept and a construct rather than an 'actual' historical personage.[13]

But Shakespeare is more than just an author function. Shakespeare as a concept far exceeds the notion of an individual figure writing. Shakespeare, as *The Bard*, exists for much of the Western world as a 'meta-author function', as the muse of English letters, as synonymous with art itself. For, as Stephen considers, 'After God Shakespeare has created most' (p. 204). More than any other author, Shakespeare the person has been effaced by his own fame. The ghost of Shakespeare is thus paradoxically never the ghost of Shakespeare. The ghost is a simulacrum, a repetition without an original. As a metaphor for the Artist in general, the figure of Shakespeare exceeds the boundaries of any single individual. Shakespeare is not *an* author function but *the* author function. His many ghosts all serve to mask the unknowable void which is the truth of the man himself.

DA(d) (or Shakespère)

However, if Stephen's Shakespeare theory tells us very little about Shakespeare the man, it speaks volumes about Stephen Dedalus. Stephen, in the 'Scylla and Charybdis' chapter, struggles with the same questions with which both his Shakespeare and Borges's Shakespeare struggle: the existence of an enduring, consistent self and the possibility of art.

James Maddox writes that '[Stephen's] concern with a perduring self as opposed to a succession of transient selves states in different terms the relation at the heart of the Shakespeare theory: the relation between the past that persists and the past that is left behind'.[14] The relationship that the artist has with the past is very delicate: on the one hand, experience is that from which the artist draws in the act of creation. On the other hand, the past cannot rule the present. The artist must be able to maintain a certain degree of detachment from the events of his own life. The artist thus must live the divided existence described by Cixous of the Christ figure that suffers and the God figure that makes use of the suffering for the purposes of creation.[15]

For his part, Stephen still struggles throughout *Ulysses* to distance himself from his own past enough to make use of it, to bend it to his will. He does not yet have the strength of a Shakespeare to turn his grief and guilt into art. 'History', states Stephen, 'is a nightmare from which I am trying to awake' (p. 34). The Artist is the one who can control the ghosts of her own past. Stephen believes himself able to marshal his forces in this respect: '"You have spoken of the past and its phantoms", Stephen said. "Why think of them? If I call them into life across the waters of Lethe will not the poor ghosts troop to my call?"' (p. 394). However, it is the unsolicited ghosts, those of his mother and father, as well as his schooling and religious background, that threaten to overwhelm Stephen. He can summon ghosts to his command, but he cannot make them go away.

The ostensible focus of Stephen's Shakespeare theory is the relationship between fathers and sons. To the question of 'Who is King Hamlet', Stephen's answer is William Shakespeare himself, not Shakespeare's father John, as some have suggested. This being the case, Hamlet then logically represents Shakespeare's dead son Hamnet, Gertrude represents his wife Anne, and Claudius represents one or both of Shakespeare's brothers who have cuckolded him with Anne. In this scenario, William Shakespeare as King Hamlet is *not* haunted by the ghost of his father and all that the father-function represents: authority, tradition, culture, society, etc. As Stephen puts it, 'No. The corpse of John Shakespeare does not walk the night' (p. 198).

Stephen then continues by explaining how fatherhood itself is 'a legal fiction', founded 'upon incertitude, upon unlikelihood' (p. 199). He concludes that 'Fatherhood, in the sense of conscious begetting, is unknown to man' (p. 199). This certainly seems to be the reaction of a young man attempting to distance/detach himself from his own father. Maddox reads Stephen's insistence that the ghost is not the ghost of Shakespeare's father as 'one of [Stephen's] strongest statements of transcendence: the son can achieve absolute freedom from the father-past'.[16] If this is the point, however, it is quickly subverted two pages later, when the conversation turns to the subject of names.

Shakespeare's father may lie rotting in the grave, but Stephen's father does not. As much as Stephen would like to (or thinks he would like to) be free of the constraints of the past, of his position as son, his own self-consciousness of his name, Dedalus, the name of the father, indicates the extent to which Stephen is trapped by societal constraints. Stephen still feels himself Icarus to his father's Dedalus (p. 202). His desire to distance himself from his father is part of his desire for an independent, coherent self, which Stephen thinks he can attain through his art, i.e., by becoming a 'father' himself. The figure of his father still looms large in his life and Stephen feels the need to deny his father's presence, as he does with much of the present, to 'free' himself from certain societal constraints.

However, the name of the father, according to Lacan, is exactly that from which the subject cannot free himself; it is the 'notion of the father' that serves as the pre-eminent *point de capiton*, the primary anchoring point buttoning down the subject's signifying chain and thereby allowing it to take on a relatively fixed meaning.'[17] According to Jonathan Scott Lee,

> The name that the child learns to speak properly and to take as his own through the resolution of the Oedipus complex is '*the name of the father*' (*le nom de père*). ... It is the child's acceptance of a particular signifier which confers upon him an identity (that bound up with the father's name [nom]) and also signifies the child's recognition of the prohibition of incest (the father's 'no' [non]) and of the father's standing as 'the figure of the law'.[18]

Stephen, in fighting against his own name, is engaged in an impossible struggle to free himself from culture. He needs not to forget his father, but to accept his father and thereby accept his own limited autonomy as a subject born into and constituted by language.

Shakesmère

The more horrific figure for Stephen, and the 'true' ghost of Joyce's text, is the spectre of Stephen's mother. May Dedalus née Goulding (*Ghoul*-ding), in typical ghost fashion, appears again and again to

Stephen in dreams, thoughts, and hallucinations – an agent of the past, of Stephen's psyche, come to remind him of his failures of filial devotion and transgressions of cultural imperatives.[19] The appearance of the ghost in this respect serves as a symptom, the manifestation of psychic conflict, including guilt, as well as repressed wishes and desires, which have not yet been 'worked through'.[20]

Cixous writes that 'The ghost is in fact one who is represented in this world by the power of the speaking voice'.[21] May Dedalus, however, contrary to the usual appearances of spectres, is not defined in Stephen's dream recollections by ambiguous form and commanding voice, but by quite the reverse. She comes to Stephen in all her appearances excepting 'Circe', 'silently', and is defined not by her recognisable voice (as is Hamlet *père*), but by an intense *physicality*, an overwhelming sensuality; she is nothing but flesh and bones, air and fluids; her breath smells of wetted ashes, bile trickles from her mouth, and her body smells of the wax which Bloom indicates is used to seal up the orifices of the dead (p. 95). She is *body*: scant, lank hair, toothless mouth, 'bluecircled hollow eyesockets' (p. 539). Her 'wasted body', emaciated, garbed as it is in its 'loose graveclothes', recalls the 'famished ghosts' of Ulysses's sojourn into the underworld (and Bloom's musings [p. 163]), who require blood to speak. Indeed, in as much as we can attribute the line 'Ghoul! Chewer of corpses!' (p. 10) to Stephen, the ghost of his mother appears as a cannibal ghost, one who has come to devour Stephen. In this respect, the figure of the ghost and the vampire merge in the mother, as Stephen conjoins the two in his poem on the beach in 'Proteus'.

However, the attribution of the line 'Ghoul! Chewer of corpses!' to Stephen is more uncertain than it may first appear, followed immediately as it is by another indented line unambiguously uttered by Stephen: 'No, mother. Let me be and let me live.' (p. 10). Stephen in this line seems to be responding to the prior line, rejecting the epithets of ghoul and chewer of corpses seemingly attributed to him. After all, the mother is the corpse, later to appear noseless (chewed). The ambiguity surrounding the epithet 'chewer of corpses' (which later will be unambiguously applied by Stephen to his mother in 'Circe' [p. 541]), must give us pause to stop and consider who indeed is the vampire that appears on the beach in Stephen's poem.

The embraced woman is both Woman, in the sense of the archetypal woman, as well as, as Maddox points out, Stephen's mother,

May Dedalus.[22] It seems somewhat of a critical commonplace to assume that the vampire that comes to embrace her is a poetic figuration of death itself. However, is it not Stephen who harbours a certain guilt for having killed his mother? Like the vampire, Stephen is the figure who comes across the water, back from Paris, to the bedside of his dying mother and, once there, refuses to grant her dying wish, the disappointment of which perhaps hastened her demise. As Mulligan is quick to remind him in 'Telemachus'. 'The aunt thinks you killed your mother ...' (p. 5). 'Someone killed her', Stephen replies as Mulligan's chastisement for Stephen's refusal to pray for his dying mother elicits Stephen's recollection of the ghost dream. From this perspective, Stephen is the vampire who has drained the life out of his mother and the emphasis on the ghost of his mother as repulsive body manifests, in disguised form, Stephen's repressed desire for the carnal encounter, for the 'mouth to her mouth's kiss (p. 47).[23]

Stephen is also depicted as a vampire in another sense: as child drawing life and sustenance from the body of the mother: 'She had loved his weak watery blood drained from her own' (p. 28), 'with her weak blood and wheysour milk she had fed him ...' (p. 28). Throughout, the mother as flesh, as body, is associated with fluids: blood, milk, bile. And woman as flesh, as nature, is by extension related to the sea: 'Tides, myriadislanded, within her ... a winedark sea' (p. 47). In the same way that the moon controls the tides, the cyclical nature of the moon is related to the woman's menstrual cycle. Blood and water come together in the image of the 'winedark sea'. Bile and water equally are connected with woman, with the mother, by Stephen's association of the ring of the bay holding a 'dull green mass of liquid' (p. 6) with the white china bowl of 'sluggish green bile' by his mother's deathbed. However, it is Mulligan who makes the connection between the sea, body fluids, and male sexuality on the second page of the text, juxtaposing 'the snotgreen sea' with 'the scrotum-tightening sea' (p. 5).

Stephen's mother, as body and fluids, as sensual, and yet as agent of order, or the law, is exactly that which both repels and attracts Stephen. Benstock describes the ghost of Stephen's mother as 'typifying the strictures of motherhood and Catholicism which threaten to trap Stephen's soul',[24] and her appearance in 'Circe', commanding Stephen to repent and to 'Beware! God's hand!' (p. 541) certainly fulfils this description. Yet, May Dedalus is not an angel descended from Heaven; she does not promise Stephen a glorious afterlife of the soul if he returns to the mandates of Catholicism. The ghost of Stephen's mother is rather a figuration of death and decomposition, of mortality and sensuality. She signifies to Stephen not the immortality of the soul, but the physicality of the body; her ambiguous statement, 'All must go through it, Stephen. More women than men in the world. You too. Time will come' (p. 540), ostensibly relates to death but also suggests sexual intercourse. The line 'More women than men in the world' points toward the latter interpretation, as does the reference back to Stephen's question in 'Scylla and Charybdis', 'And my turn? When?' (p. 183).

Thus, Stephen's mother appears, commanding him to repent, ostensibly for refusing to pray at her bedside, for renouncing his religion, but also, on a deeper level, for his attraction to the sensual, and, if one accepts Freud, for the repressed incestuous desire. Stephen's reaction formation, his psychological defence to avoid recognising his lust for the sensual, is to be repulsed by the physical. His insecurity with his own split persona, his fear that the self is merely a chain of 'flickering serial manifestations' rather than an 'enduring entity',[25] prohibits him from embracing the present world of sensual experience and dissolution in the moment that it offers. Stephen is afraid of losing himself through connecting with another, hence his solipsism and extreme reflexive consciousness.

To bolster his insecure walls of selfhood, Stephen must reject all that threatens to overwhelm him, to make him forget himself. Thus, the sensual, the fleshy, the carnal must be eschewed, resisted, denied. The body of his mother becomes a vile, repulsive form, and water, which he associates with woman, must be avoided. Yet Stephen, as much as he fears the flesh, also longs for the sensual and for connection. This comes out not only in his stray thought of 'And my turn? When?' but most evidently on the beach in 'Proteus', after his vampire vision.

Shortly after envisioning the vampire locked in an embrace with a woman, arguably his mother, Stephen thinks to himself, 'Touch me. Soft eyes. Soft soft soft hand. I am lonely here. O, touch me soon, now. What is that word known to all men? I am quiet here alone. Sad too. Touch, touch me' (p. 48). He seems to remember the answer to the question 'What is that word known to all men?' in 'Scylla and Charybdis' before again asking it of his mother in the 'Circe' vision. In addition to this conjunction of the vampire's kiss, Stephen's desire to be touched, and his attempt to elicit the word love from his mother, to the extent that one wishes to cast Stephen in the role of the melancholy Prince (an association he himself makes in the same paragraph with the vampire vision noting his own 'Hamlet hat'), the notion of Stephen harbouring an incestuous wish toward his mother is a possible interpretation. The vampire is a figure of death, but it is also Stephen-in-death, Stephen giving in to his own repressed sensual desires, Stephen giving the kiss of death to his own mother. The vampire is his artistic creation, a part of himself emerging from his subconscious and expressing the forbidden wish, the desire for the carnal, the desire for the mother.

While the ghost of John Shakespeare does not walk the night, the ghost of May Dedalus most certainly does; however, it is not that she won't stay buried, but that Stephen, as the 'thirsty fox' who probably killed his grand-mother (p. 521) will not leave her buried, but scrapes and scrapes up the earth (p. 28), commanding her to appear again and again. In contrast to the figure of Simon Dedalus, against whom Stephen struggles to construct his own independent identity, May Dedalus, as the figure of motherhood and Catholicism, incarnates Stephen's guilt at betraying his up-bringing, at having moved too far away from the cultural expectations of how he should act, and at entertaining sensual desires. Stephen is trapped between two poles, the need to distance himself from his culture and his guilt at doing so. The return of his mother seems to support Mulligan's assertion that Stephen can never be a poet, that 'They drove his wits astray ... by visions of hell' (p. 239). The question of whether Stephen can ever be an artist, can ever know '[t]he joy of creation' (p. 239), depends upon whether or not he can put the ghosts of his parents to rest.

Stephen, of course, is not the only major character to be 'haunted' by ghosts; Bloom as well has his visits from the dead. In many ways, the ghost of Bloom's son Rudy is one of the most important presences hovering over Bloom's life and the text as a whole. Bloom's period of abstinence with Molly dates back to the death of Rudy and, if one correlates Leopold and Molly's sexual dissatisfaction with Bloom's fear of having and losing another child, then the death of Rudy is the touchstone leading to the events of Bloom's day on June 16th.

Although there are frequent references to Rudy throughout the text, Bloom has only one 'real' vision of Rudy; at the end of 'Circe', after having acted paternally in aiding and defending the intoxicated and distracted Stephen, Bloom is 'graced' with a vision of his son, who has aged as if naturally. Other than the fact that Bloom is 'wonderstruck', his reaction is not recorded by Joyce.

Bloom's vision of Rudy seems straight-forward (or at least as straight-forward as anything in *Ulysses* can be!). Bloom, who demonstrates tender and paternal feelings toward Stephen, has acted the role of the father. Stephen's face reminds Bloom of the former's 'poor mother', and the chain of associations leads him to think of his own dead son Rudy. That the vision is benign, if not happy, suggests a contrast with Stephen's visions of his dead mother. Bloom, who has played the role of the father and reached out to a younger man with tender paternal feelings, is granted a calm vision which seems to suggest that he may be able to overcome the trauma of his own child's death.

Intriguingly, Rudy, in the vision, is smiling over, reading, and kissing a book. Since the book is being read from right to left, it is written in Hebrew, thus connecting the son Rudy with the ghosts of Bloom's childhood by way of his renounced Judaism. Indeed, the Rudy 'of the book' at the end of the 'Circe' chapter is tied to the figure of Bloom's father, Rudolph, who appears at the start of the chapter 'garbed in the long caftan of an elder in Zion' (p. 416), speaks with a stereotypical Jewish accent, and plays the equally stereotypical role of Jewish miser. Both ghosts, father and son, seem to function as 'signposts', as sentries guarding the perimeters of Nighttown. Bloom's father appears to warn him off, his son appears to welcome him back; both are ghosts, paralleling Stephen's situation with his mother, that Bloom must put to rest if he wishes to re-establish (or perhaps in Bloom's case simply establish) self-control.

If there is one character in the text as a whole whom one would expect to return as a ghost from a traditional folkloric perspective, it is Bloom's father, the suicide. The subject carelessly having been brought up in the carriage on the way to the cemetery, Bloom himself observes how suicides are excluded from the sanctified space of the graveyard and 'they used to drive a stake of wood through his heart in the grave' (p. 93). The suicide, having committed the hubristic act of unmaking, of thwarting God's design, is the figure in many folklore traditions most likely to rest uneasily, most likely to return from the grave as either a ghost or vampire (hence the stake of wood through the heart).[26]

However, Bloom is not bothered noticeably by the ghost of his father in the way that the trauma surrounding the death of his son seems to govern the momentum of the text. The admonitory figure of the father, as well as that of Bloom's mother, Ellen, who plays even less of a role in the text, are quickly bypassed, left behind, in Bloom's descent into Nighttown. Perhaps this is a function of Bloom's unwillingness to engage anxiety-producing subject matter, of his 'closeness to the physical world' which 'robs him of his ability to conceptualise his own fate and thereby redirect it effectively'.[27] In contrast to Stephen, who is afraid to give himself over to the sensual world, Bloom is the hedonist who enjoys spicy food and sexual excitation. However, if Bloom is 'held by the perception of sheer process itself',[28] the hold is tenuous; Bloom gives himself over to sensual events as distractions, as ways to avoid dealing with the deep-seated traumas of his personal life. He is constantly crossing the street to avoid Boylan or forcing himself to think of subjects other than Molly's suspected infidelity. As soon as the forbidden thought pops into Bloom's head, he actively changes the subject so as not to have to deal with the discomforting material.

There is, however, no hiding in Nighttown. Like a light sleeper, periodically disturbed and influenced by events in the waking world, Bloom fantasises and the reader descends with him again and again into the depths of his subconscious, where repressed desires and fears seethe and bubble. The figures of Bloom's parents are on the surface, as it were, generic and generally ineffective guilt figures, (representing both Judaism and Catholicism, two great traditions of guilt!) that fail to maintain any hold on Bloom; they are quickly left behind in the descent toward the darker, colder depths.

In as much as all Stephen's and Bloom's ghosts are generated from their unconsciouses, as the ghost always functions as symptom for some unresolved trauma, Nighttown is a world of ghosts, a true underworld, the analysis of which would necessitate much more time and space than is available to me here. I do however draw a (perhaps contestable) distinction between the ghost characters I have examined, Stephen's father and mother, Bloom's son and parents, and the majority of the other phantoms that appear in 'Circe', in that the figures I have addressed represent 'real-world' characters with whom Stephen or Bloom had blood relationships and who have died (with the exception of Stephen's father who is a ghost by absence). Presumably, these relationships (son/mother, father/son, etc.) have been especially formative in the lives of Stephen and Bloom and thus deserve somewhat more attention than many of the individual phantoms of 'Circe' which traipse across the page in seemingly endless succession. In any case, an analysis of all the phantom figures in 'Circe' is beyond the scope of this essay.

Starting at the level of the individual word, this essay has spiralled progressively outwards considering how Stephen's Shakespeare is haunted, and then considering the ghosts haunting Stephen himself, as well as Bloom. Having moved from word to character, the final level that now needs to be addressed is that of the text as a whole. Our final ghost will be that of Joyce himself.

While many critics suggest that Joyce actively inserted himself into his own text, most notably in the guise of the mysterious thirteenth mourner, M'Intosh,[29] Brook Thomas makes the more salient point that

> ... the ghostly presence of creator Joyce presiding over his creation is everywhere felt or, should we say, heard. Just as Shakespeare returns to *Hamlet* as the voice of the ghost, so Joyce calls attention to his return through the increasingly obtrusive narrative voices that dominate the second half of the book. It is through these stylistic capers that Joyce finds a way to haunt the world of *Ulysses*.[30]

Thomas is correct in his observation that the stylistic gymnastics of *Ulysses* call attention away from the content of the pages to the text *qua* text, to the text as constructed object. Marilyn French comments in reference to the 'Sirens' chapter (though the comment, with slight modifications is generalisable to the text as a whole), that,

> By using language that is for the most part recognisable English and recognisable syntactic units, yet arranging those units so that they make no sense at all, Joyce is again thrusting in the reader's face the arbitrariness of language, the void at its core ... The reader begins to feel that he is being treated high-handedly by a malicious ringmaster.[31]

And it is Joyce, the author, the creator, that is this ringmaster, the ghostly presence directing the whole show.

Or rather, it is Joyce the author *function* that manifests itself in the gaps and margins of the text. Benstock concurs with Thomas that it is the ghost of Joyce that hovers over the text, writing,

> ... Stephen argues that the ghosts in *Hamlet* are Shakespeare's personal ghosts, and that the process of writing the play is an attempt of exorcism; by extension we may conclude, I think, that Joyce has written the book of himself in *Ulysses* (that the ghosts which populate it are personal ones) ... [32]

Yet, if Stephen's Shakespeare theory teaches us anything, it is that we must be careful in reading back from the text to the person. Joyce has not written *the* book of himself, but *a* book of himself. Even *Ulysses*, in all its depth, does not contain all of Joyce, the essential Joyce (if such a thing can be said ever to have existed).

And Joyce, as author function haunting the text, is not a ghost that exists independently of the reader. Cixous writes that 'it is the work that writes the author, the creation that guarantees the existence of the creator ... '.[33] However, she discounts the complicity of the reader in this process of author creation. Just as, as Edward Duncan, citing Edmund Wilson, notes, Stephen's Shakespeare theory 'has little to do with Shakespeare, but a good deal to do with Stephen himself',[34] the reader/critic's 'Joyce theory' invariably is imbricated with his or her own prejudices, bias, interpretive strategies, etc. Just as the ghost is always a subconscious projection, a symptom, a psychic manifestation, so too is the author. This explains, at least in part, why the language of ghosts and hauntings lends itself so readily (as evinced in the Thomas and Benstock quotations above) to discussions of the author's 'presence' in the text itself.

DaDa?

The problem we are now left with is the very expansiveness of the ghost metaphor itself. If signifiers are ghosts by virtue of their separation from their signifieds, if humans are metaphorical ghosts by virtue of their 'fading' beneath the signifying chain, i.e. by life, as well as by death, absence, and 'change of manners', if memories are ghosts and authors are ghosts – what isn't a ghost? If language, as well as humans, memories, and authors (subsets of language), are all ghosts, what value does such an amorphous and expansive designation maintain?

The answers to these questions lie in the fact that the application of the term 'ghost' to words, to humans, to memories and authors, is merely the metaphorical extension of a term which has certain specific meanings. The 'primary' contemporary definition of the term remains 'a disembodied soul; *esp*: the soul of a dead person believed to be an inhabitant of the unseen world or to appear to the living in a bodily likeness'.[35] To the extent that this definition connotes incompleteness, absence, death, and 'fading', the term becomes generalisable to a broad spectrum of phenomena. If we accept this definition of the term ghost, words, humans, memories, authors, are not really ghosts, but the desire to call them so reveals something about our perceptions of the world and the human condition. I have argued throughout that ghosts are projections, symptoms pointing to repressed traumas. The disappointed bridging of the ghost between worlds points to a crime to be redressed, an act still to be performed, a failed burial. Where we see ghosts, we must dig for the body.

Ulysses finally is a ghoststory because it self-conciously dramatises the uncertainty and lack at the core of the human subject. As French observes, '*Ulysses* is an epic of relativity. The games played with language undermine every apparent certitude. Every act occurs in the void, every person lives there'.[36] The body of the text gestures toward not only the absent body of Joyce, but the profusion of quotations, allusions, and references which compose the text summon into being a host of other authors and historical figures – the 'return of the expressed', as Garber cleverly phrases it.[37] Daniel Ferrer even considers how each word of the 'Circe' chapter acts as a ghost. He writes:

> ... Every word in 'Circe' has its own past and must be considered, individually, as a kind of ghost, haunting the text, returning with a whole network of associations, woven during its previous occurrences in *Ulysses*. Each sentence recalls a host of other sentences which are superimposed upon it, and which, in turn, recall yet more sentences.[38]

The text thus dialogically exceeds its boundaries, pointing toward a multitude of other written works, and internally subverts a linear progression, as the reappearance of words sends the reader off on a tangent, back toward another context and part of the book.

DA

The ghosts of words and the ghosts of authors lead us back finally to Eliot's wasteland and the ghost of the real. *Ulysses*, as an 'epic of relativity', reminds us that although we can approach any given object from an unlimited number of perspectives, we can never capture the thing-in-itself, the essence of the object. All knowledge is mediated through a particular mode of perception from a particular standpoint. Thus, the thunder speaks and, in the hospital refectory, Stephen and Bloom listen to what it says. The usually controlled Stephen cowers as the voice of nature commands him to give in to the experience of the moment, to embrace the flesh he so abhors, to revel in the sensual coolness of the rain upon his parched lips. Stephen is not yet able to hear the thunder, to breach his solipsistic circle, to give, to sympathise, to love. The thunder unnerves him.

Stephen, however, is comforted by another who also hears the thunder. Bloom, the new apostle to the gentiles, the one who speaks the word known to all men, who gives in to the moment and sympathises with others, stands by and attempts to comfort the anxious Stephen. To Bloom however, the thunder speaks *damyata*, control. Bloom, who floats along on a tide of sensations and memories, seeks the controlled reflection that Stephen has in abundance.

Finally, the thunder speaks three things, and many things, and nothing all at once. Bloom and Stephen, haunted by their ghosts, ghosted themselves by their entrance into the symbolic register, riddled by lack, take their place in text without a centre, a presence pointing toward an absence and multiple absences: a ghoststory.

From *Journal of the Fantastic in the Arts*, 8:3 (1997), 347–69.

Notes

[Jeffrey Weinstock's essay argues that the significance of ghosts in *Ulysses* encompasses much more than the souls of dead persons. It sets out to demonstrate that in its role as a trace, a presence pointing towards an absence, ghosts become a deconstructive gesture in Joyce's novel that challenges the hierarchical binary oppositions of presence and absence, life and death, speech and writing, voice and silence as well as linear notions of time. At the same time, ghosts remind the subjects of the text of their entanglement with and subjection under signification, which is ultimately ruled by the ghostly 'name of the father'. Creation and autonomy thus become impossible challenges, yet also the driving forces behind the movements and motivations of characters in the novel. All page references to *Ulysses* are to the Oxford World's Classics edition, ed. Jeri Johnson (1993). Ed.]

1. For more on metaphors of incompleteness, see James H. Maddox Jr, *Joyce's 'Ulysses' and the Assault upon Character* (New Brunswick, NJ, 1978), p. 177.

2. Marjorie Garber, *Shakespeare's Ghost Writers: Literature as Uncanny Causality* (New York, 1987), p. 129.

3. I recognise that there are more nihilistic readings of *The Waste Land.* My own interpretation is that the thunder and its promise of rain support optimistic prospects for rejuvenation.

4. Freud recounts his observation of his grandson engaged in a repetitive game with a wooden reel with a piece of string tied around it. The child would hold on to the string and toss the reel out of sight, while uttering 'o-o-o-o', which Freud interprets as 'fort', the German word for 'gone'. The child would then pull the string and hail the reappearance of the reel with a joyful 'da', German for 'there'. See Sigmund Freud, *On Metapsychology: The Theory of Psychoanalysis*, trans. James Strachey, ed. Angela Richards, Pelican Freud Library, 11 (London, 1984), pp. 283–7.

5. Kaja Silverman, *The Subject of Semiotics* (New York, 1983), pp. 167–74. As detailed by Silverman, Lacan refers to '*fort*' as the solitary signifier, as a signifier which 'as yet lacks any paradigmatic or syntagmatic "company" – as the "unary" signifier' (p. 170). The unary signifier does not participate in meaning because there is neither a linguistic system nor a discourse to support it. 'It is both nonsensical and irreducible – nonsensical because there is no other signifier into which it can be translated, or to which it can be referred, and irreducible because it does not represent it, cannot be reduced to the drives' (pp. 170–1). When the child utters '*da*', however, the situation is altogether different, since it refers back to '*fort*'. Lacan refers to this second signifier as the 'binary' and attributes it to the momentous results indicated above. A closed system of language based on endless displacements and substitutions is established, a system in which there are no positive values, only differences. Since the binary signifier refers back to the unary signifier instead of the drives, it effects a complete rupture with them, which Lacan describes as the ' "fading" of the subject's being in the face of its meaning' (p. 171).

6. Maud Ellmann makes a similar point, 'The ghost, then, could be seen as the first pure symbol in that it bespeaks the absence rather than the presence of its referent; just as language recreates its objects in their absence, both affirming and denying their propensity to disappear. In this sense, words are the ghosts of things, their chattering afterlife'; 'The Ghosts of Ulysses', in *James Joyce: The Artist and the Labyrinth*, ed. Augustine Martin (London, 1990), pp. 193–227 (p. 197).

7. Jacques Lacan, *Four Fundamental Concepts of Psychoanalysis*, trans. Alan Sheridan, ed. Jacques-Alain Miller (New York, 1978), p. 62.

8. Silverman, *Subject of Semiotics*, p. 172.

9. Here, as throughout the essay, I use the term 'castration' in the Lacanian psychoanalytic sense of the situation of the speaker of language riddled by lack. To the extent that speech is viewed by Lacan as a metonymic attempt to cover a constitutive lack in the subject, all

human speech, as noted by Jonathan Scott Lee, is 'figuratively linked to the phallus as the central *point de capiton* ["buttoning point", a signifier that "fixes" the meaning of a signifying chain] of our discourse'; *Jacques Lacan* (Amherst, MA, 1990), p. 67. Kaja Silverman observes that the term 'phallus' (which assumes discursive rather than biological status) is used by Lacan to designate 'all those values opposed to lack', *Subject of Semiotics*, pp. 182–3. She continues:

> ... the phallus is a signifier for those things which have been partitioned off from the subject during the various stages of its constitution, and which will never be restored to it, all of which could be summarised as 'fullness of being'. ... Lacan stresses in particular the castrating effect of language, associating the phallus with those losses inflicted by signification ... The phallus is ... a signifier for the organic reality or needs which the subject relinquishes in order to achieve meaning, in order to gain access to the symbolic register. It signifies that thing whose loss inaugurates desire. (p. 183)

10. Shari Benstock, '*Ulysses* as Ghoststory', *James Joyce Quarterly*, 12 (Summer 1975), 396–413 (397).
11. Garber, *Shakespeare's Ghost Writers*, p. 26
12. Ibid., p. xii.
13. Ibid., p. 175.
14. Maddox, *Joyce's 'Ulysses'*, p. 196.
15. Hélène Cixous, *The Exile of James Joyce*, trans. Sally A. Purcell (New York, 1972), pp. 579–82.
16. Maddox, *Joyce's 'Ulysses'*, p. 105.
17. Lacan, *Four Fundamental Concepts*, p. 304.
18. Lee, *Lacan*, pp. 64–5.
19. Maud Ellmann also identifies the ghost of May as a guilt figure intertwined with desire, writing '[Stephen] has not yet murdered his mother sufficiently to rid his mind of the tormenting image of her wasting flesh. It is in "Circe" that the mother he has tried to murder, first with silence, then with words rises up to teach him *amor matris* and remind him of love's bitter mystery'; 'Ghosts of Ulysses', p. 213.
20. One such 'repressed desire' which suggests itself (as noted above), given the loose psychoanalytic framework governing this interrogation of ghosts and the hyperpresence of May's body as a source of both revulsion and desire for Stephen, is the Oedipal desire for the incestuous encounter. That Stephen at times consciously considers himself a Hamlet figure, and that critics have positioned him as such, reinforces such a reading given the frequent attention to Hamlet's own unresolved sexual conflict towards Gertrude.

21. Cixous, *Exile*, p. 495.

22. Maddox, *Joyce's 'Ulysses'*, p. 40.

23. Vampires are, of course, among the most sexual of supernatural creatures. The encounter with the vampire involves bodily contact and penetration – mouth on flesh – and the exchange of bodily fluid. Regardless of the extent to which one is willing to consider Stephen in the place of the vampire, Stephen is imagining a sexually-charged scene with a persistent emphasis on the kiss, which subsequently elicits his own desire to be touched.

24. Benstock, '*Ulysses*', p. 401.

25. Maddox, *Joyce's 'Ulysses'*, p. 34.

26. Some vampire myths require that the stake be made of wood from an ash tree, suggestive both of Stephen's ash plant walking stick, which he uses to ward off the ghost of his mother in 'Circe', and of the ghost of his mother, who smells of 'wetted ashes' (p. 5).

27. Maddox, *Joyce's 'Ulysses'*, p. 45.

28. Ibid., p. 64.

29. See Brook Thomas, *James Joyce's 'Ulysses': A Book of Many Happy Returns* (Baton Rouge, LA, 1982), p. 74 and Marilyn French, *The Book as World: James Joyce's 'Ulysses'* (New York, 1976), p. 192.

30. Thomas, *Joyce's 'Ulysses'*, p. 69.

31. French, *Book as World*, p. 128.

32. Benstock, '*Ulysses*', p. 406.

33. Cixous, *Exile*, p. 586.

34. Edward Duncan, 'Unsubstantial Father: A Study of the *Hamlet* Symbolism in Joyce's *Ulysses*', *University of Toronto Quarterly*, 2 (January 1950), 126–40 (127).

35. *Webster's Ninth New Collegiate Dictionary* (Springfield, MA, 1988), p. 516.

36. French, *Book as World*, p. 17.

37. Garber, *Shakespeare's Ghost Writers*, p. 52.

38. Daniel Ferrer, 'Circe, Regret and Regression', in Derek Attridge and Daniel Ferrer (eds), *Post-structuralist Joyce: Essays from the French* (New York, 1984), pp. 127–44 (p. 133).

4

Nobody at Home: Bloom's Outlandish Retreat in the 'Cyclops' Episode of *Ulysses*

ADAM WOODRUFF

As Seamus Deane has commented, Joyce's largely self-cultivated apolitical image has helped to obscure both his keen interest in Irish politics and the fictive nature of his political imagination.[1] What passes for apathy might be better described as disillusionment: for, in the words of David Fitzpatrick, 'if revolutions are what happens to wheels, then Ireland underwent a revolution between 1916 and 1922 ... social and political institutions were turned upside down, only to revert to full circle upon the establishment of the Irish Free State'.[2] Joyce's general approval of Arthur Griffith and the anti-parliamentarianist Sinn Féin had been tempered (from at least as early as 1906) by Griffith's cautious appeasement of the Church, and the rhetoric of venereal contamination characteristic of the *United Irishman*'s robust polemics.[3] However, Joyce's supposed indifference to the Irish struggle for independence (whether a conflation of authorial and textual politics or a projection of Stephen's '*non serviam*' onto the author), his apparent distance from the Irish Literary Revival, and the presumedly disinterested character of his work have faced increasing critical scrutiny, led by a wave of postcolonial studies.[4] As Deane remarks, paradoxically 'Joyce remained faithful to the original conception of the Revival. His Dublin became the Holy City of which Yeats had despaired.'[5] But despite some warm early reviews of *Ulysses*, Joyce was more than a little wary of making a return to that Holy City he had reconstructed through memories from afar – fearing (apart from the risk of entanglement in factional violence) that he might, like Parnell, suffer quicklime thrown in his eyes for his novel's controversial acclaim.[6]

In the light of this insight, it is tempting to gesture with automatic hand towards Freud's contemporaneous essay 'The "Uncanny"'.[7] Who is that 'Sandman' waiting for Joyce in the Holy City? However pertinent the threat to Joyce's ailing eyesight may have been, his reconstruction of Dublin from memory in exile is brimming with bogeymen for Bloom and Stephen – Mr Deasy, Blazes Boylan, Mackintosh, the Citizen, Bella/Bello, Private Carr – who interchange, blur and ultimately seem to exceed the demands of the novel's Homeric and Christian symbolic frameworks. Most of these characters are either implicitly or explicitly linked to the overbearing British colonial presence: Stephen's senior Mr Deasy, a Unionist, holds forth with platitudes about the virtues of British civilisation (pp. 30–3); Blazes Boylan's father is rumoured to have sold horses to the British (twice over) during the Boer War (p. 306); the obscure Mackintosh pops up in the New Bloomusalem to denounce Bloom as a 'notorious fire-raiser' (p. 458); later on in 'Circe', the 'despot' Bello engages Bloom as 'bondslave' in a sado-masochistic hallucinogenic fantasy (p. 498); and backed up by an apparition of Tennyson, Private Carr metes out violent punishment to Stephen in the name of King Edward the Seventh (p. 553). However, one notable exception to this trend is the 'Cyclops' episode, where the Citizen's repeated oscillation between patriotism and racism lends the novel an air of political as well as religious profanity.

If *Ulysses* shifts across political divides in its depiction of cynicism, profiteering and bigotry, then the excessive licentiousness of these prominent figures suggests something more than an attempt to see both sides of the story. Moreover, if *Ulysses* is laced with the full range of uncanny motifs detailed in Freud's study of Hoffmann's tale – ghosts, doubles, eerie premonitions and repetitions, the phallic satyr and the blind stripling – then it is important to remember the distinctions and qualifications that Freud makes: Homer's 'jovial world of gods' cannot be considered uncanny by any stretch of the imagination, and no ghost, though it scares its fictional counterparts witless, can withstand a sustained onslaught of authorial irony.[8] The spectres of *Ulysses* (which appear to be less the *victims* of the novel's multiform irony than the *products* of it) are of course possessed of limited capacity to unsettle long before the carnivalesque crescendo of 'Circe' is reached. That more privileged version of the uncanny featuring the robbing of eyesight, and (as a return of repressed infantile complexes) crucially dissociated by Freud from belief,[9] has perhaps a greater resonance with the uncanny facets of the novel, but the question of who this implied threat of castration might make more disturbing reading for remains. Perhaps the genuinely uncanny feature of the text is rather its very acknowledgement of its incompleteness, of its (permanent) destination in future readings from which, rather than from an assumed past, its symptomatic fragments and silences return.

The very unsettling force of the novel in general – and of the 'Cyclops' episode in particular – can be located in the way that it stages those processes of national identification which allow certain citizens, but not others, to feel *at home*. Joyce is certainly no apologist for British cultural imperialism, but in the same movement (to put it in the terms of Walter Benjamin) he 'views with cautious detachment' the 'cultural treasures' with which Irish nationalism installs its own hegemonic myth of origins.[10] Whether or not Joyce's monadic snapshot of a day in Dublin might have endangered his person (while ultimately reinforcing the nomadic isolation of his artistic persona), *Ulysses* is a novel that refuses to be buried under the dead weight of history, gesturing obscenely at its readers from its 'graveyard of quotations'.[11] As Slavoj Žižek has noted, both '*Ulysses* and *Finnegans Wake* are not simply external to their interpretation but, as it were, in advance take into account their possible interpretations and enter into dialogue with them'.[12]

Narrated by an impersonal figure, the 'Cyclops' episode catches nationalist rhetoric in the act of staging its conflicts of repression. The bar-room of Barney Kiernan's is awash with historical recollection when Bloom arrives: with the Citizen holding court, the talk circles around political events ranging from the contemporary enforced slaughter of cattle with foot-and-mouth disease, to the Invincibles, the Famine and emigration of 1847, Cromwell's mass-murders at Drogheda and beyond. John Wyse Nolan's report on the latest from the 'scene of action' at the City Council Meeting at the City Hall on the Irish language is curtailed by the Citizen's assertion that 'It's on the march' (p. 311). Soon after Bloom's entry into the general discussion, however, he is singled out as the butt of snide remarks and racist stereotyping amplified by the narrator (for example, by the notion that Bloom somehow secretes an odour that repels dogs) (p. 292). When Bloom makes an exit for a short while, his absence is quickly imputed to the collection of funds gained from speculation on the races – the stealthy execution of which would confirm his stereotypical status as a 'Jew' financially shrewd enough to avoid buying a round of drinks, the son of a 'robbing bagman', Virag, who is swiftly indicted for 'swamping the country with his baubles and his penny diamonds' (p. 321). Nolan's defence of Bloom on the grounds of his suggestions to Arthur Griffith (for revelations of British corruption in the *Freeman*) counts for very little with the Citizen and his acolytes. Clearly, Bloom has been allotted a very specific role in the unfolding drama.

As Franco Moretti has pointed out, one of the most curious features of *Ulysses* (and one which contrasts directly with Kafka's novel *The Trial*) is 'precisely the Law Court is absent'.[13] The insignia of colonial rule (such as the 'viceregal cavalcade' in 'Wandering Rocks') appear bloated and ridiculous, commodities and the abundant images of advertisements mingle within the polyphonic babble of countless institutions. However, while Moretti uses this as evidence to ground his premise that a psychoanalytic reading is inappropriate to the study of *Ulysses* (because its stream of consciousness corresponds at best to the neglected Freudian category of the preconscious, and its polyphony manifests an irreducible randomness),[14] the conspicuous laxity of the law can be seen to invite rather than preclude just such a reading. If, as Moretti airily claims, one would be hard pressed to maintain that '*Ulysses* is not frivolous',[15] then its frivolity is certainly tinged with desperate irony rather than contented cynicism. It is perhaps more productive to suggest that the novel's stylistic 'frivolity' recalls Freud's image of an 'unpractical' hysteric crying before a monument to the Great Fire of London, out of step with the amnesiac procession of a 'destiny on the march'.[16]

As Richard Kearney has observed, the literary-historical transposition of Ireland from a fatherland to a motherland parallels the process of Ireland's colonisation, and it is possible to view the spread of idioms connoting the mother as the manifestation of the political unconscious of a lost sovereignty.[17] However, the depiction of a virginal Irish motherhood (epitomised by Caitlain ni Houlihan) threatened by a ravishing invader has never been far removed from images of whoredom and feminine complicity. The remembrance of past events in *Ulysses* – whatever the degree of accuracy – is shown to be governed by the present context of their articulation, and the 'Cyclops' episode implies that the politics of national affiliation are played out in pubs rather than in parliaments: 'A dishonoured wife,' hectors the Citizen, 'that's what's the cause of all our misfortunes' (p. 310).[18]

The motif of an untethered female sexuality rampant in the absence of home rule is of course a recurring theme throughout *Ulysses*: for example, in 'Aeolus', Stephen counters Professor MacHugh's romantic nationalism by offering 'A Pisgah Sight of Palestine', a skit in which two vestal virgins, Anne Kearns and Flo MacCabe, sate their hunger with plums below the statue of 'the one-handled adulterer' Admiral Nelson (pp. 142–3). Stephen's light-hearted attempt to deflate the vision of a Promised Land and Mother Eire conjures up the opposite stereotype of whoredom and mobilises the same mode of representation deployed by Bloom's antagonists in 'Cyclops'; but it is easy to overlook the subtle inflections of narrative form that characterise each section: the clubby banter of the men in 'Aeolus' is arranged under mock newspaper headings, and the drunken quotidian *schadenfreude* of the men inside Barney Kiernan's in the 'Cyclops' episode is amplified by several parodic passages of journalism. At the end of the day Bloom has resisted the urge to assume the role of a jealous husband and sabotage the adulterous liaison of Boylan and Molly, and although one could cite many possible motivations for this stoical reaction (as some critical commentaries have had no hesitation in doing),[19] the novel's constant shifting of focus and perspective prompts a less precipitously speculative response; for whether or not he is correct in supposing that an act of infidelity has taken place, what is certain is that it *will have* taken place in the countless symbolic fictions that structure his waking life.[20] The coupling of degenerate tyranny and complicit betrayal that menaces on the horizon of the nationalist imagination is played out and traversed in the novel, rather than sacrificed to conventions of realist narrative form and aesthetic closure.

The shadowy milieu of Barney Kiernan's, not far from the courthouse, thus forms an alternative domain of law where Bloom stands trial in the kangaroo court of the Citizen. Alf Bergan's unsettling insistence (before Bloom's arrival) that he has just seen the freshly inhumed Paddy Dignam 'not five minutes ago' in Capel Street (p. 288), arising as it does in the wake of the glimpses of Parnell's brother offered by the parallactic narrative of 'Wandering Rocks' is perhaps the episode's clearest reminder that the past events of an individual or a nation are never peacefully laid to rest when they are engraved in memory, where the ghostly signifier *walks abroad*, animated by the exigencies of the present. In a similar manner to the way in which the ritual and rhetoric of mourning conducted by Father Coffey leads to ever more unsavoury visions of Dignam's corpse spilling forth in 'Hades', the recitation of historical grievances presided over by the Citizen in 'Cyclops' seems to stir up an increasingly intemperate series of graphic racist asides:

> – Those are nice things, says the citizen, coming over here to Ireland filling the country with bugs.
> So Bloom lets on he heard nothing and he starts talking with Joe, telling him he needn't trouble about that little matter till the first but if he would just say a word to Mr Crawford. And so Joe swore high and holy by this and by that he'd do the devil and all.
> – Because, you see, says Bloom, for an advertisement you must have repetition. That's the whole secret.
> – Rely on me, says Joe.
> – Swindling the peasants, says the citizen, and the poor of Ireland. We want no more strangers in our house.
>
> (p. 310)

Whilst the Citizen relives the traumas of the past and represents Ireland as a perpetual victim governed by forces beyond its control, the performative movement of this version of events (irrespective of its accuracy) must be simultaneously disavowed, projected as a foreign body. Leopold Bloom, the Jewish advertising agent who embodies ethnic difference as well as the ephemeral commercial concerns of a present crisis of overproduction, is thus a primary target for a rhetoric of essence and belonging condemned to ground itself through a negative frame of reference and ultimately sheer tautology. It is no coincidence that when Bloom tells Joe Hynes 'for an advertisement you must have repetition. That's the whole secret', the Citizen pointedly remarks, 'We want no more strangers in our house'. Cast as the 'blot on the landscape' of a nationalist imagination that substitutes the all too familiar tropes of anti-Semitism for the unutterable conditions of its construction, Bloom embodies a decadent complicity and instability that must be expurgated so that a lost 'Golden Age' of Ireland lamented by the Citizen can be regained.[21]

Bloom's attempts to define a 'nation' to Nolan lead him into the greatest danger. Initially proclaiming that 'A nation is the same people living in the same place', and then adding, in response to mockery from Ned and Joe, 'Or also living in different places'

(p. 317), Bloom lacks the awareness that no amount of rational argument can establish a common ground with the Citizen. Bloom's flawed attempt to appear 'More Irish than the Irish', like the printer Mr Nanetti (p. 115), coupled with his pious quest to implement the renewal of the Keyes advertisement (with its connotation of the Manx parliament and 'Home Rule') is conducted in the face of indifference and mounting derision, and discloses the anomaly that sometimes nationalist ideologies can be effectively (and unintentionally) undermined by those who take them too seriously.[22] In any case, with their interest in the picture of a racial lynching in America, their speculation over the virile qualities of hanged Republican revolutionaries, as well as the flow of disparaging jokes ridiculing the use of concepts such as 'God' and 'love' with which Britain has extended its hegemony, the pub crowd are no strangers to large measures of cynicism and jocular self-parody.[23] The narrator, the source of some of the most spiteful criticisms of Bloom, scoffs at one of the Citizen's more elaborate visions of sovereignty, dismissing it as '[a]ll wind and piss like a tanyard cat' (p. 314).

Notwithstanding the guilty consciences of John Wyse Nolan and Martin Cunningham, Bloom all too quickly becomes the scapegoat, the 'sacrificial butter' (p. 178), through which the all-male gathering subsumes other differences (such as Crofton's Presbyterianism), in a situation far more critical than Stephen's scholarly self-defence in the National Library in 'Scylla and Charybdis'. It is Bloom's final gesture, however, that spectacularly 'blinds' the Cyclopean Citizen just as Homer's Odysseus blinded his monstrous antagonist: by finally declaring himself a 'Jew' and adding that 'the Saviour was a Jew and his father was a Jew. Your God' (p. 327), Bloom sharply turns the tables on his persecutors, demonstrating that the 'Jew' is another of those terms (such as Devorgilla, Parnell's failure, the syphilitic Saxon robber) that nationalist rhetoric deploys to paper over the fissure opened up between the organic community it locates in the past and the ongoing repetitious and synchronous task of its reaffirmation.[24] Bloom has admonished the Citizen earlier in the chapter that 'Some people ... can see the mote in others' eyes but they can't see the beam in their own' (p. 312); a poignant commonplace suggesting that the figure of Bloom the Citizen so vehemently strives to chase away is none other than a projection of his own absence from the past/future imagined national utopia he describes; and accordingly, Bloom's expansion of the scope of the 'Jew' provokes such a psychotic reaction because it articulates the truth that, within the framework of the nationalist fantasy, Bloom *is* the Citizen, in the sense that he has become the support of the Citizen's symbolic existence, the symptom of what he cannot say. The Citizen's violent attempt to 'murder' Bloom with a biscuit box is narrated in a parody of a journalistic register:

> The catastrophe was terrific and instantaneous in its effect. The observatory of Dunsink registered in all eleven shocks, all of the fifth grade of Mercalli's scale, and there is no record extant of a similar seismic disturbance in our island since the earthquake of 1534, the year of the rebellion of Silken Thomas. The epicentre appears to have been that part of the metropolis which constitutes the Inn's Quay ward and parish of Saint Michan covering a surface of fortyone acres, two roods and one square pole or perch. All the lordly residences in the vicinity of the palace of justice were demolished and that noble edifice itself, in which at the time of the catastrophe important legal debates were in progress, is literally a mass of ruins beneath which it is to be feared all the occupants have been buried alive.
>
> (p. 329)

The penultimate of the chapter's burlesque interpolations indicates their function throughout: less as part of a general displacement of all meaning amidst a 'voyage through all the discourses available in English in 1904'[25] than as an ironic acknowledgement of the non-identity of the present with itself, of the fact that the event of Bloom's persecution forms a set of literary fragments, a 'mass of ruins' out of which a *version of events* may be constructed. Bloom's act of resistance amidst the everyday histrionics of national identification cannot make cyclonic, earth-shattering news, least of all when the minutiae of a humdrum Dublin day in 1904 are being assembled during the revolutionary upheavals of 1916 and beyond; but it does articulate the possibility of a different national imagination – beyond the dictatorial parody of a 'New Bloomusalem' or the parochial domesticity of a 'Flowerville' – where the more permanent revolution of a radical democracy might begin to take shape.

Like Stephen's playful defiance of the intimidating threats of the English soldiers in 'Circe' and Molly's unrepentant affirmation of her extramarital affair with Boylan in 'Penelope', Bloom's gesture forms part of the novel's trio of 'yes''s which marks the crucial blind spot of the novel itself – the point from which it is hollowed out by the future, the chink in a symbolic armour that ranges from Hamlet to 'Plumtree's Potted Meat'. Furthermore these moments, foreclosed from Moretti's account of 'polyphonic accumulation', return to reveal his confinement of *Ulysses* to the homogeneous emptiness of a literary-historical period as an oversight of near-epic proportions. As a national epic that refuses to sacrifice or domesticate the *unheimlich* character of its own movement of remembrance, Joyce's novel cannot be wholly overwhelmed by the 'nightmare of history'. Reframed as a question of the reconstruction of the past rather than historical fact, *Ulysses* begins to articulate, across the symbolic terrain of Dublin, the stirrings of '*a new perceptual and symbolic horizon*',[26] but only through cryptic, ironic gestures towards the future of its interpretation, where it might become, *nachträglich*, what it always already was.

A different version of this essay appeared in *Postcolonial Ireland?*, ed. Claire Connolly, special issue of *European Journal of English Studies* (December 1999).

Notes

[Adam Woodruff's essay tries to bridge the gap between postcolonial readings of *Ulysses* and psychoanalytic approaches. Inspired by the writings of Slavoj Žižek, it reads the crucial 'Cyclops' episode as a Freudian encounter of Irish nationalism with its own repressed but necessary Other, in this case Bloom's Jewishness. By representing simultaneously the forcefully excluded alien of nationalism's mythmaking and the familiar, Bloom fulfils a similar role as the 'Sandman' in Freud's analysis of the uncanny in Hoffmann's tale. Nationalism, like the uncanny, is a ritualistic repetition of a fictional 'knowledge', but also the emergence of repressed existential anxieties. Its ground is as shaky as that of a novel that tries to unhinge the familiarity of fiction, but also – despite itself – becomes a familiarised element in the canon of English literature, while refusing to act the part of a 'national epic' for England's Irish Other. All page references to *Ulysses* are to the Oxford World's Classics edition, ed. Jeri Johnson (1993). Ed.]

1. Seamus Deane, 'Joyce and Nationalism', in *James Joyce: New Perspectives*, ed. Colin MacCabe (London, 1982), pp. 168–83.
2. Quoted in David Cairns and Shaun Richards, *Writing Ireland: Colonialism, Nationalism and Culture* (Manchester, 1988), p. 114.
3. See Richard Ellmann, *James Joyce* (New York, 1959), pp. 245–8.
4. See for example Vincent Cheng's study, *Joyce, Race and Empire* (Cambridge, 1995) and Enda Duffy's work *The Subaltern Ulysses* (Minneapolis, 1994).

5. Deane, 'Joyce and Nationalism', p. 172.
6. Ellmann, *James Joyce*, p. 547.
7. Sigmund Freud, 'The "Uncanny" ', in *The Pelican Freud Library*, ed. Angela Richards and Andrew Dickson, vol. 14, *Art and Literature* (London, 1985), pp. 335–76.
8. Freud, 'The "Uncanny" ', pp. 373, 376.
9. Ibid., p. 372.
10. Walter Benjamin, 'Theses on the Philosophy of History', *Illuminations*, ed. Hannah Arendt, trans. Harry Zohn (London, 1992), pp. 245–55 (p. 248).
11. Maud Ellmann, 'The Ghosts of *Ulysses*', in *James Joyce: The Artist and the Labyrinth*, ed. Augustine Martin (London, 1990), pp. 193–227 (p. 195).
12. Slavoj Žižek, 'From Joyce-the-Symptom to the symptom of Power', *Lacanian Ink*, 11 (1997), 13–25 (p. 13).
13. Franco Moretti, *Modern Epic: The World-System from Goethe to García Márquez*, trans. Quintin Hoare (London, 1996), p. 198.
14. Moretti, *Modern Epic*, pp. 164–7.
15. Ibid., p. 95. Moretti is taking his cue here from Carl Gustav Jung and Fredric Jameson.
16. Sigmund Freud, *Two Short Accounts of Psycho-Analysis*, trans. and ed. James Strachey (London, 1962), p. 40.
17. Richard Kearney, *Postnationalist Ireland: Politics, Culture, Philosophy* (London, 1997), pp. 119–21.
18. The citizen is blaming the elopement of Devorgilla in the twelfth century as the primal betrayal that 'brought the Saxon robbers here'.
19. See for example Harry Blamires, *The New Bloomsday Book: A Guide Through Ulysses* (London, 1996). Though a useful sourcebook for the novel's cross-references, Blamires's attempt to 'translate' the novel chapter by chapter into a coherent narrative frequently ponders over 'the most secret desires of Bloom for recognition, acceptance and approval' (p. 172).
20. Motioning to the 'deadlock of desire' that motivates anti-Semitic caricatures, Žižek recites a Lacanian proposition concerning the pathologically jealous husband: 'even if all the facts he quotes in support of his jealousy are true, even if his wife really is sleeping around with other men, this does not change one bit the fact that his jealousy is a paranoid, pathological construction' (Slavoj Žižek, *The Sublime Object of Ideology* [London, 1989], p. 48).

21. Žižek puts it this way: 'In other words, what appears as the hindrance to society's full identity with itself is actually its positive condition: by transposing onto the Jew the role of the foreign body which introduces in the social organism disintegration and antagonism, the fantasy-image of society *qua* consistent, harmonious whole is rendered possible' (Slavoj Žižek, *Enjoy Your Symptom! Jacques Lacan in Hollywood and Out* [London, 1992], p. 90).

22. This notion of cynical ideology and its paradoxical aversion towards being taken seriously has been developed by Žižck (see for example Žižek, *The Sublime Object of Ideology*, pp. 27–33).

23. It is interesting to recall here that 'dismemberment' of the Bible in Bengal in 1817 which Bhabha motions to as an emblem of the distortion produced 'on the margins of metropolitan desire' (Homi K. Bhabha, 'Of Mimicry and Man: The Ambivalence of Colonial Discourse', *The Location of Culture* [London, 1994], pp. 85–92, p. 92): for when the Citizen reads out the newspaper account of the Zulu chief's visit to the 'Cottonopolis' of Manchester, and the pride with which he keeps an 'illuminated Bible' presented by Queen Victoria, Ned comments, 'Wonder did he put that Bible to the same use as I would' (Joyce, *Ulysses*, p. 320). Nonetheless, the proliferation of anti-Semitism in Barney Kierman's is perhaps (negative) confirmation of the profound ambivalence that Bhabha locates at the heart of colonial discourse, and out of which no oppositional community of the marginalised can be guaranteed.

24. Homi Bhabha terms this phenomenon 'the articulation of "nation*ness*" in which the anxiety of national identification switches from the domestic "unchosen" of people and homeland to the domestic "unchosen" of the marginalised' (Bhabha, 'Anxious Nations, Nervous States', in *Supposing the Subject*, ed. Joan Copjec [London, 1994], pp. 201–17 [p. 207]). Historically the figure of the Jew has of course performed a similar role in the nationalist rhetoric of any number of countries.

25. Colin MacCabe, *James Joyce and the Revolution of the Word* (London, 1979), p. 104.

26. Moretti, *Modern Epic*, p. 178.

5

'The void awaits surely all them that weave the wind': 'Penelope' and 'Sirens' in *Ulysses*

MICHAEL STANIER

Dubliners begins with the figure of a boy gazing into a dying priest's house through a 'lighted square of window' that shines 'faintly and evenly'. *Ulysses* ends in a similarly voyeuristic vein as the reader gazes illicitly into Molly's thoughts. While one sees a boy muttering 'paralysis' and the other has the critics clamouring 'flow',[1] it is important to recognise that the objects in question – Penelope as well as the window – are crafted and framed, cultural artifacts. This is particularly vital in 'Penelope', and it should be the basis for grounding any criticism of the Earth Mother and her language. Without such a basis any approach rapidly gains a Wakean circularity, forever looping the lemniscate figure eight[2] as if on a Möbius-strip treadmill. When you court Penelope, be wary of the tapestry unravelling in your hands just as quickly as it is woven.

In 'Penelope' the reader can be seduced into thinking that Molly's monologue is somehow unmediated: that tacked on to the real stuff of the topic is the 'natural', mind-speech of the excluded 'Other'. It is, for instance, the only chapter that is fully in the present tense and stands seemingly free-form, away from the ministrations of the arranger.[3] It is her language in particular, 'language of flow' (p. 253), that attracts the tag of 'archetypally feminine', more than her eroticism and apparent fertility (after all, Molly is menstruating which means, to her relief, that she is not pregnant: 'not what any self-respecting fertility symbol would be expected to feel').[4] The French feminists Hélène Cixous and Luce Irigaray appear to have used this chapter to inform their notion of *écriture féminine*. This passage of Irigaray which 'lauds the feminine signature'[5] might have been written for or inspired by Molly:

> 'She' is indefinitely other in herself. This is doubtless why she is said to be whimsical, incomprehensible, agitated, capricious ... not to mention her language, in which 'she' sets off in all directions leaving 'him' unable to discern the coherence of any meaning. Hers are contradictory words. ... For in what she says, too, at least when she dares, woman is constantly touching herself. She steps ever so slightly aside from herself with a murmur, an exclamation, a whisper, a sentence left unfinished. ... When she returns, it is to set off again from elsewhere.[6]

Others, verbosely, have followed the lead:

> [Molly's] subvocal iterations seem to imitate the amorphous and irrational utterances of hysterical speech. Her unpunctuated soliloquy flows out of a rich and capacious unconscious, drawing on those preverbal, prediscursive dimensions of language that Julia Kristeva describes as semiotic – a threatening and subversive discourse associated with preoedipal attachment to the body, voice and pulsions of the imaginary, maternal figure. Molly's lyrical prose poetry offers a paradigm of *écriture féminine*, as *jouissance* is deferred by a free play of the female imagination over the elusive terrain of enigmatic sexual difference. ... Molly Bloom's discourse is fluid and feminine, deracinated and polymorphic, uncontained by the limits of logocentric authority.[7]

Nevertheless, for all her apparent bursting of the mind-forged manacles, Molly is a construction of the 'natural', similar to the flowers on her wallpaper.[8] Joyce's attempt to portray the essential feminine as destabilising, undermining, and 'unweaving' the world of phallocentric language and presence is ultimately doomed to failure. Representation is inherently phallocentric, so that any portrayal as Other paradoxically excludes it from being Other. Otherness

> always remains and, to preserve intelligibility and meaning, must remain part of, enclosed within, conventional, 'educated' discourse. The discourse of the 'other' is never truly other.[9]

For instance, on the one hand Molly appears to subvert the notion of closure; she is the unweaver. On the other hand, even though Joyce has written that it is 'Ithaca' that really closes the book, her chapter is the culmination, filling in details and 'add[ing] to the reader's insight into the events of the day'.[10]

In this article I examine the role of 'Penelope' in *Ulysses* by trying to trace to what extent Molly's language is subversive and deconstructive to the whole. Primarily, this means exploring the full extent of her feminine 'language of flow'. I do this in part by looking at 'Sirens', a chapter that occurs literally in the middle of Bloom's Odyssean day, and I argue that it is in fact this chapter that is the most destabilising section of the novel. Rather than Penelope unravelling her tapestry from the end, unweaving her day, it unravels from the middle, from the 'omphalos' (p. 7) of the text, although, paradoxically, she continues to weave.

For Irigaray the feminine in writing is 'always fluid',[11] and one quickly sees how the connection is made between Molly's apparently flowing language and, from there, *écriture féminine*. But in a text that works to deconstruct our preconceptions about language, gender identity, and self-identity, a text whose hero is the 'new womanly man', we are unlikely to find the simplistic binaries of 'flow as against fixity, overflow as against the observance of limits: ... one of the commonest figurations of gender opposition in our culture'.[12] Rather, Stephen, Bloom, and Molly have complex and ambiguous relationships which all feature attraction to and repulsion of, as well as attempted control over, the polyvalent cluster of images that contains water and flow.

The very first sentence of *Ulysses* has the precious, priestly Buck Mulligan 'bearing a bowl of lather', neatly prefiguring the unambiguous and standard cultural stereotyping and control he later uses in naming the sea 'a great sweet mother' (p. 5). However, for Stephen the sea is as much death as it is life. Mulligan's brayings initiate for Stephen a reverie about the terminal illness of his own mother:

> The ring of bay and skyline held a dull green mass of liquid. A bowl of white china had stood beside her deathbed holding the green sluggish bile which she had torn up from her rotting liver by fits of loud groaning vomiting.
>
> (p. 6)

Stephen fails, as Mulligan does not, to control his relationship with the sea as it interwines with the claustrophobia of the sick room and the violence of his mother's death.

This is in contrast to the other two characters of 'Telemachus'. Haines, the conqueror, is '[T]he seas' ruler' (pp. 18, 30). His control, for all his apparent geniality to Stephen, lies in his 'Eyes, pale as the sea the wind had freshened, paler, firm and prudent' (p. 18) and as he offers a cigarette in a symbolic 'smooth silver case in which twinkled a green stone' (p. 19). So too, unproblematic Buck Mulligan has an unproblematic relationship to water from the bowl of lather through the risqué banter with Haines – 'When I makes tea I makes tea, as old mother Grogan said. And when I makes water I makes water' (p. 12) – to his enthusiasm for his morning swim. For Stephen it is different. He is hydrophobic: he may wash but once a month and even when calm will turn from water feeling 'the fever of his cheeks' (p. 9). He will later admit he is 'not a strong swimmer', fearing the 'Water cold soft' (p. 45), and is haunted by the image of the nine-days-dead man, 'a puffy face, salt white' (p. 21) a 'bag of corpsegas sopping in foul brine. A quiver of minnows, fat of a spongy titbit, flash through the slits of his buttoned trouserfly' (p. 49), images strongly linked with the ghost of his mother 'Ghoul! Chewer of corpses' (p. 10).

Yet while Stephen is repelled by this seeming insidious destruction and chaos, he has already rejected in the phallic, ordered tower of Buck Mulligan its apparent antithesis: 'I will not sleep there when this night comes' (p. 44). Though he leaves Mulligan swimming he returns to the beach in 'Proteus' at eleven a.m. after he has taught his class and 'broken a lance' with the bigoted (and shell-collecting [p. 30]) Mr Deasy. In this final chapter of the Telemachiad the interior monologue style is dominant, but the few times we do see Stephen 'objectively' he appears again to be beleaguered and destabilised by the sea. He declaims the 'ineluctable modality of the visible' and his 'boots crush crackling wrack and shells' (p. 37) but in the first picture we see of Stephen he is under attack: 'Airs romped around him, nipping and eager airs. They are coming, waves' (p. 38). He attempts to control this through language but never fully succeeds. Against the midwife carrying 'a misbirth with a trailing navelcord' in her bag (again, life and death) he conjures a 'belly without blemish, bulging big, a buckler of taut vellum' (p. 38). When he is pictured as having 'come nearer the edge of the sea and wet sand slapped at his boots ... his feet beginning to sink slowly in the quaking soil', he employs the defence of 'These heavy sands are language tide and wind have silted here' (p. 44) and reads 'herds of seamorse' (p. 46).

This sea-front siege is intensified by the appearance of the woman. 'Loose sand and shellgrit crusted her bare feet' (p. 47), whom be sees walking with a man and their dog. The undeniable physical presence of the dog, its 'rag of wolf's tongue redpanting from his jaws' (p. 46) links up with Stephen's previous night's dream of a '[s]treet of harlots' and a [r]ed carpet spread' (p. 46) and returns once more to his mother, the blood within her and the 'winedark sea' (p. 47). Again he seeks sanctuary from sexuality in words: he imagines the kiss, the 'mouth to her womb', but to do so must turn his back to the sea and the woman, and leaning 'over far to a table of rock ... scribble[s] words' (pp. 47–8); with his desire for touch, 'Touch, touch me', he writes, then quickly lies 'back at full stretch over the sharp rocks, cramming the scribbled note and pencil in a pocket' (p. 48). Yet there seems to be no defence; or rather, Stephen's body must unwittingly acknowledge 'the enemy'. He must urinate and watches as '[i]t flows purling, widely flowing, floating foampool, flower unfurling' (p. 49). This 'wavespeech' is very similar to that used by Bloom imagining himself in the bath in 'Calypso'. And then, as the 'snotgreen sea' (p. 5) continues to whisper in the background, Stephen lays 'the dry snot picked from his nostril on a ledge of rock, carefully' (p. 50), and, unwittingly it seems, 'countersigns his carefully constructed patriarchal universe'.[13]

The way in which water swirls through 16 June 1904 for Leopold Bloom is as complex, although different, as it is for Stephen. Whereas the latter is (bladder-) pressured into revealing his attraction to water, for Bloom it is a matter of luxury, fantasy, and somehow destiny: lying in a bath (which immediately puts him at odds with Stephen) where he foresees 'his navel, bud of flesh: and saw the dark tangled curls of his bush floating, floating hair of the stream around the limp father of thousands, a languid floating flower' (p. 83). Flowers, of course, blossom everywhere in this literary jungle: in the bath and as Bloom's *nom de plume*,[14] for two examples. In 'Sirens', in a bar of shells (p. 248), 'wavyavyeavyheavyeavyevyevy hair un comb'd' (p. 266) and the liquid letters of 'Lugugugubrious' (p. 271), Bloom's name seems to take on the heavy constant echo of the sea-breakers while at the same time he is cuckolded by the (evaporating?) Blazes Boylan (Boiling?). In the penultimate chapter 'Ithaca' it is 'Bloom, waterlover, drawer of water, watercarrier' (p. 624) who, interestingly enough, sparks what truly *might* be a language of flow. In response to the questions

'What in water did Bloom ... admire?' and 'Did it flow?' he answers in two of the longest sentences in the book,[15] a surplus of language brought about by an overload of details, a 'hyperfactuality'.[16] And yet in 'Calypso', with its clear link to the figure of Woman, Bloom has talked of:

> A dead sea in a dead land, grey and old. Old now. It bore the oldest, the first race ... [t]he oldest people. Wandered far away over all the earth, captivity to captivity, multiplying, dying, being born everywhere. It lay there now. Now it could bear no more. Dead: an old woman's: the grey sunken cunt of the world.
>
> (p. 59)

The complexity is increased when one recalls the letter from Joyce to Budger[17] in which he explicitly links 'cunt', one of the four cardinal points of the sphere of 'Penelope', to 'Yes' (p. 732), Molly's final and apparently optimistic and uplifting word.

Of all three, it is Molly's relationship with water which is probably the most complex, if only because of the stereotype that she, as Woman (and particularly Woman as Other), speaks fluid in a 'language of flow'.[18] Derek Attridge in his excellent and provocative article reveals how:

> Descriptions of the style of Molly Bloom's interior monologue by critics, female or male, feminist or patriarchal, seem to be fixated on one particular metaphor, a metaphor usually signalled by the word 'flow'.[19]

After quoting something like fifteen different examples of this critical proliferation, he argues that, while not 'erroneous or wilful ... the language of this episode is relatively conventional [and] is not particularly transgressive'.[20] Whereas it is true that Molly menstruates, urinates, and says things like 'that awful deep down torrent O and the sea the sea' (p. 732), nevertheless Attridge persuasively dismisses the arguments either that her 'sentences override the syntactic rules normally observed by language' or that 'they run on much longer than is usual' because they do not 'survive any scrutiny of the text'.[21] For instance, a commonly acknowledged aspect of Molly's language is that:

> her words change their references constantly. Pronouns have unclear antecedents and words that start with one grammatical connection can end by shifting to another one in the flow of her language.[22]

Yet as Attridge points out, these are ambiguities only to the reader and not to Molly,[23] and certainly the displacement between signified and signifier is not nearly as fundamental in the ambiguous use of 'he' in 'Penelope' as it is, for instance, in Virginia Woolf's use of 'I' in *The Waves*.

After showing that 'the interior monologues of Stephen and Leopold infringe grammatical conventions far more radically' than Molly's, and that her sentences, 'syntactically defined, are on the whole fairly short', Attridge concludes:

> The sense of an unstoppable onward movement ignoring all conventional limits is derived from the language, not as it supposedly takes shape in a human brain, but as it is presented (unknown to Molly) on the page.[24]

This conclusion is affirmed by textual evidence that this is a chapter to be read:

> Absent from the printed page are not only the punctuation marks and upper-case sentence-beginnings that might make a difference to the way we speak the words, but also the apostrophes in possessive and abbreviated forms that can make no difference to oral realisation at all.[25]

Similarly, there is the use of numerals instead of spelling out the numbers (for example, 'the oysters 2/6 per doz' [p. 691] and 'it was 1/4 after 3 when I saw the 2 Dedalus girls coming from school' ([p. 699]); the use of words like 'Xmas' (p. 702); and, as Derrida points out, the random capitalisation of words such as the last word of the text, 'Yes'.[26]

The point I take from this is that it is not so much Molly's style of thought that need be examined but rather the assumptions we bring to the text as readers. Is it our desire to see Molly using the 'language of flow', signposted for us in 'Sirens', that makes us read 'Penelope' as if it is the 'always fluid',[27] feminine language that Irigaray posits? Initially it seems that Molly's language in its Otherness may be meant to destabilise the phallocentric nature of the world that has been depicted. But some critics argue that this style of language, rather than doing this, merely shores up this world by being contained and assimilated into it: that Joyce's 'struggle to unsettle the logos of difference paradoxically proves in the final analysis to be inspired by a desire for totality and wholeness',[28] and that this 'reversal from absence to presence is not the breakdown of the patriarchal project, but its more sophisticated inscription'.[29] But perhaps another way to read 'Penelope' is not as Other at all. To reverse one of Molly's recollections, it is not the penis that has 'a kind of eye in it' (p. 711) but the eye that has a kind of phallus in it. We read this chapter with the desire to see it as Other because it is an Other we can control and assimilate.

It seems then that 'Penelope' is not nearly as Other as has been generally thought. The chapter both subverts and confirms the notion of closure: it is not an example of 'the language of flow' and consequently neither is it *écriture féminine*. It is written by the male pen(is) and thus '*Ulysses* is resolved by the presentation of a woman with phallic qualities'.[30] Molly is as much insider as outsider. To read Other is, paradoxically, to read with a phallocentric eye.

This is not to say that *Ulysses* is a novel that does nothing but stabilise and confirm our phallocentric, patriarchal world, a world of unproblematic mimesis. But where does this destabilising influence come from? It is foolish to argue that it comes from just one source, because it is found throughout the book, although more so in chapters such as 'Ithaca', where the implosion of mimesis and the sheer bulk of facts obscures any sense of representation, and 'Circe', with its vivid crudity of the subconscious. But the most predominant source of instability comes from 'Sirens'. This chapter takes place in the very centre of Bloom's day, four p.m. (eight hours after he 'ate with relish' [p. 53]; eight hours before 'He rests. He has travelled' [p. 689]). This is the omphalos of the text, the eye of the hurricane, the eye of the phallus, and it is from here that the world unweaves as body and language unravels.

From the cacophony of noise that opens 'Sirens' – bewildering, disorienting, alluring, siren voices indeed – the reader should realise that this chapter is one to be read with eyes closed. After the fifty-seven pre-echoing 'sound-bites' which shell-spiral down to 'Begin!' (p. 246), 'Sirens' takes on a form more recognisable and comforting for the reader. But the chapter still rings loud. It echoes with assonance, dissonance, word-play, and puns in an atmosphere of duplicity and multiplicity. Words are repeated, slightly distorted, one after another:

> Miss Kennedy sauntered sadly from bright light, twining a loose hair behind an ear. Sauntering sadly, gold no more, she twisted twined a hair. Sadly she twined in sauntering gold hair behind a curving ear. (p. 247)

> – With the greatest alacrity, Miss Douce agreed. With grace of alacrity towards the mirror ...
>
> (p. 250)
>
> Miss Douce reached high to take a flagon, stretching her satin arm, her bust, that all but burst, so high.
>
> (p. 254)

Diffraction is dominant: Simon Dedalus blows through the flute 'two husky lifenotes' (p. 250): the human voice is 'two tiny silky cords' (p. 266), all of which finds play in liquid word-painting: 'endlessnessnessness ...' (p. 265), 'wavyavyeavyheavyeavyevyevy hair un comb:'d (p. 266) and 'Lugugugubrious' (p. 271). Duplicity there is in duplicity itself: the pythagorean numbers 2, 4 and 8.[31] In a sense these underlie the multiplicity of the chapter; as Bloom puts it, 'Numbers it is. All music when you come to think' (p. 267). Their illusory quality is emphasised by their ambiguity: two; to (to and fro); too; for; four (four o'clock; 4 Lismore terrace; fourfold; nineteen four); eight; ate; and they breed, multiply, cubed: two, by two, by two. Bloom faces most overtly this progression when tied to the mast:

> Bloom unwound slowly the elastic band of his packet. Love's old sweet *sonnez la* gold. Bloom wound a skein round four forkfingers, stretched it, relaxed, and wound it round his troubled double, fourfold, in octave, gyved them fast.
>
> (p. 263)

This stands somewhat in contrast with 'Penelope', which, in its use of the figure 8, is more unified, more 'gyved ... fast'. Infinity is not defraction and multiplication.

The sirens' song is deceptive and sweet indeed, but with it goes the dazzle of 'bronze from anear, by gold from afar' (p. 248), a Byzantian illusive metallic shimmer, Egyptian splendour, sun on oceangreen shadow, that fills the bar and that reflects (echoes) in the mirrors and the glasses that line the walls:

> spellbound eyes went after her gliding head as it went down the bar by mirrors, gilded arch for ginger ale, hock and claret glasses shimmering, a spiky shell, where it concerted, mirrored, bronze with sunnier bronze.
>
> (p. 256)

The sense of decentring, echo, and multiplicity is further emphasised by the differing narrative points of view that occur, from the parade outside to the anecdote about Molly's second-hand clothes business.

The differing narrative positions are complemented in 'Sirens' by the corporeal disintegration, 'dislocation and fragmentation'[32] that occur. As language unravels, so does its source. Ironically, for it is now that Blazes Boylan and Molly unite in their illicit physical bliss, the chapter is synecdochic and metonymic,[33] parts standing for the whole of the body. The reader's 'untroubled belief in the human subject as unitary, unconstrained, and capable of originating action from a single centre of consciousness'[34] is challenged as we see bodily organs, predominantly lips but also various other parts, seductively strut their stuff in the bar:

> The 'Sirens' episode insists that neither language (in its materiality) nor the body (in its physicality) can be seen as merely secondary and subservient to a nonmaterial, transcendent, controlling principle, whether that principle is called 'meaning' or 'the self'.[35]

One of the effects of this 'organic liberation is erotic arousal: sexuality thrives on the separation of the body into independent parts, whereas a sexually repressive morality insists on the wholeness and singleness of body and mind or soul'.[36] This chapter drips sexuality; the *entendre* in Lydia Douce's 'wet lips' (p. 247), and her complaint after her laughing spree that 'I feel all wet' (p. 250) is clear enough. In this chapter there are echoes of all the women Bloom admires throughout the day, giving a coherence and structure to this chapter of diffraction.[37] Knowles chronicles the appearance in 'Sirens' of all of the fifteen women that Bloom encounters (one per chapter) and shows their siren qualities. The major focus is of course the principal siren Lydia Douce. However, there are references to Raoul's mistress, the Virgin Mary, Venus Kallipyge, the smoking mermaid, Daly's shopgirl, Cleopatra, Marion Tweedy (the young Molly), Martha Clifford, Milly Bloom, Mr Wood's servant-girl, Mary Driscoll, the silk-stockinged lady, Gerty MacDowell, and the frowsy whore. One gets an idea of Joyce's craftsmanship when we find in Lydia qualities that link her with the other women, from the manipulation of the beerpull, a narrative gesture toward Gerty and 'Nausicaa', to *eau de Nil* and Cleopatra, a 'wholly narrative siren'.[38] Perhaps even more remarkable is that in thinking of these women, Bloom links them all, including Lydia, back to Molly, which gives him the strength to survive the sirens and '[p]ass by her' (p. 274). If

Bloom is sometimes symbolised as 'Black wary hecat' (p. 254), then Molly proves to be the binding 'catgut thong' (p. 266).

Bloom resists the sirens and the allure of their false sexuality, which from the first they build with the pseudo-climactic O's (pp. 245–51). He is like the piano tuner, acute of hearing but blind, who comes tap tap tapping back into the picture, and Pat, the tap-palindrome, who waiting waits, deaf but alert for signs. The linking between the tapping tuner and Bloom is explicit in:

> Bloom. Flood of warm jimjam lickitup secretness flowed to flow in music out, in desire, dark to lick flow, invading. Tipping her tepping her tapping her topping her. Tup. Pores to dilate dilating. Tup. The joy the feel the warm the. Tup. To pour o'er sluices pouring gushes. Flood, gush, flow, joygush, tupthrop. Now! Language of love.
>
> (p. 263)

However, this has been prefigured by Bloom's own tapping: the repetitive, constant sea-breaker boom (or shuttle-loom-bang) of his own name. It has resounded throughout the chapter, gradually overpowering and encompassing not only the weaker 'Boylan' but also the sense of dislocation and diffraction that is so predominant. More important, it reveals Molly at the centre of 'Sirens': the very unweaving of the chapter reveals the weaver.

The two chapters 'Sirens' and 'Penelope' have a complex relationship that is not easy to tease out. In many ways they are complementary in a similar way that Leopold Bloom and his wife Molly are complementary: warp and weft of a tapestry. 'Sirens' takes place largely in Bloom's head. It takes place in the middle of his day, the furthest point from his homecoming, and might be, you would think, a phallogocentric 'masculine' chapter, one where Bloom is able most to express himself. Yet it is a cacophony of noise, 'the audible against the visible',[39] and Bloom's difficulty in writing to Martha Clifford reflects the difficulty in reading it. It is a chapter of unravelling and unweaving both of language and of self, a chapter of flow imagery: diffraction and duplicity. All echo all. And yet, again, it is not chaos. Throughout the chapter is the comforting thud of 'Bloom' and the presence, hidden, of Molly working her loom. 'Penelope', on the other hand, takes place in Molly's head in the sanctuary of her bedroom with her husband asleep beside her. A time for Woman? Critics have seized on this chapter as exemplifying language of the Other, the 'language of flow' as *écriture féminine*. But Molly's language is one of 'plain words', simplistic rather than transgressive. Molly seems a unified self centred in her body. Rather than destabilising *Ulysses* the lemniscate feel of this chapter sets it firm.

Maud Ellmann in a wonderfully succinct article argues that 'Bloom, the new womanly man, must uncover a new language which eludes both voice and eyes, both music and writing: a language which evades antithesis of itself'.[40] I think Molly has found this language, perhaps unwittingly, already. It is not in 'Penelope'. For Molly unweaves the language and the bodies[41] of *Ulysses* with wind, language without sound, voice without words: her siren voice sings a song of silence. She weaves and unweaves the text from the omphalos, manipulating her windy (B)loom who farts voidance[42] 'prrpffrrppfff' (p. 279).

From *Twentieth-Century Literature*, 41: 3 (Autumn 1995), 319–31.

Notes

[Michael Stanier criticises the ideas that Molly Bloom's monologue in 'Penelope' represents the 'natural' discourse of the Other, as is claimed by theoreticians of *écriture féminine* such as Luce Irigaray. Since representation is inherently phallocentric, attempts to represent Otherness are doomed. By comparing the closing (or unclosing) 'Penelope' section with the earlier 'Sirens' episode, Stanier demonstrates that the most radical unravelling in the text is not undertaken from its end, but its middle, the navel or *omphalos* of the novel. While *Ulysses*' beginning provides multiple representations of masculinity, all of whom are in an Oedipal relation to water and the sea, 'Sirens' gives language to this sea. Situated in the middle of Bloom's day, the section doubles and distorts language – rather than producing a clearly objectified Other. This is mirrored in linguistic distortions and disintegrations that are more radical than the stable descriptions of Molly at rest at the novel's conclusion. When Bloom resists the 'Sirens', he demonstrates that text and reader achieve the stability of their positions by ultimately opting for a 'phallogocentric' order where the stable masculine weave of the text is preferred to the uncertainties of unweaving. All page references to *Ulysses* are to the Oxford World's Classics edition, ed. Jeri Johnson (1993). Ed.]

1. James Joyce, *Dubliners* (London, 1977), p. 7. It may be that these reactions are not as polar as they first seem. The connection may be 'evenly', used to describe both the quality of the light in the opening of 'The Sisters' and, as Joyce wrote to Frank Budgen, the quality of 'Penelope' which 'turns like the huge earth ball slowly surely evenly

round and round spinning'; James Joyce, *Selected Letters*, ed. Richard Ellmann (New York, 1975), p. 285.

2. The use of this symbolism is well documented. For instance, Restuccia mentions the eight 'sentences' and the eight negatives that 'begin' the last of these as well as the famous eight 'yeses' that end it; Frances L. Restuccia, *Joyce and the Law of the Father* (New Haven, CT, 1989), p. 149. Henke draws attention to Molly's birthday – 8 November – which links her with the Virgin Mary, whose number is also eight, and mentions the eight poppies Bloom gave her while courting; Suzette A. Henke, 'A Speculum of the Other Molly: A Feminist/Psychoanalytical Inquiry into James Joyce's Politics of Desire', *Mosaic*, 21:3 (1988), 149–64 (155). In addition, Molly's marriage was in 1888, so that on the 16th day of June in '04 (and here are multiples of 8) she will have been married sixteen years. Molly's breasts and buttocks also make the lemniscate [geometrical figure resembling the number eight – Ed.]. Boyle argues that this figure is also represented by her genitalia; Robert Boyle, 'Penelope', in Clive Hart and David Hayman (eds), *James Joyce's 'Ulysses': Critical Essays* (Berkeley, CA, 1974), p. 412.

3. There is, however, the curious appeal to 'Jamesy' in 'Penelope', which is presumably to Joyce, and extra-textual reference to the author in a work that surely sets about deconstructing the notion of authority. The absence of the arranger is explicable if she is Molly: absence is thus really presence. Thickstun, in an otherwise unremarkable book, claims that ' "Penelope" retrospectively shapes and informs the rest of *Ulysses*'; William R. Thickstun, *Visionary Closure in the Modern Novel* (Basingstoke, 1988), p. 77. Christine van Boheemen asks, 'Is *Ulysses* ventriloquated through the womb of Molly Bloom?'; van Boheemen, ' "The Language of Flow": Joyce's Dispossession of the Feminine in *Ulysses*', *Modern Fiction Studies*, 35:3 (1989), 153–67 (166).

4. Derek Attridge, 'Molly's Flow: The Writing of "Penelope" and the Question of Woman's Language', *Modern Fiction Studies*, 35:3 (1989), 543–65 (561).

5. Diana E. Henderson, 'Joyce's Modernist Women: Whose Last Word?', *Modern Fiction Studies*, 35:3 (1989), 517–28 (518).

6. Luce Irigaray, *This Sex Which Is Not One*, trans. Catherine Porter (Ithaca, NY, 1985), pp. 28–9.

7. Henke, 'Speculum', 149–52.

8. Annette Shandler Levitt, 'The Pattern out of the Wallpaper: Luce Irigaray and Molly Bloom', *Modern Fiction Studies*, 35:3 (1989), 507–16.

9. Christine van Boheemen, *The Novel as Family Romance: Language, Gender and Authority from Fielding to Joyce* (Ithaca, NY, 1987), p. 177.

10. Ibid., p. 173
11. Irigaray, *This Sex*, p. 79.
12. Attridge, 'Molly's Flow', p. 553.
13. Maud Ellmann, 'To Sing or to Sign', in *The Centennial Symposium*, ed. Morris Beja et al. (Chicago, 1986), p. 68.
14. Which of course puns on flow-er, another connection with water.
15. I agree with Attridge when he argues that the eight lengths of Molly's discourse are not sentences: 'whether we think in terms of syntactic structure or graphic markings, the only unit they approximate to is the paragraph, and then only by virtue of some white space on the page'; 'Molly's Flow', p. 546.
16. Restuccia, *Joyce*, p. 63.
17. '["Penelope"] begins and ends with the female word *yes*. It turns like the huge earth ball slowly surely evenly round and round spinning, its four cardinal points being the female breasts, arse, womb and cunt expressed by the words *because*, *bottom* (in all senses bottom, button, bottom of the class, bottom of the sea, bottom of his heart), *woman*, *yes*'; *Selected Letters*, p. 285.
18. Ironically, though, 'Penelope' is one of the few (five) episodes in the book where the word 'flow' does *not* appear.
19. Attridge, 'Molly's Flow', p. 543.
20. Ibid., pp. 544–5.
21. Ibid., p. 545.
22. Sheldon Brivic, 'The Veil of Signs: Perception as Language in Joyce's *Ulysses*', *ELH*, 37 (1990), 737–55 (746).
23. Attridge, 'Molly's Flow', p. 548.
24. Ibid., pp. 546–7.
25. Ibid., p. 551.
26. Jacques Derrida, 'Ulysses Gramophone: Hear say yes in Joyce', trans. Tina Kendall, in Bernard Benstock (ed.), *James Joyce: The Augmented Ninth* (Syracuse, NY, 1988), p. 46.
27. Irigaray, *This Sex*, p. 79.
28. van Boheemen, *The Novel*, p. 184.
29. Ibid., p. 40.
30. Ibid., pp. 180–1.
31. Bloom's day begins at eight, 'Sirens' is at four, and 'Penelope' is at two in the morning.

32. André Topia, ' "Sirens": The Emblematic Vibration', in *The Centennial Symposium*, ed. Morris Beja et al. (Chicago, 1986), pp. 76–81 (p. 76).

33. The idea of metonym, where 'You/I are always several at the same time. How would one dominate the other?' (Luce Irigaray, 'When Our Lips Speak Together', trans. Carolyn Burke, *Signs: Journal of Women in Culture and Society*, 6:1 [1980], 69–79 [72]), is important for Irigaray's ideal of multiplicity.

34. Derek Attridge, *Peculiar Language: Literature as Difference from the Renaissance to James Joyce* (London, 1988), p. 161.

35. Derek Attridge, 'Joyce's Lipspeech: Syntax and the Subject in "Sirens" ', in Beja, *Centennial Symposium*, pp. 59–65 (pp. 64–5).

36. Attridge, *Peculiar Language*, p. 167.

37. Sebastian Knowles, 'The Substructure of "Sirens": Molly as *Nexus Omnia Ligans*', *James Joyce Quarterly*, 23:4 (1986), 447–63 (449).

38. Ibid., p. 454.

39. Ellmann, 'To Sing', p. 66.

40. Ibid., p. 67.

41. 'As we, our mother Dana, weave and unweave our bodies, Stephen said, from day to day, their molecules shuttled to and fro, so does the artist weave and unweave his image' (p. 186).

42. 'The void surely awaits all of the that weave the wind' (p. 21).

6

Wasted Words: The Body Language of Joyce's 'Nausicaa'

CLARA D. MCLEAN

> Swollen from head to foot he was, and seawater gushed from his mouth and nostrils.
>
> (Homer, *The Odyssey*)
>
> Sir, sir, thou art so leaky
>
> (Shakespeare, *Antony and Cleopatra)*

'Lord, I am wet' (p. 355), Bloom says to himself in the 'Nausicaa' episode of *Ulysses*. This adjective could easily be applied to the whole episode, which, throughout its narrative fluctuations, its ebb and flow of style and perspective, its turgid 'tumescence' and ejaculatory 'detumescence', exhibits a relentless obsession with bodily fluids. Bloom is indeed wet when he makes this statement: having just manoeuvred a clandestine ejaculation to the sight of Gerty MacDowell, he sits submerged in his own silent narrative, his semen seeping up through his shirt, mentally and physically stewing in his own juice. '[W]aterlover, drawer of water, watercarrier' (p. 624) though Bloom may be, the inner wetness of the human body is nonetheless highly problematic for him, a point hinted at in 'Ithaca', where the narrative tribute to water winds down to this ominous ending: 'the noxiousness of its effluvia in lacustrine marshes, pestilential fens, faded flowerwater, stagnant pools in the waning moon' (p. 625). Bloom is water-fearer also, and in

'Nausicaa' appears suspended between these contradictory feelings toward bodily fluids. Fluids here are both precious and threatening, essential and potentially noxious. His semen seems especially suspect, inspiring mixed impulses. It is the '[S]ource of life' (p. 358), masculinity's special essence: 'The strength it gives a man', Bloom says, '[t]hat's the secret of it' (p. 353). As such, it is a precious fluid, limited in supply, a life force to hold in: Bloom complains after ejaculation that Gerty has '[d]rained all the manhood out of me, little wretch' (p. 359). At the same time, semen is something demanding expulsion, an excess pressing on the body's boundaries, needing release; as Bloom says, 'you have to get rid of it someway' (p. 353). Under cover of clothing, Bloom's veiled masturbation becomes a kind of clever compromise, a concealed exhibitionism by which he attempts to release the pressing 'excess' of bodily fluid and guard its vital 'essence' for himself. Throughout the episode, the paradoxical nature of the body's wet interior is a central problem of the text. At once vital and threatening, bodily fluids must be concealed and uncovered, protected within the body, and somehow expelled, flushed out of it. For the individual characters and for the narrative as a whole, coping with the ubiquitous ambiguity of fluids demands elaborate mechanisms of control.

Bloom's battle with bodily fluids is waged with both body and words. In a paradoxical gesture much like his contained ejaculation, Bloom's narrative both reveals and conceals his semen, repeatedly evoking its wetness but refusing to ever call it by name. '*That* diffuses itself all through the body', says Bloom (my emphasis), 'permeates. Source of life and it's extremely curious the smell. Celery sauce' (p. 358). Again and again, the various narrative voices of 'Nausicaa' call up the body's interior wetness but at the same time suppress, cover, and disguise it with words. Bloom's meticulous measuring of fluid, we see, is not really successful: the precious life fluid he hoped to protect leaks out through his shirt, becoming in spite of him a wet unpleasantness, waste to be rinsed out: 'Mr Bloom with careful hand recomposed his wet shirt. ... Begins to feel cold and clammy. After effect not pleasant' (p. 353). I will argue here that, ultimately, the dirty secret that the narrative and characters strive so hard to conceal is precisely this troubling property of the body: its inner fluids are both life and waste, sustenance and poison. Any verbal or bodily effort to filter, to separate these contradictory properties, to align the body definitively with one or the other, is consistently undermined in this episode. The paradoxical nature of bodily fluids inevitably seeps to the surface of body and text.

The attempt to guard this secret through language becomes especially problematic in a text where language is so self-consciously permeable – even 'flowing'[1] – where words blend and narrative voices spill into each other. In 'Nausicaa', Joyce develops the relationship between the flows of bodily liquids and language, showing them to be at once linked and parallel. Both 'flows' at once demand control and refuse it. In both, the pure, life-affirming stream is inextricably entwined with the poisonous and dirty one. In both, attempts at control repeatedly unravel as the secret leaks out and the interior threat to bodies and narratives is revealed.

The structure of 'Nausicaa' presents a progression of related strategies of resistance to the problem of waste inside the body. This problem is introduced through the children, in whose various stages of development we first see the link between the imperatives to control fluids and language. The chapter's first spoken words are a dialogue between Cissy Caffrey and baby Boardman:

> – Now, baby, Cissy Caffrey said. Say out big, big. I want a drink of water.
> And baby prattled after her:
> – A jink a jink a jawbo.
>
> (pp. 331–2)

From the outset of the episode, the baby's need for the essential fluid – water – is explicitly connected to the imperative to speak. To control the vital flow of fluids through his body, Cissy shows him, he will have to learn to control language. Baby, so much a prelingual being that his own name is never pronounced in the text, is both unspoken and essentially unspeaking. Instead of words, he emits an uncontrolled, fluid run of sounds. Still a stranger to the world of names, he is presented in the text simply as a leaking body, a hole-filled bag of fluids:

> Cissy wiped his little mouth with the dribbling bib and wanted him to sit up properly and say pa pa pa but when she undid the strap she cried out, holy saint Denis, that he was possing wet. ... Of course his infant majesty was most obstreperous at such toilet formalities and he let everyone know it:
> – Habaa baaaahabaaa baaaa.
> And two great big lovely big tears coursing down his cheeks. It was all no use soothering him with no, nono, baby, no and telling

> him about the geegee and where was the puffpuff but Ciss, always, readywitted, gave him in his mouth the teat of the suckingbottle and the young heathen was quickly appeased.
>
> (p. 341)

Cissy labours throughout this passage, as elsewhere, to coax baby toward language, but it is clear that his relation to the world is still based on an exchange of fluids rather than of words. Instead of articulating, he spits, cries, urinates. Cissy tries diligently to replace his fluid emissions with verbal ones. She encourages him to use language; she wipes, changes, and covers his fluids; she masks his fluids with words: when he spits up on his bib, she exclaims, 'O my! Puddeny pie!' (p. 347), using verbal magic to convert the unspeakable fluid into a sweeter, premasticated form. But baby, at eleven months, is still largely unreachable by language, impervious to its soothing, sweetening powers – at this stage, only the bottle can move him.

Baby Boardman, casually emitting fluids, shamelessly desiring to sit in his own filth, has not yet learned to distinguish good fluids from bad ones, life-giving fluids from waste. He cannot yet distinguish, that is, between those fluids which he is encouraged to speak, and those which must remain unspeakable. All of Cissy's dealings with him reflect this division: good fluids, like water, are painstakingly pronounced, while bad fluids – the sullied waste fluids of the body – are physically and verbally covered over, cleaned up, disguised by omission or euphemism. This inability to distinguish is what keeps baby nameless in the text: he still revels in the unspeakable, inhabits its realm; he is still unaware of the problem of waste. He has not yet been converted from dirty, unintelligible heathen to the 'Master Boardman junior' (p. 347) that he will someday be, master of his fluids and of the language that both accompanies and facilitates this mastery.

The next leaking child we encounter in the chapter is Tommy Caffrey, whose leaks are of a far more controlled order. In accordance with the digestive logic of the episode, he too, like baby, is introduced as a receptacle for fluid, and he later passes it out. The narrator tells us:

> Tommy Caffrey could never be got to take his castor oil unless it was Cissy Caffrey that held his nose and promised him the scatty heel of the loaf or brown bread with golden syrup on. What a persuasive power that girl had!
>
> (p. 332)

Unlike baby Boardman, Tommy understands and responds to language's magical conversions. No longer a babbling heathen, he has come to believe the Word. The narrative cooperates in this distinction, separating him from baby by naming him directly, placing him firmly in the world of the spoken. Tommy is capable of distinguishing bad fluids from good ones according to his society's designations; and significantly, it is language, and not any inherent property of the fluid, that allows him to do so. He knows castor oil is good only because his sister *says* so – and, believer that he is, he obligingly opens his mouth to it. Tommy Caffrey has quite clearly accomplished the transition to the Symbolic, of which Kristeva writes simply, 'there is language instead of the good breast'.[2] Language for him has become the privileged system, overriding, masking, and converting the baby's system of fluid response.

A short while later, Tommy speaks his first words in the text; here again the imperative to use language is driven by the need to regulate fluids. Significantly, though, this necessary use of language consists of a careful balance between the need to speak and the need to keep silent. 'His eyes misty with unshed tears', Tommy approaches Cissy and can respond only 'Nao ... Nao' to her teasing inquisition. Eventually Cissy guesses what the matter is, and whispers to Edy Boardman 'to take him there behind the pushcar where the gentlemen couldn't see and to mind he didn't wet his new tan shoes' (p. 333). Here again Tommy shows his nascent understanding of the complex relation between the control of fluids and language. He knows that inner fluids – tears, urine – must be 'unshed', contained, held back; he knows likewise that some fluids must be unspoken, cannot be named by name. His initiation into language has involved grasping the nature of the verbal taboo. Still needing assistance to urinate, he must manipulate his verbal emissions to say without saying. Tommy is on the threshold of leaking babyhood: in a second his 'hot tears' might 'well up' (p. 332), his 'new tan shoes' might get wet – the liquid system threatens to surface, to spill over, if words should fail. Still, he has come to understand the dual nature of fluids and hence the need to fight such leakage. As a member of the world of language, Tommy has become part of the world of waste, understanding what it represents and hence the imperative to control it. It is this understanding that forms the primary marker of adulthood – its painstaking separation of the good, clean body from the inner fluids that could defile it: 'O, he was a man already was little Tommy Caffrey since he was out of pinnies' (p. 337). Dressed in his little 'sailor suit' – a would-be Master of the waves – the leak for him has become an unspeakable secret. Leaking carefully, in secret behind the pushcar, Tommy conceals and controls the threat of immersion, of sinking back in.

In 'Nausicaa', the women are presented as the true masters of the art of concealment, the boys as their young trainees. Here, children leak; woman's job is to stop or clean up their leaking. Like the young princess in the *Odyssey*, in Joyce's 'Nausicaa' the three marriageable women are drubbers and cleaners, laundresses of the world. Much like Homer's Nausicaa, Gerty obsessively launders her own underwear in an attempt to fulfil her womanly role and catch a husband. So too the women of the episode attend to their language, whitening it and working out the soiled spots with care. In their dealings with the children and with each other, their language is veiled, euphemistic, marked by decoratively insinuating wordplay: we learn of Cissy, for example, that 'when she wanted to go where you know she said she wanted to run and pay a visit to the Miss White' (p. 338). In this same vein, one of Gerty MacDowell's jobs at home is apparently the actual cleaning of the outhouse; like Cissy, she cleans it verbally as well: it is referred to only as 'that place where she never forgot every fortnight the chlorate of lime' (p. 340). As elsewhere in Joyce, the third-person narrator here stands in uncertain relation to the characters, moving in and out of their consciousness at will and affecting, from a quasi-omniscient perspective, the narrative style associated with them. Thus, in the first half of 'Nausicaa', the narrative cooperates with the women's project to 'launder' language by stylistically reinforcing their verbal manoeuvres. Like Gerty, the narrative is obsessed with clothing: in her long introduction into the narrative, Gerty's body is often supplanted by the clothes that cover it, as though textiles had finally achieved supremacy over the flesh. Thus her 'skirt cut to the stride showed off her slim graceful figure to perfection', '[h]er wellturned ankle displayed its perfect proportions beneath her skirt and just the proper amount and no more of her shapely limbs encased in finespun hose' (p. 335). Functioning much in the manner of Gerty's underwear, frilly and meticulously washed, the narrative's decorative layers clothe the implicit dirtiness of the underlying body, containing its fluids and masking its desires. By calling attention to itself as a cover, decked with stylistic frills and euphemisms, the language distracts from, and even attempts to replace, the unspeakable body beneath, much as Cissy's 'puddeny pie' replaced the filth of the baby's soiling body.

The sentimental narrative covering of 'Nausicaa' reveals, in spite of itself, its own irreducible entanglement with the very things it tries to conceal. By its very association with the body it hopes to disguise, it becomes both soiled and soiling. The underside of the covering and cleaning so apparent in Gerty's half of the narrative is that beneath its careful language, her life, like Cissy's and Edy's, largely consists of attending to the body's troubling interior. Hers is the working-class woman's role that Bloom later describes as 'No soft job ... Nature. Washing child, washing corpse' (p. 356). Gerty, like countless other women in her position, names herself the 'ministering angel' (p. 339) of the house who, because of her compulsory ministering to the dirty body, finds a means of escape by narratively floating above it. Joyce sets up a striking contrast here between the dainty language associated with the women of 'Nausicaa' and the pervasive corporeal filthiness of their lives. The women's evening on the beach, for all its idyllic narrative potential, is constantly being interrupted by the filth of the children's bodily overflow. The women's verbal impulse to prettify and sanitise their world can be seen, in this context, not so much as frivolous or narcissistic covering, as many critics have argued,[3] but as their express job in life, and a dirty job at that. Joyce thus vividly contrasts the 'covering' of the women's language to the fluid-soaked reality it covers, suggesting a reading that scrutinises not just the surface of the narrative, but what drives its imperative to conceal.

In the very act of verbal concealment, then, Gerty betrays the sordidness of her life, a sordidness that motivates her verbal artistry and her appeal to the only 'high art' available in her world – romantic fiction and trite poetry – to provide the tools for escape. The sentimental language of 'Nausicaa' thus does more than merely parody a popular genre; it also, through Gerty, exposes the dirty reality behind the pristine dream of the romance heroine, the corporeality behind the cliché. We see, as Margot Norris points out, that it is 'because of this squalor, and not in spite of it, [that] Gerty dreams the dream of art' and longs 'for beauty and significance forever outside [her] ken'.[4] In 'Nausicaa', Joyce reveals the filth that lies behind the drive to art, behind the need to fictionalise.

Throughout, Gerty's narrative is hopelessly mixed with the waste it attempts to transcend. Indeed, Gerty's introduction into the text occurs through a bodily leak: it is not until Tommy Caffrey begins to urinate that the narrative turns to her, asking. 'But who was Gerty?' (p. 333), as though modestly diverting its eyes. Here as elsewhere, the narrative allows Gerty the most room for her verbal artistry when she is hiding something. The vacillating narrative perspective cooperates with Gerty's own ladylike modesty by allowing her reverently descriptive inventory of clothing to stretch across the whole unpleasant flow of the boy's urination, shielding it thus from her eyes and the reader's. Yet this same fluctuation of perspective also strangely entangles the flow of Gerty's narrative, the 'stream' of her consciousness, with that of Tommy's urine: her voice seems to emerge from Tommy's body with the flow of waste, cut off neatly when he buttons up. Thus the ambiguous flow of the narrative at once assists Gerty's verbal repressions and undermines them, keeping her (and our) eyes off the filth and all the while implicating itself within it. The narrative plays peekaboo with the reader, moving without warning from exteriority to interiority, from the narrative and the fluid flows outside to those inside the body. Again and again, it covers the dirty secret only to let it leak into the text.

The leakage of the unspeakable is played out in the central 'event' of the chapter, the cloaked sexual exchange between Gerty and Bloom. As in the romance literature its style emulates, Gerty's sexuality in 'Nausicaa' is unspoken, repressed, covert. She seduces Bloom with veiled glances, peeks from under her hat (p. 340), a game of peekaboo in which what she ultimately reveals to Bloom is only more clothing: carefully swinging and lifting her leg, she exposes 'her shapely limbs encased in finespun hose' (p. 335) and 'nainsook knickers, the fabric that caresses the skin' (p. 350). In Gerty's half of the narrative, the entire exchange occurs without any direct acknowledgement of its sexual nature. There is a nearby allusion to 'something not very nice' that a 'gentleman lodger' did alone at night, something Bertha Supple told Gerty about 'in dead secret' (p. 349). But she immediately distances this deadly secret from what Bloom is doing, saying 'But this was altogether different' (p. 349). Gerty's narrative practises a deliberate verbal coquetry much like that of the romance novel, wherein sexuality is at once aroused and elided, revealed and concealed.[5] The erotic for Gerty, as packaged for women through the popular media of her time, is only possible if it is hidden:

> And she wasn't ashamed and he wasn't either to look in that immodest way like that because he couldn't resist the sight of the wondrous revealment half offered ...
>
> (p. 350)

Gerty is not ashamed because sex remains unnamed, concealed, and unaired in her half of the text. In this way she can keep her hands clean, experiencing pleasure without the crippling effect of shame, keeping the dirty secrets of the body separate from her good, clean self.

Ultimately, though, even this apparent triumph of bodily purity cannot be maintained in 'Nausicaa''s world of flowing, intermingling narratives. Right after the moment of sexual ecstasy so cleverly disguised in Gerty's narrative, Bloom's narrative voice spills into the text as though released through his orgasm from a subterranean realm. Bloom's ejaculation is the final bodily leak to interrupt Gerty's narrative, to break through its concealing folds. With it, the narrative at last names Bloom, and in so doing seems to abandon any complicity with Gerty's project of concealment, turning finally against her. Suddenly the secret sordidness of their sexual encounter is brought out into the text: 'Leopold Bloom (for it is he) stands silent ... What a brute he had been! At it again?' (p. 350). At once the 'difference' that Gerty had maintained between Bloom and the lecherous 'gentleman lodger' is rendered suspect: not only is this particular event made more 'brutal' than romantic, but Bloom has apparently done this before! And immediately after this, as Gerty and her narrative style retreat into the background and Bloom's voice comes to dominate, the final, most poisonous secret of all is leaked into the narrative:

> She walked with a certain quiet dignity characteristic of her but with care and very slowly because, because Gerty MacDowell was ...
>
> Tight boots? No. She's lame! O!
>
> (p. 351)

Assisted by the vacillating narrative, Bloom spills the bad secret of the ruined leg, laying waste in an instant to the carefully constructed purity of Gerty's beautiful body.

The shift in narrative style that marks the second half of 'Nausicaa' has often been read as an unmasking of the first half; Bloom, in this view, becomes the truth-teller, unveiling all that Gerty's frilly words have covered and repressed. Gilbert's schema of 'tumescence: detumescence'[6] encourages such a reading: Gerty's half becomes the 'tumescent' half, a taut narrative covering full to bursting with unacknowledged truths; Bloom's is 'detumescent', releasing into the text all that had been held back. Ellmann follows this tradition, claiming that Joyce set up 'Nausicaa' as he did in order to 'oppose to Gerty's floridly imaginative consciousness the realistic observation of Bloom'.[7] This reading privileges Bloom's narrative as the 'final word' on the events in the chapter, and relegates the feminine half of the narrative to little more than frills and excess over the story's essential, masculine core. If Gerty's half clothes the secret, then, Bloom's half is said to disrobe it, tearing the 'drawers' off its 'drawersy'[8] narrative.

As we have seen, though, Gerty's narrative is not an unproblematic cover; neither is Bloom's an unproblematic release. The idea that Bloom's half is somehow 'realistic' or truthful, as opposed to Gerty's, seems to rest upon the dubious assumption that Bloom's half is not itself manipulating language, filtering its 'reality' through a style. Yet Bloom's half does have a style of its own, a style that earlier chapters have established as associated with Bloom via the 'Uncle Charles Principle'. Just as it is perhaps more fruitful to look at what Gerty's narrative *cannot* cover, it is, I think, more productive to look at what Bloom's *does not* willingly release, what it is trying not to say. Bloom's physical release of fluids is itself only a half-release – it too is a 'wondrous revealment half offered'. Bloom contains his sexual fluid under cover of clothing; he also refuses to name it: calling it 'Celery sauce' (p. 358), he purifies it, much as Cissy's 'puddeny pie' converted baby's unspeakable vomit into sweetness. Bloom also conceals his semen by omission, dropping the dirty substantiality of the noun right out of his text, referring to it as 'that' (p. 358) just as Gerty refers to her menstrual fluids as 'that thing' (p. 345). On the one hand, Bloom feels the imperative to ejaculate, and to speak directly and even crudely about sex, as an essential pressure of manhood: women, he says,

> Dress up and look and suggest and let you see and see more and defy you if you're a man to see that and, like a sneeze coming, legs, look, look and if you have any guts in you. Tip. Have to let fly.
>
> (p. 357)

The need to speak sex and expose sexual fluids is counterbalanced, in Bloom's half, by the need to hide and suppress them. Like the 'French letter' (p. 354) he carries in his pocket – like, also, the clandestine letter he has from Martha, its dirtiness protected under a pseudonym – Bloom's narrative both releases and contains its flows with a paradoxical impulse suggestive of Shari Benstock's claim that '*Ulysses* thematises the desire to name and the resistance to naming'.[9]

As with Gerty, Bloom's own naming in the text is concurrent with a bodily emission; here, though, it is his own ejaculation, rather than a leaking child, that names him. Gerty's naming allowed the narrative to turn away from Tommy's urine; conversely, with Bloom's naming, the narrative seems to turn *toward* the source of the leak, the wet spot. In Gerty's narrative, as in the spoken language of the women in the chapter, the division between speakable and unspeakable is more clearly designated, and the troubling stuff of the body is more uniformly censored. In Bloom's more 'masculine' narrative there is, instead, an overt war going on between a *compulsion* to leak and a compulsion to cover that leaking. The wet body is spoken and not, released and not, in a strange, halting motion echoed in the measured rhythms of his discourse.

Bloom's narrative style throughout *Ulysses* is characterised by sentence fragments, the flow of language released and then cut off. In contrast to Gerty's more even, decorative flow, Bloom's words emerge in measured spurts:

> Still I feel. The strength it gives a man. That's the secret of it. Good job I let off there behind coming out of Dignam's. Cider that was. Otherwise I couldn't have.
>
> (p. 353)

Bloom exerts a supreme control over liquids and language, attempting to regulate both to his advantage. This control is equally notable in his approach to conversations with women: Bloom wonders about Gerty, 'Suppose I spoke to her. What about? Bad plan however if you don't know how to end the conversation' (p. 353). Self-preservation, for Bloom, involves conserving language, not saying too much, not letting the conversation slip out of his hands. He would have made a 'worse fool' of himself, Bloom thinks, by 'talking about nothing' (p. 355) than by not talking at all. Bloom's careful containment of language corresponds to the contained ejaculation that is the central event of the episode. Both are driven by a powerful fear of waste. Bloom's veiled masturbation attempts to release semen without wasting it, to somehow let it out without diluting its life-giving, man-enriching purity. Bloom's verbal frugality represents a fear of wasted words: intemperate words threaten to become excess, a soiling, threatening spill. The problem with women is that they undermine this control, making Bloom say what he does not want to say, spill more than he intended. They compel him to 'let fly', coaxing out his precious fluids and steering language in threatening directions: 'Worst is beginning', he complains. 'How they change the venue when it's not what they like' (p. 354). So too they drain the body of its life, leaving poor Bloom soaked and exhausted on the rocks, moaning, 'O! Exhausted that female has me' (p. 363). A 'little man' much like Tommy Caffrey, Bloom in 'Nausicaa' still struggles to master his fluids, aware that bodily and verbal overflow threaten both his cleanness and his autonomy from the ever-present, invasive hands of women.

Bloom's narrative, while measuring and regulating his own self-exposure, does not hesitate, in 'Nausicaa', to 'expose' women. As the 'revealer' or 'truth-teller' of the episode, Bloom leaks the painful secret of Gerty's withered leg into the text – revealing the part of her body that is culturally defiling, corrupted, dead. Throughout this narrative, Bloom labours to expose female secrets; again and again his words bring up their bodily functions, their weaknesses. He leaks the secret of Gerty's lameness, then says with uncharacteristic cruelty, 'Glad I didn't know it when she was on show', calling her a 'Curiosity' (p. 351). He pointedly distinguishes himself from the 'they' of women, usually at women's expense: 'That's what they enjoy. Taking a man from another woman. Or even hear of it. Different with me' (p. 354). Repeatedly, Gerty and women in general are named 'devils': 'that little limping devil', 'Devil you are', 'Devils they are when that's coming on them. Dark devilish appearance' (pp. 353, 355, 352). Bloom attaches unpleasant and even evil associations to menstruation, nonetheless a topic of endless fascination in his narrative: 'Turns milk, makes fiddlestrings snap. Something about withering plants I read in a garden' (p. 352). Magical poisoning powers are associated with these female fluids; they are also sexually repellant, exuding a bad smell, a 'hogo you could hang your hat on' (p. 358) that sends men into recoil. This foul smell is in sharp contrast to the 'mansmell', 'celery sauce', that follows it in the narrative. Bloom's exposure of the interiors of women's bodies and minds operates here as a motion of expulsion, where the bad, defiling fluids, so carefully filtered from his own body, are narratively ejected onto theirs. Like Gerty's whitening language, Bloom's dirty talk, too, has a cleaning function, as it projects all bodily defilement onto the other.

Like Gerty's, Bloom's narrative works to conceal, though in different, perhaps more characteristically 'masculine' ways. What Bloom conceals with his professed 'understandings' (p. 355)[10] of women *is* understanding, empathy, a sense of being of the same mind and flesh. He conceals, also, his own sentimentality, his nostalgia in overlooking 'dear old Howth' (p. 331) and the painful thoughts it brings of a purer union with Molly, by rudely ejecting from his narrative any identification with the female. He thinks of Howth:

> Ye crags and peaks I'm with you once again. Life, love, voyage round your own little world. And now? Sad about her lame of course but must be on your guard not to feel too much pity. They take advantage.
>
> (p. 359)

The rejecting *they* cuts off the inadmissible flow of emotion, suppressing any emotional or physical entanglement with the poisonous bodies of women.[11]

The uncertain narrative perspective of 'Nausicaa' works against Bloom's project of ejecting the defiling feminine from his half. The crucial, central point in the narrative, in fact, is a moment of narrative spilling, when the two distinct voices conspicuously converge. The 'Uncle Charles Principle' takes a strange twist here: Bloom's consciousness emerges in the text embedded within Gerty's style, as the two narratives briefly overlap. Bloom is introduced thus:

> Leopold Bloom (for it is he) stands silent, with bowed head before those young guileless eyes. What a brute he had been! At it again? A fair unsullied soul had called to him and, wretch that he was, how had he answered? An utter cad he had been.
>
> (p. 350)

It takes half a page for Bloom's style to assert itself; in the meantime his 'brutish' perspective seems marooned within her sentimental 'feminine' language. Bloom's embedding in the stream of Gerty's interior monologue repeats Gerty's own introduction into the text, mired in Tommy's bodily stream. Thus for Bloom, as for Gerty, the careful extrication of his body from defiling influences is undercut at every textual level. This narrative slipperiness in 'Nausicaa' collapses boundaries, breaking down any traditional notions of bodily, sexual, or characterological intactness. The threat of this leakage to the characters' wholeness, to their independent 'lives' in the text, is a direct extension of the threat of bodily leakage that haunts the whole chapter.

When Bloom's well-guarded semen seeps up through his shirt, the troubling mixing of life and waste presents itself, finally, as a problem of his own body, interior and inescapable. That which is the 'source of life', that which makes a baby's body, is also filth, unpleasantness, maker of dirty laundry. This could provide a clue to the aversion to intercourse that, as we learn in 'Ithaca', has sexually paralysed Bloom for many years. Points in *Ulysses* suggest that Bloom's sexual horror is connected to the death of his infant son, Rudy: 'Could never like it again after Rudy' (p. 160), Bloom thinks. He speculates on the cause of Rudy's death, sometimes quite explicitly pointing to himself as its possible poisonous source: 'Our. Little. Beggar. Baby. Meant nothing. Mistake of nature. If it's healthy it's from the mother. If not the man' (p. 92). A 'mistake of nature': the implication surfaces that something killed Rudy from the inside, a terrible secret of the blood. And Bloom's ruminations suggest that he links the baby's dead body with his own life-giving fluids, suspecting that its mysterious death came from him.

Kristeva formulates the *abject* as 'the bad object that inhabits the body' and 'something rejected from which one does not part'.[12] The problem of the abject, the filth integral to the body, the dead thing contained within life, is central to the 'Nausicaa' episode. Bloom's horror of the dead body that emerged from his own interior leads him to attempt to reject and eject the waste of his body, through language, onto the bodies of women. His response resembles Kristeva's *abjection*, whose subjects feel 'a collapse of the border between inside and outside', wherein 'it is as if the skin, a fragile container, no longer guaranteed the integrity of one's "own and clean self" but, scraped or transparent, gave way before the dejection of its contents'.[13] Abjection, in its preoccupation with the paradox of bodily waste, often fetishises this waste, much as Bloom does, eroticising it in 'an attempt at stopping the hemorrhage'.[14] 'Suspended in the uncertainty of abjection, Bloom in *Ulysses* is sexually paralysed by his fear of his own bodily interiors. Afraid to create life for fear of the waste inside it, Bloom, at some inarticulate level, would have found truth in Temple's statement in *Portrait* that 'reproduction is the beginning of death'.[15]

Kristeva asks, 'Does one write under any other condition than being possessed by abjection, in an indefinite catharsis?'.[16] The urge to 'fictionalise experience', to cleverly manipulate the flow of language, is linked in 'Nausicaa' to the need to control, conceal, and expel the unwanted wastes of the body. The catharsis of each narrative voice is impelled by the need to drive the bad object from view, to make the body whole, alive, and clean. Bloom in *Ulysses* is paralysed by the dark suspicion that such catharsis is always inadequate, for the horror of waste regenerates in the body, and language absorbs rather than purifies it. At the end of 'Nausicaa' Bloom starts to write a message in the sand, then gives up:

> Mr Bloom effaced the letters with his slow boot. Hopeless thing sand.
> Nothing grows in it. All fades ...
> He flung his wooden pen away.
>
> (p. 364)

Bloom aborts his writing for fear of its effacement, for fear of the wet tide that might overtake his language, corrupting it into wasted words.

'Nausicaa' suggests that defilement is implicit in the body and in language. While 'Nausicaa' 's characters fight valiantly against this situation, there is some suggestion of another possible response. Toward the end of the episode, Bloom's narrative turns more toward Milly, his living child. In Milly, Bloom's narrative harshness toward women seems to lessen, acknowledging a continuity between his own, clean flesh and hers: 'Little paps to begin with', he thinks. 'Left one is more sensitive, I think. Mine too. Nearer the heart' (p. 362). At other points, thoughts of the dead Rudy are often countered by thoughts of Milly, as in 'Hades', when his memory of his son's conception is followed by, 'Molly. Milly. Same thing watered down. ... Yes, yes: a woman too. Life. Life' (p. 86). The bad waters of the body, bearing waste, are entangled with those which bring life, and this realisation can have either a paralysing or a liberating effect. The point in the novel at which Bloom and Stephen seem to achieve their moment of deepest communion comes when they 'in penumbra urinated, their sides contiguous' (p. 655). Bloom in *Ulysses* echoes the pun that Joyce used in his own book of poems: 'Chamber music. Could make a kind of pun on that. It is a kind of music I often thought when she. Acoustics that is. Tinkling' (p. 271). Joyce's own work suggests a way out of Bloom's troubling impasse: that the body's waste waters can be cherished, rather than feared, for their paradoxical properties. They are, in part, an artful trajectory, their leakage a life-affirming stream.

From *Joycean Cultures/Culturing Joyce*, ed. Vincent J. Cheng, Kimberley J. Devlin and Margot Norris (Newark and London, 1998), pp. 44–58.

Notes

[Clara McLean employs Julia Kristeva's concept of the 'abject' for her reading of 'Nausicaa'. It describes the ambivalence of the self towards the Other first experienced when the child realises that it can neither be nor control nor incorporate its mother. The effect is the transformation of the object of desire into the goal of aggression. McLean's reading applies this concept to the tensions between pleasure and fear of excess in *Ulysses*. The need to regulate this ambivalence produces contradictions between display and hiding, expression and repression, value and waste. The body and its fluids become a crucial metaphor for the way in which subjectivity and meaning require the 'proper' use of this flow of signification. The uneasy position of the narratorial voice in 'Nausicaa' mirrors the tensions, conflicts and contradictions created by the competing demands of stability and fluidity. Gender positions and power depend on the access to and control of the body and its secretions and their metaphoric equivalents in language. All page references to *Ulysses* are to the Oxford World's Classics edition, ed. Jeri Johnson (1993). Ed.]

1. Suggestive liquid language has often been used to describe *Ulysses*' narrative: David Lodge has argued, for example, that the narrative style of *Ulysses* 'plunges the reader into a flowing stream of experience' (*Metaphor, Metonym, and the Typology of Modern Literature* [Ithaca, NY, 1977], p. 45). Stuart Gilbert has perhaps taken this the farthest, writing that in *Ulysses* 'a stream of thought from a lower level suddenly usurps the bed of the stream which flowed on the highest plane of consciousness ... At every instant of conscious life we are aware of such simultaneity and multiplicity of thought-streams'; Stuart Gilbert, *James Joyce's 'Ulysses': A Study* (New York, 1958), p. 15.
2. Julia Kristeva, *Powers of Horror: An Essay on Abjection*, trans. Leon S. Roudiez (New York, 1982), p. 45.
3. Criticism of the 'Nausicaa' episode has often reduced Gerty's entire narrative to its apparent 'covering' function. Seemingly seduced by the hypnotic magic of the advertising language its style often imitates, many critics have kept their eyes focused on the narrative's attempt to

cover at the expense of what it is trying to hide. There has been a long critical tradition – including both Richard Ellmann and Stuart Gilbert – of perceiving Gerty's narrative as simple parody; in these readings Gerty's character starts to look like an empty dress, a frilly ensemble with no body beneath. A recent adherent to this view is Thomas Karr Richards, who writes that Gerty was created to 'represent' the superficiality of consumer culture, and asserts unequivocally that 'Joyce made Gerty MacDowell one dimensional ... No other character in *Ulysses* can be so summarily pigeonholed' ('Gerty MacDowell and the Irish Common Reader', *ELH* [Autumn 1985], 52:3, 755–76). I find it significant that Gerty is so eagerly made the target of the critical 'pigeonholing' that Richards both acknowledges and repeats.

4. Margot Norris, 'Modernism, Myth, and Desire in "Nausicaa" ', *James Joyce Quarterly* (Autumn 1988), 26:1, 37–50 (48).
5. See Kimberley Devlin, 'The Romance Heroine Exposed: "Nausicaa" and *The Lamplighter*', *James Joyce Quarterly*, 22:4 (Summer 1985), 383–97 (392). Devlin writes that the romance novel of the time 'implicitly encourages the transcendence of sexuality, while subliminally awakening erotic desire.'
6. Gilbert, *Joyce's 'Ulysses'*, p. 278.
7. Richard Ellmann, *James Joyce*, revd edn (New York, 1982), p. 473.
8. Joyce famously described 'Nausicaa' 's style as 'namby-pamby jammy mamalady drawersy' (Stuart Gilbert and Richard Ellmann [eds], *Letters of James Joyce*, 2nd edn [New York, 1966], vol. 1, p. 135).
9. Shari Benstock, *Textualizing the Feminine: On the Limits of Genre* (Norman, OK, 1991), p. 188.
10. When Bloom mentions a woman he saw walking upstairs 'two at a time to show her understandings' (p. 355), we are reminded of Tommy's 'unmentionables' (p. 332), so delicately referred to in the first half of the narrative. Bloom's professed 'understanding' of women is, like the 'unmentionables', itself a covering.
11. Linda Williams writes of male-oriented pornography that 'even its obsessive focus on the female body proves to be a narcissistic evasion of the feminine "other" deflected back on the masculine self' (*Hard Core: Power, Pleasure, and the 'Frenzy of the Visible'* [Berkeley, CA 1989], p. 267). Bloom, in his paradoxical verbal penetration of and distancing from the female body, executes just such a scheme. Pretending to 'reveal' female sexuality, to leak its secrets, Bloom instead conceals it under the titillating folds of his own language. His efforts at verbal control thus subtly repeat the eroticism of concealment that Gerty's narrative practises more overtly.
12. Kristeva, *Powers of Horror*, p. 54.

13. Ibid., p. 53.

14. Ibid., p. 55. We are not told much about Bloom's sexual dysfunction, but it is hinted that his current predilections tend toward the scatological, as several references toward the end of the novel would indicate; see, for example pp. 686 and 730.

15. James Joyce, *A Portrait of the Artist as a Young Man* (London, 1977), p. 208.

16. Kristeva, *Powers of Horror*, p. 208.

7

Cribs in the Countinghouse: Plagiarism, Proliferation, and Labour in 'Oxen of the Sun'

MARK OSTEEN

The 'Oxen of the Sun' episode of Joyce's *Ulysses* presents, on several levels, a debate about human proliferation and its effects on the political economy and on the quality of life. Depicting the painful and prolonged delivery of a child to Mina and Theodore Purefoy by means of a capsule history of English prose style, the episode first confronts the inescapable fact of literary debtorship and then demonstrates how Joyce both acknowledges the debts to his predecessors and makes literary capital from them. The episode's two thematic planes intersect in Joyce's borrowings from nineteenth-century writers, particularly John Ruskin, whose writings on value, labour, and political economy reveal the same conflicts displayed in the *Ulysses* episode. Like the 'Scylla and Charybdis' episode that anticipates it, 'Oxen of the Sun' uses homologies between physical and artistic generation to translate the debate about human proliferation into a self-reflexive questioning of Joyce's own artistic practice. As it explores parallels between Mr Purefoy's work in a bank and Joyce's management of the intertextual economy, the episode also discloses relationships between the Purefoys' prolific childbearing and Joyce's prolixity and textual extravagance. By pairing the intertextual and political economies,

'Oxen' ultimately illustrates how Joyce privileges artistic labour – an Irish labour of excess that emerges from debt – over both the female labour of childbearing and the male labour of physical and financial begetting.

'Oxen of the Sun' is merely the most extreme example of a typical Joycean strategy that Richard Ellmann has called 'inspired cribbing'.[1] The dual meanings in the word *crib* – it signifies both plagiarism and a baby's bed – punningly embody Joyce's achievement in 'Oxen'. An instance of what Michael Riffaterre calls syllepsis (a pun that combines different etymological levels and that may incorporate opposite meanings), *crib* denotes both licit and illicit creation, and forms of it are used in both senses in the episode. In the 'Ruskin' section it describes the bed of the Christ child (p. 401); later Mulligan comments that Stephen's sardonic telegram ('the sentimentalist is he who would enjoy without incurring the immense debtorship for a thing done') has been '[c]ribbed out of Meredith' (p. 404). Joyce's cribbing is more systematic than Stephen's; throughout the episode, in fact, he kidnaps the literary offspring of his forebears and places them in his own textual crib. Since he borrows not only their stylistic mannerisms but also many of their words, Joyce's strategy in 'Oxen' may be seen as bold plagiarism. The latter term also befits the episode's concern with offspring, since *plagiary* was originally a word for kidnapping a child.[2] By appropriating others' textual progeny and becoming their foster father, Joyce aims to beget his own literary progenitors in a manner similar to the one Stephen describes in 'Scylla and Charybdis'.

These syllepses on *crib* and *plagiary* more generally invoke the problem of intertextuality, two versions of which have gained prominence in literary theory since the 1960s. The first and most radical depicts an infinite citationality that affects not only texts but also the consciousnesses of authors and readers. Jacques Derrida, among others who have developed the notion, employs another syllepsis, iterability, to define the linguistic condition in which repetition and alterity operate simultaneously; for him this means that 'every sign ... can be cited ... thereby it can break with every given context, and engender infinitely new contexts in an absolutely nonsaturatable fashion'.[3] An 'iterable' text is thus an original tissue of citations. To search for specific sources is precisely to miss the point: the intertextual citing (and siting) of a text in relation to the discourses of others is both ongoing and irrecoverable. In one sense. 'Oxen of the Sun' seems to exemplify iterability, as it undermines barriers between text and context by enveloping within its frame precisely those historical discourses that have produced the conditions for reading it. It deconstructs the difference between borrowing and originality by making the latter a function of the citationality of the text: an original author is one who cribs successfully and extravagantly. According to this reading, Joyce announces himself as artistic criminal and heretic, a plunderer of copyrights and archives, a Shem-like forger armed with a 'pelagiarist pen' who means to 'utter an epical forged cheque on the public for his own private profit'.[4] In addition to challenging legal definitions of words as property and shattering the linear version of literary history that depends upon tracing influences, such extravagant cribbing violates the author–reader contract, in which the reader's labour is rewarded with original artistic currency. If Joyce commits a 'crime against [literary] fecundity'[5] by stealing words and reneging on his contract, he cannot be prosecuted, since all authors are guilty of plagiary. Some are just better at it than others. Indeed, according to this theory there *are* no authors, only circulating and recirculating texts.

The other school of intertextuality argues, by contrast, that tracing specific textual debts is not only helpful but, according to Riffaterre, its most systematic theorist, compulsory. For him the intertext consists only of those texts the reader 'may legitimately connect with the one before his eyes'.[6] His use of 'legitimately' is telling: Riffaterre's intertextuality seeks to sanction authorial power and ownership – the same functions overturned by general citationality – by recognising the author's ingenuity and by restoring intertexts to their rightful 'owners'. Riffaterre regards the intertextual stock as a kind of fund, and the author's role as resembling that of bank manager or notary. For him an author is a 'guarantor, witness to a verbal contract. Intertextuality is to the hypogram [i.e., the precursor text] and its palimpsest what escrow is to the lender and the borrower'.[7] The writer may take interest on these deposits by borrowing the words of others, but this operation, like financial usury, is subject to regulations.

Where does 'Oxen' fit into these competing schemas? Although the episode seems to exemplify infinite citationality, it also bears the stylistic signatures of its originals: Joyce wants his readers to recognise his specific intertextual sources (he named them to certain friends) and invites us to try to recover the historical conditions of the discourses he imitates. But we cannot truly recover them.

Instead, the borrowed styles impose upon the events a moral discourse alien to them, as for example in the famous 'Bunyan' passage, in which the episode's characters are transformed into allegorical figures such as 'Young Boasthard', 'Mr Cautious Calmer', 'Mr Sometimes Godly', and so on (p. 378). The styles thus demonstrate the irrecoverability not of sources but of the sociohistorical framework within which each style operates; though a style may be imitated, such imitation cannot restore to power the ideology that begets and is begotten by that style.

This fact suggests that we must further historicise plagiarism and intertextuality. When we do, we learn that plagiarism as literary theft was seldom recognised until the late sixteenth century, when economic factors (the ability for writers to live by the pen) and aesthetic movements (the new premium on originality) led writers to view words as individual property.[8] Obviously, the 'crime against fecundity' we call plagiarism became a 'crime' only after it was perceived to be violating a law. In a sense, then, texts begin to have authors only when, as Foucault states, 'authors became subject to punishment' for illicit appropriation.[9] That is, the 'crime' of plagiarism defines the modern notion of authorship as much as authorship defines plagiarism. Only when texts are implicated in the 'system of ownership' or 'system of property' do they become subject to legal and economic regulation.[10] Thus, everything preceding the 'Milton–Taylor–Hooker' passage (about line 333 in 'Oxen') is public domain, since the 'authors' of this passage would not have conceived of themselves as authors (owners) in the modern sense. The earlier passages represent, rather than a signed investment, a kind of collective fund of circulating capital available to all later linguistic workers.[11]

In 'Oxen', then, plagiarism and originality are the poles around which the intertextual economy circulates. To be true to the historical definitions of authorship, however, we must see the episode's words as both (or first) freely circulating in a general economy of citation and (or then) manifesting the restricted economy of ownership that generated the concept of authorship. 'Oxen' invokes both versions of intertextuality and in so doing weaves and unweaves itself, its catalogue of plagiarised authors at once constructing the system of authority and tearing it down. 'Oxen' thus invites us to examine the economic and legal foundations of authorship, and thereby reveals what both models of intertextuality share: the recognition that authors are readers before they are writers. In foregrounding the relationship between authorship and the appropriations necessary to reading, 'Oxen' valorises the labour of reading by suggesting that readers are co-creators. The redefinition and redistribution of authorship Joyce performs here thus undermines the ideology that grounds plagiarism even as it seems to canonise those who have created it. The cataloguing of the 'fathers' of English prose style actually deconstructs the models upon which such lists are based by implying that original authorship and cribbing are themselves historical constructs. In its place it proffers a paradoxical intertextual economy in which originality and authority are functions of the proliferation of plagiarism.

This leads us to my second, related topic. That the overt subject of 'Oxen' is human proliferation is both stated and illustrated in the opening Latinate paragraphs, which announce that 'by no exterior splendour is the prosperity of a nation more efficaciously asserted than by the measure ... of its solicitude for ... proliferent continuance' (p. 366). Thus all should 'be fruitful and multiply'. But because the passage embodies its content, its periphrastic style and tortured syntax exemplify the dangers of verbal proliferation, thus by analogy undercutting its praise for physical proliferation. Mere abundance enhances neither the quality of life nor the clarity of style. It seems, then, that the subject of 'proliferent continuance' refers both to reproduction and literary production (as Robert Bell has recently noted).[12]

The tensions in the episode's treatment of proliferation are made manifest through a pun on 'labour' which I want to develop a bit later. In any case, the early paragraphs seem to offer unqualified praise for proliferation, using the Purefoy family as exemplars and the idle and drunken medical students (and their cronies) as antagonists. The latter are repeatedly associated with poverty and infertility, as if to suggest negatively the connection between proliferation and prosperity. For example, the leech Lenehan is 'mean in fortunes' and fraternises with con-men and criminals. Therefore both his purse and his scrotum are merely 'bare tester[s]'. Similarly, 'donought' Costello, though he has conspired to commit plagiary ('kidnapping a squire's heir'), has only 'naked pockets' to show for his criminal enterprises (p. 380).

The debate about reproduction is most apparent, however, in the passages adopted from nineteenth-century writers. This foregrounding is historically appropriate since, as Mary Lowe-Evans has shown in detail, nineteenth-century society was preoccupied with issues of population and reproduction. Both passages in question describe the Purefoys and seem to applaud their fecundity. The first announces the birth of the baby in a parody of Dickens's *David Copperfield*. It lauds mother Mina for 'manfully' helping, congratulates father Theodore (Doady) and ends with 'Well done, thou good and faithful servant' (pp. 399–400). Of course, 'Doady' is not here to help his wife endure her pain; moreover, the ironies of describing Mina's labour as 'manful' or 'helping' are excruciating. 'Dickens' represses Mina's agony while aggrandising Theodore's labour, but it is difficult to see what the latter has done that is so worthy of praise. The narrator's articulation of patriarchal values emerges plainly in his ventriloquism of the voice of Christ as master in the final lines, which are quoted from the parable of the talents. In it a master praises his good servants for multiplying what they have been given, while condemning the bad servant for failing to increase his store by trade or usury (Matthew 25:14–30). When we consider that the Dickens passage also reveals that Purefoy works as the 'conscientious second accountant of the Ulster bank' (p. 400), Joyce's multiple intertexts converge brilliantly: like the good servants in the parable, Purefoy's labour is to earn interest, to multiply what he has been given. Like Shakespeare's Shylock, he breeds money as well as children, but unlike the good servants and Shakespeare's merchant, he gains nothing from his chrematistic generation.[13] The new baby will be christened Mortimer, 'after the influential third cousin of Mr Purefoy in the Treasury Remembrancer's office, Dublin castle' (p. 400). The parents will use this baby – like many of his siblings, named for British nobility or members of the Anglo-Protestant elite – to ingratiate themselves with wealthier relatives. This mercenary motive collides with the cloying tone of the passage; indeed, it implies that the Purefoys have used their children as currency, as ladders to class mobility. Ironically, however, by having more children than they can easily provide for, their efforts produce the opposite result.

The last of the historical pastiches (and the only one out of chronological order) mimics another nineteenth-century writer, Thomas Carlyle. Praising Mr Purefoy for doing a 'doughty deed', it names him 'the remarkablest progenitor ... in this chaffering allincluding most farraginous chronicle' (p. 402). Since I will be discussing the passage in some detail, it is worth quoting at length:

> [L]et scholarment and all Malthusiasts go hang. Thou art all their daddies, Theodore. Art drooping under thy load, bemoiled with butcher's bills at home and ingots (not thine!) in the countinghouse?

> Head up! For every newbegotten thou shalt gather thy homer of ripe wheat. See, thy fleece is drenched. ... Copulation without population! No, say I! Herod's slaughter of the innocents were the truer name. ... She is a hoary pandemonium of ills, enlarged glands, mumps, quinsy, bunions, hayfever, bedsores, ringworm, floating kidney, Derbyshire neck, warts, bilious attacks, gallstones, cold feet, varicose veins. ... Twenty years of it, regret them not. ... Thou sawest thy America, thy lifetask, and didst charge to cover like the transpontine bison.
>
> (pp. 402–3)

'Malthusiasts' are accused of encouraging 'copulation without population', and thus of sterilising the act of coition. A discussion of Malthusian doctrines is outside of my scope here; but it is clear that in 'Oxen' Joyce has borrowed Malthus's implication that 'economic laws of commercial production have an allegorical relation to the economics of human (sexual) production', a relation in which 'production and reproduction contradict each other'.[14]

More pertinent perhaps are the Carlylean intertexts that circulate here. Robert Janusko shows that Joyce's primary stylistic model for the passage was Carlyle's *Past and Present* (also a fitting title for the episode).[15] I would suggest that Joyce has adopted some of the content as well as the style. For example, *Past and Present* condemns in turn the gospels of Mammonism and dilettantism, both of which are on display in 'Oxen': the Purefoys (unsuccessfully) practise the former, while the medicals exemplify the latter. But unlike Joyce's 'Carlyle', the real Carlyle criticised laissez-faire economics for leading precisely to what Malthus predicted: 'such world ends, and by Law of Nature must end, in "over-population"; in howling universal famine, "impossibility", and suicidal madness'.[16]

Borrowing Carlyle's style, Joyce inverts his views on political economy. Carlyle's remedy for such misguided credos is, of course, labour, which he praises indiscriminately and redundantly, especially in the section called 'Labour', which, I submit, was Joyce's primary Carlylean intertext for the pastiche. One excerpt from the section typifies both the real Carlyle's style and his ideology: 'Doubt, Desire, Sorrow, Remorse, Indignation, Despair itself, all these like helldogs lie beleaguering the soul of the poor dayworker ... but he bends himself with free valour against his task and all these are stilled'.[17] Ironically, Joyce's 'Carlyle', unlike his evangelical original, praises as 'man's work' only Theodore's labour of sexual intercourse, not his banking job; but though her labour is virtually ignored, it is Mina who is tortured by sorrow and pain. At any rate, for the original Carlyle, the value of labour is limitless: 'labour is life'.[18]

The Joycean Carlyle's words, however, owe more to Ruskin's economic ideas than to the real Carlyle's. Joyce's familiarity with Ruskin has been well documented, and it appears initially that he borrowed Ruskin's definitions of value and labour as the cornerstones of the episode's anticontraceptive preachments.[19] In *Unto This Last* (1862) Ruskin defines value as that which 'avails toward life'.[20] This enables him to divide labour into positive and negative kinds: 'the positive, that which produces life; the negative, that which produces death; the most directly negative labour being murder, and the most directly positive, the bearing and rearing of children'.[21] Rebutting Malthusians, he asserts instead that, 'the final outcome and consummation of all wealth is in the producing as many as possible full-breathed, bright-eyed, and happy-hearted human creatures'.[22] In sum, he boldly states, 'THERE IS NO WEALTH BUT LIFE'.[23]

However, Ruskin's definitions of key terms, particularly *labour* and *life*, complicate these straightforward axioms. He immediately qualifies his distinction between positive and negative labour by noting that he means 'rearing not begetting', and implies that a person is not truly created until he or she is grown up.[24] Merely begetting a child is not particularly worthy of praise. In *Munera Pulveris* (1866) he further refines his definition of *life*. Now advocating increasing the population only 'so far as that increase is consistent with their happiness',[25] he defines the goal of political economy as 'the multiplication of human life at the highest standard'.[26] Dunned by the butcher, 'drooping' under their load of children and work, and with Mina chronically ill, the Purefoys have surpassed the number of children that Ruskin would find consistent with their happiness.

As for labour, Ruskin believed that its most unpleasant aspects were 'what is mechanical about it'.[27] If, as Leopold Bloom earlier observes, the Purefoys produce 'hardy annuals', mechanically and methodically making children as a factory manufactures goods, then for Ruskin their methods sap their labour of its positive qualities (p. 153). As the 'Carlyle' passage implies, Theodore works in the 'countinghouse' to multiply the 'ingots' (i.e., money) of others; thus his principal labour is generating interest. Drawing from Aristotle and the Bible, Ruskin condemned all taking of interest as illicit;[28] according to him, then, Theodore's bank job would be negative labour and would offset the positive aspects of his reproductive 'work'. Indeed, the Purefoys turn their house into a countinghouse by attempting to generate wealth through reproduction. Theodore's generation of financial and physical offspring are thus homologous: both are excessive and chrematistic.[29] A kind of inverse Shylock who equates ducats and daughters, Purefoy breeds more of the latter than of the former. In 'Calypso' Bloom makes his own deposits into what he calls his 'countinghouse': the jakes (p. 66). This connection between the outhouse and the countinghouse further suggests that the Purefoy children, used as 'ingots' by their parents, are little more than excremental deposits, at once precious and worthless. Thus Bloom consistently confuses the Purefoys with hack writer Philip Beaufoy, whose 'prize titbit' literary productions become toilet paper in Bloom's 'countinghouse'. Since the family's energy is directed toward the purgation of birth rather than toward provision, the Purefoy children, their parents' prize titbits, may seem as superfluous as Beaufoy's productions.

But what of Mina's labour? It is certainly arduous enough: even the 'Carlyle' passage acknowledges her suffering on the way to dismissing it. Upon first hearing about Mina's protracted labour from his ex-paramour, Josie Breen, Bloom is led to think of childbirth as 'Life with hard labour' (p. 154), as if it were a prison sentence. Similarly in 'Oxen' Crotthers comments ironically on 'women workers subjected to heavy labours in the workshop' (p. 398). Indeed, this birth is not only the most difficult that Mina has endured; it is the most difficult even that the experienced nurse Callan has ever witnessed. Thus she may be forgiven if her attitude toward this pregnancy is rather less joyful than the 'Carlyle' narrator's. In any case, Mina Purefoy's 'job' – bearing babies – is labour. In this respect Ruskin's definition of *labour* is highly pertinent: it is 'the quantity of "Lapse", loss, or failure of human life, caused by any effort. ... Labour is the suffering in effort. ... In brief, it is "that quantity of our toil which we die in" '.[30] For Ruskin, labour is not life-preserving, as it is for Carlyle, but rather life 'spending'.[31] Mina Purefoy's childbearing labour, which has turned her into a living encyclopaedia of disease, exemplifies Ruskin's negative definition of labour. Joyce's own views about contraception are as problematic as Ruskin's views about labour. In this regard, it is worth noting, as Lowe-Evans does, that James Joyce had observed the effects of excessive childbearing on his own mother, a woman who died at the age of forty-five, in part from exhaustion brought on by seventeen pregnancies.[32] Mrs Purefoy's labour in fact resembles Marx's description of the worker in capitalist production, who owns 'only [the] capacity for depletion ... because the capitalist has purchased his [or her] capacity for production'.[33] Mr Purefoy's juggernaut of procreation begets babies as a capitalist creates surplus value – at the cost of the labourer, who in this case is also the 'factory'. For Mrs Purefoy the result of this 'inversion of fertilities' is not wealth but, to use another of Ruskin's coinages, 'illth'.[34]

Of course, *Ulysses* elsewhere criticises the Purefoys' proliferation, through Bloom, primarily, but also by casting Mina in the role of sacrificial victim in the Black Mass staged in the Nighttown episode. Ironically, the activity of reproduction, which ostensibly leads to prosperity and life, may, when performed to excess, 'sterilise the act of coition' by robbing it of its life-enhancing sacredness. By producing more and more children without increasing their provisions or considering the mother's suffering, the Purefoys subject the act of coition to a mechanisation that imitates the depredations of capitalism. As in monetary inflation, so in physical proliferation: there are more lives, but less value in each. The intertextual and textual evidence in 'Oxen' thus collaborate to undermine the episode's apparent praise for proliferation by exposing the economic, physical, and spiritual effects it brings upon labourers, both male and female. And just as the episode appears to sanction (male) definitions of authority and authorship but actually challenges them by plagiaristic proliferation, so it appears to applaud the patriarchal values behind excessive reproduction (in which more children equal more possessions and greater proof of male ownership) but actually subverts them.

The relevance of these issues for the labour of artistic creation may not be immediately apparent. But we must remember that the homologies between artistic and physical generation were introduced in 'Scylla and Charybdis' by Stephen Dedalus, another (would-be) writer who appears in the 'Oxen' cavalcade. These homologies therefore apply to him. Unfortunately, Stephen's literary offspring so far consist of the vampire poem he scribbles in 'Proteus' and the parable of the plums he narrates in 'Aeolus'. His problem is not excessive proliferation but its opposite, artistic contraception. He *has* spent money: entering the hospital with £2 19s of his £3 12s wages (p. 573), he buys two more rounds of drinks for himself and his cronies, and he enters Nighttown with about £2 14s 7d.[35] He will spend another pound at Bella Cohen's brothel. Unlike Joyce's, however, Stephen's expenditures remain financial rather than literary or 'spiritual'. The episode's extravagant marshalling of English literary history thus merely highlights Stephen's artistic paralysis and suggests that his debts to these 'fathers' are yet another 'net' preventing his flight. Unlike Joyce, he has not learned to make interest out of his forebears' literary capital nor to pay those debts by weaving them into his own currency, nor to incorporate the female principle he describes at such length. Stephen's artistic identity is thus captured in the word he utters at the end of the Ruskin passage – 'Burke's!' (p. 401). Another syllepsis, the word *burke* (in addition to being the name of a Dublin pub owner) was derived from a famous nineteenth-century graverobber and strangler and was later expanded to denote all kinds of smothering or suppression, but especially that of a book before publication *(OED)*. Stephen's artistic birth is indeed burked, his idleness starkly contrasting with both the arduous labour of Mina Purefoy, and, I now want to argue, with the labour of James Joyce.

I have argued elsewhere that we may conceive of Joyce's extravagant methods of composition as a kind of excess expenditure of words that parallels the 'spendthrift habits' he believed he had inherited from his father.[36] If so, then in one way Joyce resembles Stephen. The major difference lies in the fact of labour: unlike Stephen's, Joyce's expenditures themselves constitute labour. Indeed, in another sense Joyce's labour resembles Theodore's: in 'Oxen' he treats English literary history as a kind of vault, an 'immense repository' or clearinghouse from which he may draw at will.[37] In storing, then borrowing from and expending this hoard, Joyce both increases his own stock and augments the value of his forebears' deposits. Labouring in his linguistic countinghouse, Joyce generates interest from his debts and begets his own 'fathers', who have now become offspring. His labour also resembles and valorises Mina's; it must, or it would merely duplicate the patriarchal ideology that the episode critiques, and thereby commit a 'crime against fecundity'. Joyce's and Mina's labour have in common an economy of excess. Joyce estimated that 'Oxen' cost him '1000 hours of work'[38] – less than Mina's nine months (multiplied by nine children) but an enormous expenditure nonetheless. At times Joyce, too, felt abused by this labour, writing that he worked at 'Oxen' 'like a galley-slave, an ass, a brute'[39] – 'like a very bandog' (p. 402). Just as the delivery of baby Mortimer is the most difficult labour

Mina has ever endured, so 'Oxen' was for Joyce 'the most difficult episode' to execute.[40] We recall that Stephen ends his description of the creative process in 'Scylla and Charybdis' with an image of 'weaving and unweaving', actions associated with Homer's Penelope and therefore with femininity. Similarly, in 'Oxen' Joyce mimics what Stephen calls the 'economy of heaven' in which the author, an androgynous angel, is simultaneously male usurer and female labourer; in revolutionising the economy of gender and thereby becoming 'a wife unto himself', Joyce brings forth his text from the intertextual economy. Joyce's delivery of the episode mimics Mina's difficult delivery of the baby; like hers, his labour is excessive, and his offspring – all the authors that he now adopts as parts of his own identity – numerous. Moreover, by legitimising cribbing as artistic labour, the episode at once unweaves Joyce's 'image' as original author and reweaves it as a female principle of collective, anti-authoritarian authority.

The debate about proliferation and economy dramatised in the episode is in fact staged on another level throughout the second half of *Ulysses*, which offers many examples of Joycean verbal proliferation (for example, the lists in 'Cyclops', or the water hymn in 'Ithaca'). Thus, although 'Oxen' critiques the excessive proliferation of families like the Purefoys and Dedaluses (and the Joyces), its own compositional economy imitates that proliferative excess. If, as Foucault writes, 'author' is the word we give to 'the principle of thrift in the proliferation of meaning',[41] then Joyce redefines the nature of authorship by violating that principle. Challenging the fear of proliferation that Foucault describes as the function of authorship, Joyce instead authorises textual excess. His banking on signs thus deconstructs the Jamesian sublime economy of art – an economy that 'saves, hoards and "banks" '[42] – with one of splendid expenditure. In short, 'Oxen' satirises the economy of proliferation on one level only to reinstate it on another as a principle of artistic composition. Hence, the textual economy of 'Oxen' reinscribes the conflict between control and expenditure, between miser and spendthrift, that Joyce's economic habits betray again and again.

Throughout Joyce's writings Dublin and Ireland are depicted as dominated by indebtedness; his characters respond to their colonised condition by a variety of economic stratagems, most of which defy the bourgeois economy of balance and acquisition by versions of excess and illegitimacy – gift exchange, gambling, extravagant expenditures. In redefining authorship as plagiarism, as proliferation and expenditure, Joyce similarly defies the principles of bourgeois artistic economy, employing instead an economy of excess that adapts Irish economic behaviour as a compositional principle. 'Oxen' exemplifies and valorises this excess, whether we conceive of it as labour or as expenditure. Extravagantly rewriting male English literary history, Joyce appropriates it for those excluded from that history: the female, the Irish. Joyce's economy of excess is thus also political, because it identifies his art as Irish labour. Moreover, if the catalogue of styles in 'Oxen' shows that all authors are readers before they are writers, then it also encourages – even demands – a Joycean expenditure of labour on the reader's part. The reader of 'Oxen' must revise his or her relationship to the textual and intertextual economies; we too must perform 'heavy labour' in the textual and intertextual countinghouse in order to bring forth *Ulysses*. The reader, too, must labour and spend in excess; the reader too must become more Irish, more female. The labour of reading thus collaborates with the labour of writing, enabling readers to become co-authors. It is this extravagant, arduous and proliferating labour of reading and writing – Irish labour – that 'Oxen' ultimately affirms.

From *Joyce in the Hibernian Metropolis*, ed. Morris Beja and David Norris (Columbus, OH, 1996), pp. 237–49.

Notes

[Mark Osteen reads 'Oxen of the Sun' as a debate about human proliferation and its relation to political economy. Economy becomes the equivalent of artistic style in *Ulysses* when Mina Purefoy's fertility is equalled to Joyce's prolixity and textual extravagance. The episode sets up a distinction between the female labour of childbirth and the masculine one of financial and artistic production and shows the latter to be by far the more problematic. Joyce's intertextual 'borrowings' in 'Oxen of the Sun' are both an acknowledgement and a critique of the laws and paradoxes of originality and cultural value. Authorship, authority and the dubious freedom of textuality are thrown into question by Joyce's aesthetic experiments. They challenge the established notions of productivity and produce a text that upholds different forms of creativity, ones that are more 'female' and 'Irish', and also urges the reader to produce meaning differently. All page references to *Ulysses* are to the Oxford World's Classics edition, ed. Jeri Johnson (1993). Ed.]

1. Richard Ellmann, Introduction to Stanislaus Joyce, *My Brother's Keeper: James Joyce's Early Years*, ed. Richard Ellmann (New York, 1958), p. xv.

2. Thomas Mallon, *Stolen Words: Forays into the Origins and Ravages of Plagiarism* (New York, 1989), p. 6. The two meanings of the word were both in currency in the seventeenth century. The first use of the word in its contemporary sense is attributed by the *OED* to Ben Jonson and dates to 1601; as a term for kidnapping the word was still in use for much of that century. Other early users of the word to mean literary theft include Browne, one of Joyce's models in 'Oxen'. Curiously, Sterne, another of Joyce's intertexts here, was himself accused of plagiarising Burton's *Anatomy of Melancholy* (see Mallon, *Stolen Words*, pp. 12–14).

3. Jacques Derrida, *Margins of Philosophy*, trans. Alan Bass (Chicago, 1982), p. 315.

4. James Joyce, *Finnegans Wake*, 3rd edn (London and Boston, 1960), pp. 182 and 181.

5. James Joyce, *Letters*, 2nd edn, ed. Stuart Gilbert and Richard Ellmann (London, 1966), 3 vols, vol. 1, p. 139.

6. Michel Riffaterre, 'Syllepsis', *Critical Inquiry*, 6 (1980), 625–38 (626).

7. Michel Riffaterre, *Semiotics of Poetry* (Bloomington, IN, 1978), pp. 85–6.

8. Mallon, *Stolen Words*, pp. 2, 39.

9. Michel Foucault, 'What is an Author?', in David Lodge (ed.), *Modern Criticism and Theory: A Reader* (Harlow and New York, 1988), pp. 197–210.

10. Ibid., p. 202.

11. I am adapting the terms 'linguistic capital' and 'linguistic work' from Ferruccio Rossi-Landi, *Linguistics and Economics* (The Hague, 1975), pp. 146–58 and 39–54 respectively.

12. Robert H. Bell, *Jocoserious Joyce: The Fate of Folly in 'Ulysses'* (Ithaca, NY, 1991), p. 150.

13. These remarks depend upon a Greek pun on *tokos* – meaning both 'interest' and 'offspring' – which I have developed, along with the notion of usury, in my essay 'The Intertextual Economy in "Scylla and Charybdis" ', *James Joyce Quarterly*, 28 (Autumn 1990), 197–208.

14. Kurt Heinzelmann, *The Economics of the Imagination* (Amherst, MA, 1980), p. 92. [Thomas Robert Malthus (1766–1834) was an economist who became famous for his views on population control – Ed.] One entry in the *'Ulysses' Notesheets* establishes Joyce's familiarity with Malthusian ideas: 'Malthus in Irel. food decreases arithm population incre geometrically' (Phillip Floyd Herring, *Joyce's 'Ulysses' Notesheets in the British Museum* [Charlottesville, VA, 1972], p. 282). It is also a

misreading of Malthus, who did not claim that subsistence decreases, but only that it increases more slowly than population.

15. Robert Janusko, *Sources and Structures of James Joyce's 'Oxen'* (Ann Arbor, MI, 1983), pp. 99, 126–32, 155.

16. Thomas Carlyle, *Past and Present* (New York, n.d.), p. 179.

17. Ibid., p. 190. The 'Labour' chapter contains not only the sentence just quoted but also an allusion to Gideon's fleece, which is used as a metaphor for the rewards gained by the 'man of nature' (p. 192). This is the same biblical passage alluded to in the 'Oxen' Carlyle pastiche. At the end of 'Labour' Carlyle also exhorts his readers to make the world bear them to 'new Americas' (p. 193), a metaphor also employed in the 'Oxen' passage.

18. Carlyle, *Past and Present*, p. 191.

19. Joyce acknowledged his debt to Ruskin in a letter to Stanislaus, in which he admitted that he had been educated 'by Father Meagher and Ruskin' (*Letters*, vol. 2, p. 108). According to Stanislaus, when Ruskin died, Joyce wrote a 'studious imitation' of him called 'A Crown of Wild Olive' (p. 89).

20. John Ruskin, *The Library Edition of the Works of John Ruskin*, ed. E. T. Cook and Alexander Wedderburn, 39 vols (London, 1903–12), vol. 17, p. 84.

21. Ruskin, *Works*, vol. 17, p. 97.

22. Ibid., p. 56.

23. Ibid., p. 105.

24. Ibid., p. 97.

25. Ibid., p. 148.

26. Ibid., p. 150.

27. P. D. Anthony, *John Ruskin's Labour* (Cambridge, 1983), p. 157.

28. Ruskin, *Works*, vol. 34, p. 417.

29. ['Chrematistic' means 'related to money making' – Ed.]

30. Ruskin, *Works*, vol. 17, p. 182.

31. Ibid.

32. Mary Lowe-Evans, *Crimes against Fecundity: Joyce and Population Control* (Syracuse, NY, 1989), p. 26. See also Joyce, *Letters*, vol. 2, p. 48.

33. Heinzelmann, *Economics of the Imagination*, p. 175. Similarly, Jean-Joseph Goux writes: 'The position of labour within the capitalist "act

of production" reproduces in its specific domain the position of female reproductive labour within a patrialist [i.e. patriarchal and philosophically idealist] reproduction. The value of the produced (children, goods) is a lost positivity, a "surplus" that becomes estranged from the producer. The relation between mother and offspring, under the father's control, is like that between worker and product under capitalist domination. There is an *inversion of fertilities*'; *Symbolic Economies: After Marx and Freud*, trans. Jennifer Curtiss Gage (Ithaca, NY, 1990), p. 233.

34. Ruskin, *Works*, vol. 17, p. 89.

35. Stephen buys two rounds of drinks in 'Oxen'. The first costs him 2s 1d ('Two bar and a wing', p. 404) and the second about 2s 4d, for a total of 4s 5d. I have arrived at the price for the second round by calculating how many half crowns his pocket holds at the beginning of 'Eumaeus', before he lends one to Corley (p. 574); the text does not specify how many, but it is probably three. I have also assumed that the expenditures must all be subtracted from £2 19s. Efforts to determine exact expenditures must remain inconclusive, however, since we never know how much money Stephen has at the end of the day, nor whether the (indeterminate number of) half crowns in 'Eumaeus' are part of the total.

36. Joyce, *Letters*, vol. 2, p. 48; see my 'Narrative Gifts: "Cyclops" and the Economy of Excess', in *Joyce Studies Annual*, ed. Thomas F. Staley (Austin, TX, 1990), pp. 162–96.

37. Karen Lawrence, *The Odyssey of Style in 'Ulysses'* (Princeton, NJ, 1981), p. 143.

38. Joyce, *Letters*, vol. 2, p. 465.

39. Ibid., vol. 1, p. 146.

40. Joyce, *Selected Letters*, p. 249.

41. Foucault, 'What is an Author?', p. 209.

42. Henry James, *The Spoils of Poynton* (New York, 1908), p. vi.

8

'Circe': Joyce's *Argumentum ad Feminam*

EWA PLONOWSKA ZIAREK

> *Argumentum ad feminam*, as we said in old Rome and ancient Greece. ... For the rest Eve's sovereign remedy.
>
> (James Joyce, *Ulysses*, p. 483)

The rapidly growing body of feminist scholarship in Joyce studies[1] can be seen as part of a larger project to rethink the complex intersections between gender and the logic of modernity.[2] As Alice Jardine argues, the often uneasy valorisation of the feminine in modern literary and theoretical texts is not an accidental but rather an intrinsic feature of modernity. The invention or recovery of new rhetorical and 'conceptual spaces' in modern texts all too often depends on coding as feminine what has been excluded or marginalised in the dominant discourse.[3] Similarly, the work of Julia Kristeva has located the source of the aesthetic 'revolution' in a desire to reach the maternal *jouissance* by violating the constraints of the symbolic exchange. The suppressed level of signification – the semiotic *chora* – is 'gendered' as maternal as if the structuralist linguistics could not be deconstructed without dismantling gender ideology.[4] From yet another perspective, Luce Irigaray responds that the articulation of female sexuality in its own specificity necessarily involves 'retraversal' and 'mimicry' of the discursive operations of the patriarchal culture, whose specular system of representation is intolerant of differences, multiplicity, and indeterminancy.[5]

In her recent *The Gender of Modernity* Rita Felski undertakes perhaps the most systematic interrogation of the complex operation of gender behind the founding categories of the 'modern', informing not only theoretical studies but also cultural and literary histories of modernity. What Felski diagnoses is the paradoxical gender dialectic of modernity – the simultaneous and contradictory positioning of femininity outside and inside modern culture. Thus, in addition to the frequently noted exclusions of women from the paradigmatic forms of modern experience – the dandy, the flâneur, the stranger, the alienated artist – her study also reveals an equally problematic feminisation of these very forms; for instance, irrationality, libidinal excesses, commodification, artificiality of everyday life, and even experimental writing have been gendered feminine. This contradictory figuration of femininity is inseparable from the antithetical representations of modernity itself. When modernity is associated with the rapid processes of industrialisation and technologisation or with the crisis of capitalist production, femininity seems to offer a nostalgic refuge from the fragmentation and disenchantment of modern life. Conversely, when modernity is identified with an aesthetic counterdiscourse to the dominant culture, femininity can become an embodiment of the very superficiality from which the modern subject wants to escape. As Felski writes, 'the superficiality and interchangeability of women symbolises ... an all-pervasive disenchantment of the world in which feminine sexuality, like art, has been deprived of its redemptive aura, contaminated by the rationalisation of everyday art'.[6]

Focusing on the 'Circe' episode of *Ulysses* as a highly idiosyncratic and yet characteristic example of the gender dialectic in modernity, I would like to examine the contradictory role of femininity in Joyce's fashioning of the 'subversive' claims of aesthetics.[7] I focus on this particular episode because it explicitly heralds the aesthetic counterdiscourse of modernity as a certain release of 'the other of reason' while, at the same time, it confines this irrationality to the excesses of female sexuality and the spectral figures of maternity. By exploring the function of 'post-creation', sublimation, and the abject in the composition of 'Circe', I will argue that the aesthetic emancipation of 'the other of reason' does not necessarily entail the cultural emancipation of femininity; on the contrary, its outcome remains profoundly ambiguous. As my reading suggests, the aesthetic innovations of modernity simultaneously reproduce and shatter the traditional representations of femininity in terms of the carnal enslavement and the paralysis of matter.

Although many Joycean critics have offered excellent accounts of the radical style in this episode, the connection between the new formulation of aesthetics in 'Circe' and the figuration of femininity is usually ignored.[8] Traditionally, the chapter has been read as a purgation of characters' obsessions, which prepares them for the meeting of the son (Stephen) with his father (Bloom).[9] However, if we follow the convoluted path of Joyce's *argumentum ad feminam*, we will notice that the rhetorical innovations in 'Circe' initiate drastic revisions of *Ulysses'* aesthetic assumptions centred on the notion of literary paternity.[10] 'Circe' becomes a strategic locus where the text stages a breakdown of its paternal metaphors, especially prevalent in Stephen's definition of artistic production and in his interpretation of literary history. Explicitly coded as feminine, the stage of representation in 'Circe' uncovers and mimics the paternal logic of postcreation. One of the most startling effects of 'Circe' is that such mimicry leads, on the one hand, to a dazzling display of textual innovations whereas, on the other, it leaves the male artist figures (including Shakespeare) paralysed and impotent. Inverting the motif of a play as a literary 'parturition' of the artist (p. 200), 'Circe' submits the autonomous 'begetter' (p. 199) to the play of insubordinate maternal spectres. Although the complexity of 'Circe' requires a rethinking of the 'revolution of the Word' in the double context of the commodification of female sexuality (the prostitute) and the fear of reproduction (the mother), my argument here will be limited to the spectral unfolding of modern aesthetics associated with the maternal body.[11]

The goddess of unreason: aesthetics and im-passes of 'postcreation'

In the final apocalyptic vision of 'Circe', Mrs Mina Purefoy, still pregnant, is crowned as the goddess of unreason and sacrificed at *altare diaboli* during a mock mass celebrated by medical students. This scene recalls and reverses the pattern of 'The Oxen of the Sun', which describes a much delayed birth of 'poor Mrs Paraph's' child whereas its style celebrates the patriarchal tradition of English letters.[12] It also alludes to the opening scene of *Ulysses* ('*Introibo ad altare Dei*')[13] but intensifies its blasphemous and mocking effect by juxtaposing the Body of Christ with the body of a pregnant woman: 'On the altarstone Mrs Mina Purefoy, goddess of unreason, lies, naked, fettered, a chalice resting on her swollen belly' (p. 556). The presence of the pregnant woman on the altar becomes the striking reversal of the Eucharist – a profane display of the carnal and physical fertility. Since the maternal body is associated with the 'fetters' of unredeemed matter, with the opposite of the spirit, it also occasions the mocking exhibitions of the cross-dressed celebrant's (wearing lace petticoat) body in place of the Body of Christ. Staging a profane transformation of the divine back into the mundane carnality, the swollen belly becomes the striking emblem of 'the other of reason' that the aesthetic counterdiscourse of modernity wants to recover and put on display.

If the swollen belly of 'unreason' seems blasphemous for the religious and philosophical sentiments, it is even more so for Stephen's artistic sensibilities, attuned to the idealistic metamorphosis of imagination. The excess of the maternal body that refuses to 'bring forth' its fruit epitomises the artist's fear of paralysis, impotence, and the suffocating burden of carnality. For Stephen, the maternal body functions, to recall Rita Felski's argument, 'as a primary symbolic site for confronting and controlling the threat of unruly nature. If the dandy-aesthete embodies an aspiration to the ideal, then woman ... represents materiality and corporeality'.[14] That the figure of the pregnant body in 'Circe' should signify for the artist a negative relation to his work becomes especially apparent if we notice that this vision irrupts between Bloom's violent solicitation of speech from Cissy Caffrey, who becomes for that occasion a mother figure ('Are you struck dumb? You are the link between nations and generations. Speak, woman, *sacred life-giver*!' [pp. 554–5; emphasis added]) and Stephen's appeal to reason ('Reason. This feast of pure reason' [p. 557]). In the context of these paternal positions of logos and speech – what Lynch calls 'dialectic, the universal language' (p. 557) – the woman appears as 'unreason', as the negativity, and an uncertain 'link'. The swollen womb is thus the figure of passing (from father to son, from logos to speech) and of the impasse, or aporia, of these religious and aesthetic transubstantiations.

The consecration of the womb of unreason in 'Circe' – the episode that as a whole revolves around the traditional association of feminine sexuality with night-time hallucinations, madness, repressed fantasies, irruptions of uncontrollable desires and obsessions, in short, with the underworld[16] of reason – not only celebrates modern aesthetics as the other of reason but also genders this irrationality as maternal. Such a descent into the underworld figured as the womb of unreason creates a radical interruption, or an impasse, in Stephen's theorising about art. Yet, if the characters feel the need to escape and defend themselves against the sexual and linguistic economy of this underworld, Joyce's text remains submerged in its web, dreaming of the other possibilities of literature – possibilities that are no longer limited to the level of the character, representation, or the romantic notion of genius as the great 'begetter'. The association of the experimental aesthetics with the irrationality of the maternal body reveals what imagination, transforming the flesh of existence into the poetics of the word, could not imagine.

I suggest that the stage of 'Circe' as the womb of unreason is the other side, the other 'post' passed over in Stephen's idea of artistic 'postcreation', yet recovered as the perilous source of modern art. Although Stephen is obsessed by the urgent desire to distinguish poetic creativity from natural procreation, he can articulate the difference of poetic language only by referring to the process of birth and incarnation, that is, by appropriating and overcoming maternal procreation. The claim that the artist's word is independent from the servitude of the maternal flesh is announced paradoxically only in the 'post' of the 'postcreation' – in its mark of secondariness, in its coming after, but also in overcoming the involuntary procreation of the maternal body. Therefore the library cannot be a sufficient locus of artistic self-definition, and the celebration of poetic language has to continue in the maternity hospital, where the difference between the pro- and postcreation can be finally heard: 'In woman's womb word is made flesh but in the spirit of the maker all flesh that passes becomes the word that shall not pass away. This is the postcreation' (p. 373). This frequently quoted aphorism[17] seeks to demarcate the contrast between the body and the spirit, between procreation and 'artist's conscious begetting', by deploying the old religious rhetoric of eucharistic transformation. We observe here, in fact, two kinds of 'transubstantiation': the maternal womb externalises the word, turns it into flesh, whereas the paternal spirit internalises the body into the immortal word. The flesh is recuperated back into a position of the living speech – the paternal logos. Yet the necessity of this contrast reveals that the spirit of the maker cannot describe itself otherwise than in the negative relation to its other: to the woman, the body, the exterior. As was the case with Mulligan's profanation of the mass, the maternal body is also an obverse coin of artistic production, its indispensable, negative, blind, and mute side.

This operation is not unusual; as Luce Irigaray points out in the context of her analysis of sexual difference, the feminine function has been constructed as the negative against which man defines and represents himself. Outside the parameters of men's self-definition, the feminine in itself is a matter of 'sexual indifference': 'Freud does not see *two sexes* whose differences are articulated in the act of intercourse, and more generally speaking, in the imaginary and symbolic processes that regulate the workings of a society and a culture. The "feminine" is always described in terms of deficiency or atrophy, as the other side of the sex that alone holds the monopoly on value: the male sex.'[18] Similarly, for Stephen maternal procreation is merely a negative and blind process against which the artist can demarcate *his* relation to language and art. There is a strange double necessity for the recurrence of maternal images in the process of Stephen's artistic self-definition – they are simultaneously evoked and expelled as if the artist could know himself only by differentiating himself from a maternal nonself. Yet, the artist's confrontation with the pregnant goddess, who not only delays but denies parturition, who does not release the 'content' of her womb, no longer works in the economy of self-knowledge or self-definition. It is indeed a confrontation with 'unreason' because, at this moment, the contrast between art and birth as well as the stable positions of the inside and the outside (on which it depends) collapse. Traditionally associated with nature, body, and its blind procreative powers, and therefore with the opposite of conscious creativity, the 'pregnant goddess of unreason' reappears in *Ulysses* as a mocking impasse of this metaphorical logic, as the paralysing limit of the artistic and sacral transubstantiation, as its *locomotor ataxia*. Yet, by blocking the transformation of the flesh into the stability of the word ('that shall not pass away'), the inscription of 'the womb of unreason' within 'the spirit of the maker' releases endless 'passing' of both the word and the flesh and marks the radical temporality of the 'post' in postcreation. It is a turn from the 'transfiguration' and the stability of truth revealed in the word to what Walter Benjamin calls 'transmissibility' – unpredictable accidents of change and transmission in the absence of the revealed truth.[19]

By breaking down the identity of the words, disturbing the logic of postcreation, and, consequently, paralysing the *figures* of male artists (Stephen, Shakespeare), the reappearance of the womb as 'the repressed matrix of language'[20] reveals nonetheless the very texture of *Ulysses'* textuality. This figure describes the most irruptive, unpredictable elements of the creative process, which are incompatible with the scheme of literary paternity. The unpredictable rhythm of hallucinations, breaking the boundaries of singular selves, shatters the logocentric vision of the artist as the great begetter: 'God, sun, Shakespeare', who in his wandering always in the end returns into himself. Let us recall here that in Stephen's aesthetic theory, paternity is invariably associated with 'a conscious begetting' of the artist, 'an apostolic succession', creation of 'aesthetic offsprings who reflect their parent immortally'.[21] Many commentators have pointed out that the notion of dominant paternity even for Stephen has, after all, a status of 'legal' fiction. But as Karen Lawrence argues, this paternal fiction nonetheless remains authoritative and legal, necessary to keep the 'maternal counterpart' in check.[22] And by stressing its 'legal', that is, normative, character, Joyce implies that it has a claim on both the writer and the reader, just as the interpretation of legal discourse has a direct impact on the situation of the interpreter.

Confirming Stephen's suspicion that 'paternity may be a legal fiction', 'Circe' re-enacts this breakdown of the paternal metaphor in an even more radical fashion: it exacerbates not only the crisis of artist's intentionality but also the crisis of the legitimation of modern art. In this context, the return of the figure of the mother does not merely represent the spectre of Stephen's guilty consciousness, but, on the contrary, it displays the limit of that consciousness and its voluntary 'begetting'. The figure of the womb as the matrix of language discloses a non-assimilable otherness interrupting the trajectory of the 'paternal postcreation'. The event of the delayed birth, the threat of the interruption in the succession from father to son, is symptomatic of the textuality of *Ulysses*, which both suppresses the figure of the woman and recalls it as a ghost in order to mark its new rhetorical spaces.

Even though the artist tries to reduce *amor matris* – this 'subjective and objective genitive, ... the only true thing in life' (p. 199) – to a simple biological fact in comparison with the 'mystery' of conscious begetting, the figure of the mother cannot be dissociated from the figuration of language. Exceeding the scope of the artist's intended meaning, the phrase *amor matris* also functions after all as an example of the genitive structure in Latin; it points simultaneously to both maternal love and the grammar of language. It is both a 'subjective and objective' generator of meaning. In this context, Stephen's attempt to bury the mother (or grandmother, as his riddle reveals on p. 27) not only bespeaks the repression of maternity on the level of the son's guilty consciousness, it also points to the suppression of maternity in the tropology of textual production. If *amor matris* evokes a loss of a dead and already foreign 'mother' tongue that is buried in the process of artistic 'postcreation', the stage of 'Circe' – the stage of the descent into the underground of culture and reason – initiates the process of excavating the forgotten maternal and linguistic resources.

In contrast to the linear temporality of succession from father to son, 'the womb of unreason' as the buried matrix of language interrupts the continuity of artistic production with unpredictable delays, deferrals of meaning, and postponements of fruition. In light of the Homeric parallels in Joyce's text, the descent into Circe's cave thematises *par excellence* the threat of irreversible delay in the hero/artist's homecoming. But in Joyce's 'Circe' such deferral and the threat of madness associated with it are explicitly linked with the figures of whores and mothers, and their everyday 'magic' of sexuality and procreation.[23] In this sense, 'Circe' is the culmination of the rhetoric of deferral operating throughout *Ulysses*. Hugh Kenner was one of the first to argue that such an 'aesthetic of delay' creates time gaps 'in the order of presentation', which prevent the semantic closure of the chains of signification.[24] The significant information about the major facts in the book (like the importance of Bloom's potato) comes late, or too late, constantly modifying our earlier comprehension of the text: 'Joyce's aesthetic of delay [produces] ... the simplest facts by parallax, one element now, one later, and leaving large orders of fact to be assembled later at another time or never.'[25]

The aesthetics of delay dramatises the temporality of poetic language. The unpredictable movement of transformations, endless 'weaving and unweaving' of figures, the fusion and decomposition of identities no longer imply a mere detour on the way home, but rather an openendedness of the text that renounces the nostalgia for a final destination. For Hélène Cixous the figures of delayed birth and the womb of unreason become crucial metaphors of textual production 'reopening' the traditional categories of self and representation: 'From father unto son, via mother, always, begun again. This delayed birth constitutes the movement of a work which playfully undermines gestation, the delay inscribing itself in the various falls, losses ... which are all the more astounding in that the goal seems accessible, is named ... (I, the Artist, the Word).'[26]

Stephen likewise associates maternal body with the weaving and unweaving process of textual production, but for him, this unsettling process of dissolution and recuperation has to be subordinated to the agency of the father securing continuity of the name and the image for the son: 'We, or mother Dana, weave and unweave our bodies ... so does the artist weave and unweave his image. And as the mole on my right breast is where it was when I was born, though all my body has been woven of new stuff time after time, so through the ghost of the unquiet father the image of the unliving son looks forth' (p. 186). The ghost of the father secures the identity for the yet unliving son in the risky process of becoming; it establishes the illusion of the final destination in the endless trajectory of 'posts' in postcreation. The ghost of the mother, on the other hand, remains a suspect mediatory figure, since she can 'unweave' the scheme of filiation entirely, or disturb it with postponements, delays, unfaithfulness.

Between sublimation and disgust: 'androgynous angels' and 'emaciated ghosts'

From the rhetorical side of Joyce's *argumentum ad feminam*, maternity and paternity appear as two different modes of *Ulysses'* textuality supplementing each other: the maternal dissipation and deferral of meaning is submitted to the paternal function securing the continuity of identity. How are these two functions of language, so explicitly infused with gender categories, played out in the text? Can those two functions – paternity and maternity – be reconciled or united? As an answer to these questions *Ulysses* tests the limits of the modernist fascination with androgyny as a more complete metaphor of textual production: 'in the economy of heaven, foretold by Hamlet, there are no more marriages, glorified man, an androgynous angel, being a wife unto himself' (p. 205). Let us notice that the figure of 'glorified' androgyny differs significantly from artistic 'postcreation' in terms of its relation to the figure of the mother. As an androgynous angel, the artist no longer needs to differentiate his art from the blind process of procreation, because now he can incorporate it as part of his own creativity. As John Paul Riquelme suggests, the artist (the male artist nonetheless) both mothers and fathers his text.[27] Androgyny appears then as a happy sublimation of the unstable dialectic between maternity and paternity on a higher level of 'the heavenly economy' of art. In such overcoming of the gender differences, the woman does not merely represent negativity in the artist's self-definition but is completely erased from the process of artistic creation. From the trope of the mother as a blind fertile genetrix, we arrive at the figure of the mother as an 'emaciated ghost': the second apparition confronting Stephen in 'Circe'.

The apparition of the maternal ghost marks the erasure on the level of aesthetic theory and poetic practice. In a brilliant definition of the ghost, Stephen reveals the structure of that erasure: 'What is a ghost? ... One who has faded into impalpability through death, through absence, through change of manners' (p. 180). According to this definition, the mother is ghostly not simply by death, but also by 'absence' and denial in the son's 'heavenly economy' of artistic creativity – she 'has faded into impalpability' through the 'change of [artistic] manners'. The sublimation of this maternal figure into the 'heavenly economy' of male begetting is a repression-through-incorporation of difference. The ghost of the mother in the Joycean text plays the role of what Derrida calls an 'intermediary figure': 'the mediation, the middle term between total absence and absolute plenitude of presence'.[28] As such, it both escapes and upsets the logic of androgynous inclusion (which subsumes otherness into sameness) by introducing the legacy of a 'ghostwoman': its mark of dissociation and decomposition, its simultaneous withdrawal and encroachment on the work that tries to contain it. The apparition of the mother as a ghost at once reflects and fractures the false unity of androgynous angels and marks the limit to the 'all-inclusiveness' of their art. Frightening and fascinating, this maternal apparition indicates a possible resistance to the voracious inclusion of all discursive resources in *Ulysses* as a whole.[29]

The male fantasy of the absolute plenitude of the androgynous creation is ridiculed by Buck Mulligan, whose joke might be a mocking announcement of the first labour pains of 'Circe': 'Wait. I am big with child. I have an unborn child in my brain. Pallas Athena! A play! The play is the thing! Let me parturiate!' (p. 200).

'Circe', a play within the novel, is a deforming reflection and a mimicry of this literary parturition. It functions as a deforming mirror, which does not confirm the identity and unity of the androgynous construct but insists on difference and otherness in their place. For Stephen such a cracked mirror is merely a metaphor for the inferiority of the colonised Irish culture: 'It is a symbol of Irish art. The cracked lookingglass of a servant' (p. 7). It is ironic that Stephen's metaphor of inferiority (which is a reversal of Hamlet's famous aphorism: a play is 'the mirror up to nature') has been frequently used to describe the mode of representation in 'Circe', the most radical part of *Ulysses*. Daniel Ferrer, for instance, suggests that the whole episode is a variation of Stephen's/Hamlet's metaphor, with the significant difference that the textual distortions are no longer predictable according to the laws of optics: 'According to this model, "Circe" is indeed a mirror, but a distorting mirror, one of those disquieting contraptions which introduce difference in the very place where one is seeking confirmation of one's identity. Such an explanation would account for the systematic repetition of elements found earlier in the novel, and for the constant transformation which they undergo; it would account for the fusion, within each image, of the strange and the familiar.'[30]

What is there in the structure of the servant's mirror that it can 'serve' as a metaphor of both the most servile and the most radical art? Not surprisingly, the distorting, cracked glass is a purloined 'possession' of a woman. First, Buck Mulligan steals the mirror from the servant girl in his aunt's house, and then Stephen, angry at his deformed reflection, commits a second theft and transforms the mirror into the emblem of the colonial servitude and, by implication, feminisation of Irish art.[31] As Colin MacCabe points out, in *Ulysses* women are too often reduced to mirrors: in order to reflect male desires, they deny their own sexuality.[32] Yet here the 'feminine' no longer serves as an instrument of the specular reflection and self-definition of man but mimics the very logic of that reflection.[33] Through that act of mimicry the servitude of the feminine is converted into a form of resistance. However, Stephen is not aware of the inherent contradiction in his aphorism: he does not notice that the servant's cracked mirror (as all women are figures of servitude in his metaphors of creativity), like the weaving and unweaving of the maternal body, like the weaving of the texture of the text, refuses to serve faithfully, to reproduce the artist's face with exactitude.

In 'Circe' Joyce transforms the metaphor of feminine servitude into the emblem of literary language liberated from its representative function. Forced to gaze into that (maternal) mirror, the young artist no longer can reassemble his portrait from the unfolding linguistic differences and transformations. Yet this liberation of the mother tongue from its servitude, from the burden of conscious begetting, also implies that the maternal ghost usurps the place of the Father–Shakespeare–Artist articulated in Stephen's interpretation of *Hamlet*. This sense of a radical displacement in the structure and the theory of textual production is usually covered over by the traditional explications of the maternal ghost in terms of the Homeric parallels (Odysseus meeting the shadow of his mother in the underworld) or in terms of Stephen's psychology (his earlier dream of the mother) because both of these interpretations corroborate the maternal as the link securing the continuity with the Homeric source and the earlier parts of the text. However, if we also see 'Circe' as a repetition and drastic refiguration of Shakespeare's *Hamlet* (as the dramatic form of the episode, the apparition of Shakespeare, and the scene of the ghost addressing the figure of the son in the text encourage us to do), then the maternal figure – the blindness of the non-origin – simultaneously usurps the place of paternal origin and withdraws itself from any sense of genealogical continuity.

The ghost of the mother as the mark of non-origin has been already 'present' at the beginning of creation, spoiling the likeness passed from father to son: 'Wombed in sin darkness I was too, made not begotten. By them, the man with my voice and my eyes and a ghostwoman with ashes on her breath' (p. 38). Reflecting on his conception through the logic of literary paternity (a father speaking to his son so that 'his namesake may live for ever' [p. 181]), Stephen stresses consubstantiality with his father as the continuity of vision ('my eyes') and speech ('my voice') in spite of the fact that for other characters this continuity is clouded by his resemblance to the mother (for instance, Bloom repeatedly asserts Stephen's matrilineal likeness: 'Face reminds me of his poor mother' [p. 565], 'the sideface of Stephen, image of his mother' [p. 616]). This erasure of the figure of the mother[34] from the moment of origin constitutes her as a non-origin, which perverts the paternal logos (from and breath of life) with the 'breath' and formlessness of ashes.

The intrusion of the excluded maternal ghost performs a violent collapse of androgynous fantasy. The maternal ghost is thus an obverse side of the poetic sublimation of the great sweet mother that Stephen discovers in the lines of 'Algy' Swinburne's poem, 'The Triumph of Time': 'I will go to the great sweet mother, / Mother and lover of men, the sea. / I will go down to her, I and not other, / Close with her, kiss her and mix her with me'.[35] If these lines, as Victor Burgin suggests,[36] bespeak the male desire for a blissful union with the mother and for the loss of identity in that fusion, the nightmarish apparition signifies the aversion to that fantasy. The horror and disgust evoked by the maternal apparition in 'Circe' imply that the androgynous unity does not hold, that the mother, non-assimilable to the design of consciousness and the text, is repeatedly expelled beyond their limits.

As Julia Kristeva persuasively argues, this experience of disgust – a synthesis of affect and judgement – points to the defensive expulsion of what cannot be assimilated to the self.[37] Consistently erased from the text as the figure of *jouissance*, the mother appears with a vengeance as a mark of abjection. The carefully orchestrated iconography of matrilinear genealogy reads as if it were a condensation of the biblical abominations, ranging from the Leviticus list of impurities (corpse, excrement, uncleanness) to a particularly Christian addition of 'the womb of sin'. The physical decay of the maternal body – 'her face worn and noseless, green with grave-mould' and 'a green rill of bile trickling from a side of her mouth', as if reinforcing her earlier associations with bitter milk, with fits of vomiting, with excrements of the rotting body (pp. 5–6) – is the other side of sublimated androgyny. The ever increasing nearness of the maternal body is associated in 'Circe' with the spreading of decomposition, with the infection of disease (leprosy, cancer), and finally, with the threat of death. Unlike the breath of life, the mother creates a choking sensation in the son. Since she cannot be reduced to the limits of signification, she violently dissociates herself from the androgynous fantasy – repelling and repulsive. From spiritual androgyny we return to the most physical sensation of abjection.

The mere memory of the maternal corpse is enough to shrink the expansion of Stephen's universe – the never ending horizon of the sea – to the bowl of excrement: 'The ring of bay and skyline held a dull green mass of liquid. A bowl of white china had stood beside her deathbed holding the green sluggish bile' (p. 6). These repressed memories structure Stephen's famous dream, yet another nightmare, from which he is trying to awake: 'Silently, in a dream she had come to him after her death, her wasted body within its loose brown graveclothes giving off an odour of wax and rosewood, her breath ... a faint odour of wetted ashes. ... A bowl of white china had stood beside her deathbed holding the green sluggish bile which she had torn up from her rotting liver by fits of loud groaning vomiting' (pp. 5–6). In 'Circe', this dreamwork does not stop until it demarcates the textual border through a peculiar metonymic chain associating the maternal body with waste, the rotting insides, a disintegrating corpse, disease, the formlessness of ashes and uncleanness of the loins – that is, with everything that threatens borders, identities, and orders, including the order of the sign.

For Kristeva, the spasm of revulsion is a defensive attitude that ejects 'beyond the scope of the possible, the tolerable, the thinkable' whatever cannot be assimilated to the outlines of the subject and the world.[38] This resistance discloses the abject as the most radical form of alterity and the primary form of exclusion. If the object evokes desires, including desires for signification, and constitutes a correlative of subjectivity, the abject points to a place where signification collapses, where the borders of the world and the self are threatened and dissolved. Abject not only reveals radical alterity par excellence (judgement) but also betrays the subject's defensive attitude to it (affect). No longer assimilable to the limits of discursivity, such otherness is expelled as waste, rejected with revulsion. Kristeva makes it clear that it is not merely a revolting sight that causes abjection but rather everything ambiguous, everything that disturbs the boundaries, identities, orders, including the autonomy of the subject and the coherence of discourse. The abject is not revolting in itself, but is considered as such only with respect to a system of signification that it threatens.[39] As the irreducible otherness, the abject not only cannot be a correlative of the self but it constantly violates the borders of the world, identity, and language.

The utmost form of abjection for both Kristeva and Joyce is the encroachment of the corpse on the space of the living consciousness: 'Deprived of world, therefore, I *fall in a faint*. In that compelling, raw, insolent thing in the morgue's full sunlight, in that thing that no longer matches and therefore signifies anything, I behold the breaking down of a world that has erased its borders: fainting away.'[40] Instead of giving birth to a new life, the maternal body consumes itself in the production of waste and death. However, for the defensive artistic imagination, the cannibalism of the mother does not stop at her body, it does not respect the boundaries between the inside and the outside, the self and the other. By invading the living space of consciousness, the maternal corpse also consumes the body of her son: 'Ghoul! Chewer of corpses! / No, mother! Let me be and let me live' (p. 10). This encroachment of the maternal corpse in 'Circe' no longer sustains the fantasy of an androgynous union but performs instead the collapse of consciousness and the world: Stephen's fits of fainting prefigure an even more threatening apocalyptic imagery of the destruction of the world.

The spasm of revulsion is a futile defence against *amor matris*. The mother dissociates herself from any sense of unity with the paternal self of the artist, yet constantly encroaches on its autonomy. Her return bespeaks both the dissociation and contiguity; even though she returns as an *empty* mother, the invisible navel cord still upsets the economy of representation based on identity: 'The cords of all link back, strandentwining cable of all flesh' (p. 38). The uncontrollable movement of such suppressed links and cords turns the short-lasting heavenly harmony – the dance of the hours – into the macabre dance of death. Stephen's final violence, his attempt to strike the ghost with Nothung/ashplant, is a desperate gesture to sever that cord and free himself from the nearness of a 'ghostwoman'. By cutting the link with his mother, Stephen wants to be reborn as an artist. Since he cannot erase the mother, he at least wants to secure his separation from her by occupying simultaneously the position of the midwife and the position of the paternal superego. In the end, this violence of self-creation masquerades as the heroism of aesthetics. Yet the maternal ghost cannot be cut off, it cannot be controlled or contained, even though it has faded into impalpability, and denotes nothing but absence (p. 180). Unlike guilty Ann Hathaway, whose ghost 'has been laid for ever', because '[s]he died, for literature at least, before she was born' (p. 182), it is the ghostwoman that embodies the spectral logic of modern aesthetics.

Referring to *Ulysses* as an example of the catharsis of the abject through the proliferation of the word, Kristeva considers the avant-garde literature to be a privileged signifier of abjection, since its 'revolutionary' aesthetics is by definition involved in questioning, testing, and crossing the limits of culture and language. We could say that for Kristeva the aesthetic counterdiscourse of modernity repeats the economy of disgust. In this confluence of the abominable and the maternal, both of which are designated by patriarchy as the dangerous limit of culture and signification, Kristeva sees not only the origin of cultural misogyny but also a source of literary experimentation. Thus, she considers *Ulysses*' preoccupation with the maternal corpse as an affirmative power of modern literature: by approaching the abject as the limit of legibility, by incorporating linguistic indeterminacy, by crossing the boundaries of pure and impure, proper and improper, moral and perverse, the text extends the parameters of culture and refigures the space of signification. Yet the fact that a modern text like *Ulysses* gives birth to itself through the abjection of the maternal body is necessarily far more problematic and ambiguous. Rather than simply affirming the subversive claims of aesthetics, *Ulysses* reproduces a familiar dilemma of modernism: does modern aesthetics convert what the dominant culture considers abominable and non-productive into a new source of linguistic proliferation, or, on the contrary, does it repeat the misogynist gesture of excluding femininity by finding it already outside the parameters of signification?

Learning midwifery with 'Circe': a note on the art of reading

As Kristeva and her critics suggest, the phenomenon of abjection is inextricably linked with the mode of reading. Tracing the interdependence between abjection and rhetoric, Cynthia Chase argues that abjection is a prototype of every act of reading and interpretation; it is a defensive rejection of everything that is not received as a sign, that is not recuperable within the horizon of meaning.[41] As a synthesis of affect and judgement, revulsion might be the first distinction between the legible and the illegible, between what makes sense and what does not. It reinforces both a subjective and a cultural repudiation of the indeterminacy of sense; in other words, it is a repudiation of the excess of the materiality of language.

By repeating and defamiliarising the past of the text, the repulsive maternal ghost in 'Circe' similarly dramatises the limits of interpretation. For Daniel Ferrer, the spectre of the mother conjures up the even more impalpable ghost of the recurring language of *Ulysses*, which resists recuperation in the act of interpretation: 'But we should not forget that every word in "Circe" has its own past and must be considered, individually, as a kind of ghost, haunting the text, returning with a whole network of associations. ... It is impossible to have any clear idea of the ghost volume or its outlines.'[42] If 'Circe' as 'the womb of unreason' is a ghostly reworking of the text's main themes, motifs, and languages, it demands that we learn midwifery as a way of reading the coils of navel cord, 'strandentwining cable of all flesh'. With its passing of cords and cables, with its discernment of the nameless marks of the flesh, midwifery comes to resemble an act of weaving rather than an act of separating and ordering. Assisting this maternal replication that both recalls and repels, transfers the likeness and deforms, drags out the apparitions and refuses to name them, midwifery is no longer the hermeneutics of the (spoken) word. It renounces the question that the sons in the text pursue with such urgency: 'Tell me the word, mother, if you know now. The word known to all men' (p. 540). Like the maternal production, midwifery is no longer devoted to the paternal authority and stability of the name. Instead of interpreting the word 'known to all *men*' it reads the mark familiar to all *men and women* – call it *omphalos* if you are dissatisfied with the mundane 'navel'. The maternal imprint of otherness and the mark of irrevocable disconnection silently defamiliarise every act of naming and signing. Tracing the coils of these marks challenges the notion that *Ulysses* is a tightly controlled, synchronised novel, built on the intricate patterns of symbols, correspondences, and mimetic details from Joyce's contemporary experience.

Interpreting 'Circe', we are placed in Stephen's situation, trying to find and untangle the links, untie and cut off the cords, learn how to separate things and identities, the interior from the exterior, but 'Midwife Most Merciful, pray for us'. Midwifery is a tricky art in *Ulysses*, and, unlike Socrates who learned from his mother (another midwife) the art of philosophy, we might never learn 'how to bring thoughts into the world' (p. 183). By converting it all too quickly into the principles of philosophical dialectic, Socrates learned the art of midwifery badly. For him, it was merely the skill in the service of paternal logos, 'a portal of discovery'. 'Circe''s midwifery, however, refuses to serve as an analogy for 'bringing the thoughts into the world'. Since the navel cords are not severed or untangled, things and beings do not gain their separate identities, do not occupy clarified positions, but they drag behind them a residue, a ghost of someone/something else, or even worse, they can be partially aborted, dismembered, or swallowed back by the cannibalistic mother into the womb/tomb of unreason:

> 'Circe' not only replays all parts of *Ulysses* in one scene but, by decompartmentalisation and by depersonalisation, decomposes each and everyone into his several selves, breaks the real into fragments ... without distinction of object, of subject, of interiority or exteriority, of property.[43]

Renouncing the mastery of the logos and the word, 'Circe' teaches us midwifery as the art of reading, attuned to the entanglement of the cords, to the endless posting and reposting of the marks and figures on the body of the text.

The figure of the mother, the mother of the figures, returns. Why should this ghost return in 'Circe' and then become a figure of the return? What aspects of unexplored tropology does this return uncover? According to Aristotle (another paternal figure evoked by Stephen as the teacher/father of philosophy and poetics), each figure implies a transfer of properties between the inside and the outside, between the interior and the exterior, between the genus and the species, or between the species by analogy. We might say that the very survival of the species and the genus of literature depends on the proper work of this analogy. Yet, 'Circe' 's locomotive apparatus is afflicted with the *locomotor ataxia:* the transfer does not work properly. This paralysis discloses the fact that the rhetoric of the text does not work according to the Aristotelian patterns of substitution and combination.[44] The spirit of associations and substitutions is accompanied by the convolutions of aversions: what is brought together is violently dissociated, turned aside. The figure of the woman, the figure reduced to transfer and mediation in the economy of paternal metaphorisation, flaws the logic of all figures on 'Circe''s stage. It collapses the distinctions, dissociates analogies, or spins endless reversals between the inside and the outside, between the word and the flesh, between paternal postcreation and maternal reproduction. Its uncontrolled, ghostly reappearance not only distorts the resemblance between the father and the son, but also by refusing to serve, it paralyses the transformation of the 'flesh' into the 'word'. Thus the reversed analogy of birth and creativity is reversed once again: the emptied figure of the mother threatens to empty out the figures of the filial metaphoric production. In Stephen's theory of artistic imagination, the figure of the woman is this 'dangerous' supplement[45] that both escapes the limits of conscious creation and refuses to be sublimated (that is misappropriated) to the level of androgynous consciousness. The stage of 'Circe' – the stage miming the textual principles of composition – is erected in the wake of this insubordinate ghost.

From *Gender in Joyce*, ed. Jolanta W. Wawrzycka and Marlena G. Corcoran, The Florida James Joyce Series (Gainesville, FL, 1997), pp. 150–69.

Notes

[Inspired by recent poststructuralist feminist positions and reassessments of femininity and modernism, Ewa Ziarek explores the possible subversion of representations of femininity in *Ulysses* through the very aesthetic mechanisms that make these representations possible in the first place. It explores how the 'Circe' episode demonstrates 'the Other of reason' while simultaneously framing it in traditional masculinist norms. Ultimately, Ziarek regards 'Circe' as a paradoxical enactment of the breakdown of masculine power when faced with its Other – a breakdown that is brought about by (and produces pleasure for) exactly the masculine positions that it seems to threaten. Out of this ostensible collapse evolves the masculine counter-creation that Joyce's novel calls 'postcreation' – of which the text itself is the prime example. Yet it also entangles *Ulysses* in a 'familiar dilemma of modernism': its simultaneous subversion and continuing attachment to dominant cultural norms, here those of originality and masculine creativity. All page references to *Ulysses* are to the Oxford World's Classics edition, ed. Jeri Johnson (1993). Ed.]

1. In addition to the works directly referred to in my paper, one should mention here such excellent feminist studies as Shari Benstock, *Women of the Left Bank: Paris 1900–1914* (Austin, TX, 1986); Christine van Boheemen, *The Novel as Family Romance Language, Gender and Authority from Fielding to Joyce* (Ithaca, NY, 1987); Maud Ellmann, 'Disremembering Dedalus: *A Portrait of the Artist as a Young Man*', in *Untying the Text: A Post-Structuralist Reader*, ed. Robert Young (London, 1981); Suzette Henke, *James Joyce and the Politics of Desire* (London, 1990); and Margot Norris, *The Decentered Universe of 'Finnegans Wake'* (Baltimore, 1974) and 'Stifled Back Answers: The Gender Politics of Art in Joyce's "The Dead" ', *Feminist Readings of Joyce*, ed. Carol Ellen Jones, *Modern Fiction Studies*, special issue, 35 (1989) 479–503. The special issue of *MFS* on Joyce and feminism represents a wide range of articles deploying feminist approaches and interpretation strategies.
2. In addition to the texts discussed directly in my essay, my study of gender in modernity has been deeply influenced by the revisionary work of Marianne DeKoven, *Rich and Strange: Gender, History, Modernism* (Princeton, NJ, 1991); Bonnie Kime Scott (ed.), *The Gender of Modernism: A Critical Anthology* (Bloomington, IN, 1991); and Bonnie Kime Scott, *Refiguring Modernism*, vol. 1 (Bloomington, IN, 1995).
3. Alice A. Jardine, *Gynesis: Configurations of Woman and Modernity* (Ithaca, NY, 1985), p. 25.
4. For elaboration of the distinction between the maternal semiotic and paternal symbolic levels of language, see Julia Kristeva, *Revolution*

in Poetic Language, trans. Margaret Waller (New York, 1984), pp. 25–30 and 68–90.

5. Luce Irigaray, *This Sex Which Is Not One*, trans. Catherine Porter (Ithaca, NY, 1985), pp. 28, 33, 72–81.
6. Rita Felski, *The Gender of Modernity* (Cambridge, 1995), p. 107.
7. One of the most recent controversial examples of the feminist 'resistance to Joyce' can be found in Sandra Gilbert and Susan Gubar (eds), *No Man's Land: The Place of the Woman Writer in the Twentieth Century* (New Haven, CT, 1988), vol. 1, pp. 232–61.
8. 'The break in form' that 'Circe' represents has been variously interpreted as a descent into the unconscious (of the characters of the text itself), as 'provisional insanity', or as a 'cathartic purgation'. See, for instance, Daniel Ferrer, 'Circe, Regret and Regression', in Derek Attridge and Daniel Ferrer (eds), *Post-structuralist Joyce: Essays from the French* (New York, 1984), p. 228; Mark Shechner, *Joyce and Nighttown* (Berkeley, CA, 1974), pp. 100–53; Hugh Kenner, *Ulysses* (London, 1980), p. 118.
9. Joyce's feminist critics take issue with such appraisal of 'Circe'. Bonnie Kime Scott, for instance, regards the death of the mother, not the meeting with Bloom, as the most defining event in Stephen's artistic development. For her discussion of 'myths of female origins' in Stephen's theory of art, see her *James Joyce* (Atlantic Highlands, 1987), pp. 86–97.
10. In contrast to critics who, after Stuart Gilbert, emphasise strict Homerian parallels in the chapter, Scott points to the fact that 'Circe' enacts important feminist revisions of the inherited mythological structures (*James Joyce*, p. 92).
11. For an excellent discussion of the commodification of femininity, see Felski, *Gender of Modernity*, pp. 61–91.
12. Suzette A. Henke, *Joyce's Moraculous Sindbook: A Study of 'Ulysses'* (Columbus, OH, 1978), p. 175.
13. For an interesting discussion of Mulligan's parody of mass as an opening of endless metamorphoses in *Ulysses*, see Fritz Senn, *Joyce's Dislocutions: Essays on Reading as Translation*, ed. John Paul Riquelme (Baltimore, 1984), pp. 124–6.
14. Felski, *Gender of Modernity*, p. 109.
15. For a discussion of logos and speech in terms of the father–son relation see Jacques Derrida, 'Plato's Pharmacy', in *Dissemination*, trans. Barbara Johnson (Chicago, 1981), pp. 84–117.
16. For a different discussion of the descent into the underworld as the leading metaphor of 'Circe''s textuality, see John Paul Riquelme,

Teller and Tale in Joyce's Fiction: Oscillating Perspectives (Baltimore, 1983), pp. 215–16.

17. See, for instance, Scott, *James Joyce*, pp. 117–18. Scott suggests that Stephen as an artist is both denigrating the mother and admitting his filiation to her.

18. Irigaray, *This Sex*, p. 69.

19. Walter Benjamin, *Illuminations*, ed. Hannah Arendt, trans. Harry Zohn (London, 1992), p. 144.

20. Patrick McGee reads the numerous references to the womb in 'Oxen of the Sun' as Joyce's attempt to uncover the matrix of language foreclosed by the symbolic construction of literature; Patrick McGee, *Paperspace: Style as Ideology in Joyce's 'Ulysses'* (Lincoln, NE, 1988), pp. 101–4.

21. Henke, *Joyce's Moraculous Sindbook*, p. 68.

22. Karen Lawrence, 'Paternity as Legal Fiction in Ulysses', in Bernard Benstock (ed.), *James Joyce – The Augmented Ninth: Proceedings of the Ninth International James Joyce Symposium, Frankfurt, 1984* (Syracuse, NY, 1988), pp. 233–43 (p. 234).

23. The episode as a whole plays on and mimics the notorious mother–whore duality, characteristic, for instance, of Otto Weininger's influential but misogynistic study *Sex and Character*, trans. from the German (London and New York, 1906).

24. For a discussion of 'the aesthetics of delay' see Hugh Kenner, *Ulysses*, Unwin Critical Library (London, 1980), pp. 72–82. Developing the implications of Kenner's analysis of delay, Restuccia interprets it as Joyce's move from patristic typology to typography. See Frances L. Restuccia, *Joyce and the Law of the Father* (New Haven, CT, 1989), pp. 53–73.

25. Kenner, *Ulysses*, p. 81.

26. Hélène Cixous, 'Joyce: The (R)use of Writing', in Derek Attridge and Daniel Ferrer (eds), *Post-Structuralist Joyce: Essays from the French* (New York, 1984), pp. 15–30 (p. 16).

27. Riquelme, *Teller and Tale*, p. 35.

28. Jacques Derrida, *Of Grammatology*, trans. Gayatri Spivak (Baltimore, 1974), p. 157.

29. This all-inclusive quality of *Ulysses* as a sign of the affirmation of the Other is discussed by Jacques Derrida in 'Ulysses Gramophone: Hear say yes in Joyce', trans. Tina Kendall, in Bernard Benstock (ed.), *James Joyce: The Augmented Ninth* (Syracuse, NY, 1988), pp. 56–71. For an excellent discussion and critique of Derrida, see Christine van

Boheemen, 'Joyce, Derrida, and the Discourse of the "Other" ', in Benstock, *Augmented Ninth*, pp. 88–102, and 'Deconstruction after Joyce', in *New Alliances in Joyce Studies*, ed. Bonnie Kime Scott (Newark, DE, 1988), pp. 29–37.

30. Ferrer, 'Circe, Regret and Regression', p. 229.

31. For an excellent discussion of Joyce's ambivalent reaction to the imperialist gender allegory associating the coloniser with masculinity and the colonised with femininity, see, for instance, Joseph Valente, *James Joyce: Negotiating Sexual and Colonial Difference* (Cambridge, 1995), pp. 38–48.

32. Colin MacCabe, *James Joyce and the Revolution of the Word* (London, 1979), p. 125.

33. Irigaray suggests that perhaps the only path of resistance to that specular logic of identity historically assigned to the feminine is mimicry, which subverts the form of subordination to that of affirmation. See *This Sex*, p. 76.

34. MacCabe interprets this erasure of the mother from the conscious begetting in terms of 'a disavowal of the mother's sexuality'; *Revolution of the Word*, p. 125. I see it rather as an exclusion of what Kristeva calls a semiotic dimension of language.

35. Frank Gifford, with Robert J. Seidman, *'Ulysses' Annotated: Notes for James Joyce's 'Ulysses'*, revd edn (Berkeley, CA, 1988), p. 15.

36. Victor Burgin, 'Geometry and Abjection', in *Abjection, Melancholia, Love*, ed., John Fletcher and Andrew Benjamin (New York, 1990), pp. 117–18.

37. Julia Kristeva, *Powers of Horror: An Essay on Abjection*, trans. Leon S. Roudiez (New York, 1982), pp. 1–31.

38. Ibid., p. 1.

39. That is why Judith Butler rethinks abject as a violent process of exclusion that constitutes the domain of the cultural norms of compulsory heterosexuality; *Bodies That Matter: On the Discursive Limits of 'Sex'* (New York, 1993), pp. 8–10.

40. Kristeva, *Powers of Horror*, p. 4.

41. Cynthia Chase, 'Primary Narcissism and the Giving of Figure: Julia Kristeva with Hertz and de Man', in Fletcher and Benjamin, *Abjection*, pp. 128–9.

42. Ferrer, 'Circe, Regret and Regression', p. 234.

43. Hélène Cixous, 'At Circe's, or the Self-Opener', trans. Carol Bove, *Boundary*, 23 (1975), 387–97 (387).

44. In his 'Semiology and Rhetoric', Paul de Man was the first to argue against the neutralisation of rhetoric to the grammatical modes of combination and substitution. This neutralisation might be seen as a defence against the disfiguration at work in every figure. See *Allegories of Reading: Figural Language in Rousseau, Nietzsche, Rilke, and Proust* (New Haven, CT, 1979), pp. 5–10.

45. For a double meaning of 'supplement' as an addition and a replacement – something that 'intervenes in-the-place-of', see Derrida, *Of Grammatology*, p. 145.

9

'Circe' and the Uncanny, or Joyce from Freud to Marx

MICHAEL BRUCE McDONALD

As Leopold Bloom half staggers through the more than merely hallucinatory milieu of 'Circe', his imaginatively prosaic sensibility is confounded by the sheer variety – and garish spectacle – of the apparitions rising to confront him. Joyce, not content merely to render a milieu *emblematic* of unconscious forces, limns a Nighttown that – fraught with overdetermination – is rather a place *in* the psyche, the constitutive nexus, determinant centre, of a true host of *unheimlich* spectres. These uncanny spectres comprise, in swirling aggregate, a necessary counterweight to the psychically-vitiated Dublin portrayed so poignantly throughout Joyce's work, the everyday Dublin demonstrably sapped by a certain 'haemiplegia of the will'.[1]

Bloom, acting as a sort of conduit between the prosaic harmonies of everyday Dublin and their suppressed dissonances – precisely the dissonances that yield to no harmony whatsoever in Nighttown – is confronted throughout the episode by a delirious succession of unnerving spectres, spectres that appear veritably to embody the uncanny. Thus the apparition of Bloom's long-dead grandfather, Virag, quickly gives way to Gerty MacDowell's sudden, uncanny advent in the guise of ruined-maiden-turned-whore, a spectre supplanted, in turn, by the abysmal, yet strangely banal transformation of Bella into Bello Cohen. Bloom is even confronted, at last, with the galling, yet indelibly comic apparition of his own feminised – and curiously self-alienated – other.[2] Given the eerily charismatic aura of degradation attending such phenomena, the episode's spectral maelstrom is tantamount, it would seem, to the moment in Joyce where the *unheimlich* is finally brought most fully, most unnervingly, into its own.

Still, the uncanniness of 'Circe' has remained *merely* spectral, however entertaining, for the overwhelming majority of the episode's critics and has thus lacked a certain affective force – a certain poignancy – in the general view. Joyce scholars have, by and large, scarcely bothered even to note the more unsettling qualities of the uncanny in 'Circe'. Critics have tended merely to gloss or virtually smirk and wink at such phenomena, even while extolling Joyce precisely *for* bringing the uncanny so brilliantly into play here. To be sure, the critical smirk is concomitant with – and an oddly inverted likeness of – the heightened attention recently accorded psychoanalytic matters in Joyce. Even so, the uncanny, as that which is at once utterly familiar and irreducibly strange, tends to disconcert even those who, with Sigmund Freud, most readily acknowledge its psychological and cultural significance. The critical smirk or hasty gloss tellingly signals the discomfort, moreover, that knowledge of the uncanny almost invariably finds in *itself*, in the unavoidable jarring dissonance of its own implications.

As Joyce criticism came into its own in the fifties and sixties, some readers – heeding T. S. Eliot's guarded celebration of Joyce's Ulyssean art as 'a way of controlling, of ordering, of giving a shape and a significance to the immense panorama of futility and anarchy which is contemporary history'[3] – acclaimed the uncanny in Joyce while avoiding the question of its irreducibility *as* the uncanny. Even Richard Ellmann's keen reading scants the uncanniness that – in the sheer frequency and intensity of its manifestation – tends to undermine, and certainly to complicate, whatever harmonies soar among the dissonances of *Ulysses*.[4] Ellmann overlooks the very qualities that make the *unheimlich* resistant to the values of inclusiveness and closure valorised by humanist traditions, even as he identifies the *nature* of the uncanny eruptions in 'Circe' with exceptional precision: 'The eye confronts no ineluctable modality of the visible, only unsought images of the invisible, lusts and loathings from within claiming autonomous existence without.'[5] Despite the incisiveness of this formulation, Ellmann – bent on arguing that Bloom's association with Stephen must ultimately describe a sort of 'profane salvation, The New Bloomusalem'[6] – spares little time for the 'unsought images' that rise to plague Bloom throughout the episode. The sort of humanism embodied in Ellmann's work, its eye always on the prize of a chaos-defying harmony, cannot afford to trouble itself very much with the darker aspects of the 'unsought images' that, if considered too long or taken *too* seriously, might reveal a harmony not so insusceptible to the inroads of dissonance after all.

To take a more contemporary instance of the generally unsatisfactory response to the uncanny in Joyce,[7] Daniel Ferrer proves unable to forego – in an otherwise most compelling essay – the virtual wink that signals an attempt to keep the uncanny at bay, even as he seeks to entertain its implications for his reading of 'Circe': 'Exploring Circe (and any other woman) is always a homecoming to familiar territory. But, inevitably, the homecoming seems uncanny.'[8] Ferrer's knowing reference to Circe (whatever her incarnation) as equivalent to 'any other woman' glosses the remarkably *particular* uncanniness inscribed in Joyce's mythography in the questionable terms of a universal masculine experience of woman. But this gloss also manages to scant a crucial aspect of Circe's role in *The Odyssey* itself, where she is potent enough – while remaining poised in her sheer, irreducible difference – effectively to terrorise Odysseus's crew, her familiar aspects as *woman* notwithstanding.

Likewise, the canny smirk occludes the intractable otherness embodied in the Sirens' scarcely *womanly* song, a song against whose potency Odysseus must stop his sailors' ears and whose irresistibly familiar – yet utterly strange – intimations of home bring him to curse himself for securing his own restraint.[9] The gesture that glosses the uncanny tends, finally, to obscure the significant fact that Penelope herself, however familiar she may seem to Odysseus upon his return, is different enough from the woman he was accustomed to that some time passes before he can think he knows her once more. She has changed in some rather dramatic ways since Odysseus reluctantly left for war, just as the Molly to whom Bloom returns at the close of *Ulysses* is not quite the same figure he left ages – though just a day – ago.

If the figurations of the uncanny in *The Odyssey* are at least somewhat removed, then, from Joyce's more determinedly comic renderings in 'Circe', this divergence might aptly be attributed to Joyce's distance from the epic world of Homer. But 'Circe' also illustrates Joyce's distance, in an important sense, from the literary milieu of Freud, whose theory of the *unheimlich* emerges in close conjunction with a fascinating reading of E. T. A. Hoffmann's 'The Sandman'.[10] While Hoffmann's tale is splendidly comic in many respects – most especially in its portrayal of the stupid infatuation of the protagonist Nathanael for an automaton – it nonetheless highlights the lurking terror implicit in the uncanny in some rather extraordinary ways. Each appearance of the demonic yet curiously prosaic Coppelius heralds a frightful catastrophe for Nathanael, from the loss of his eyes – a loss seemingly imaginary at first – to his eventual loss of sanity and, finally, life itself.[11]

Freud's painstaking exposition of the manner whereby the terrifying aspects of the uncanny are readily entwined with its more comic facets raises telling questions for readers of 'Circe': is it not strange to find hilarity *alone* among the uncanny apparitions of Nighttown? Have modernist aesthetics habituated us so readily to accede to an *unheimlich* virtually emptied of all affect? What sort of critical legacy could perpetuate so odd an habituation to – and even facile *contentment* with – that which had but recently seemed so poignant, even frightful, to the canny likes of Freud? How is it, moreover, that a criticism beholden to the defamiliarising practices of literary modernism – and to the work of Freud himself – fails to find itself unnerved or even very discomfited by the uncanny apparitions haunting 'Circe'? Perhaps Joyce himself bears some responsibility for his readers' facile habituation to the *unheimlich*. Joyce may encourage such tendencies, that is, by inscribing the uncanny in ways that *permit* its domestication, thus allowing it to lose its very identity *as* the *unheimlich*, as that which intrinsically disrupts the comforts of the familiar, the consolations of domesticity.

Perhaps the uncanny in Joyce fails, in other words, to provoke the sort of shudder which, for Theodor W. Adorno, marks the special distinction – and imperative – of art in a world that has increasingly come to deny art's ability to provoke *any* shudders but those of titillation and crude affect. Characteristically concerned with the vitiation of experience, the demystification of the world attending the Enlightenment,[12] Adorno asserts that works of art are 'truly after-images of prehistorical shudders in an age of reification, bringing back the terror of the primal world against a background of reified objects.'[13] My argument is haunted precisely by the tendency among readers of 'Circe' to miss such implications, to scant or gloss over that which might not only provoke a shudder but even preclude the sort of complacency that Joyce's work surely seeks to resist. In this regard, it is perplexing to think that readers would slight the very element in Joyce that most aptly suggests 'the terror of the primal world' and that might thereby recall us, to echo Stephen in *A Portrait*, to suffering's 'secret cause'.[14]

Freud's understanding of the uncanny might *seem* to render such fuss rather beside the point. Freud asserts, after all, that the uncanny can *never* truly evoke the terror of that which is utterly alien, for the uncanny comprises 'that class of the frightening which leads back to what is known of old and long familiar'.[15] Freud notes, in his exacting study of the philological record, that the *unheimlich* has usually been understood as the antonym of *heimlich* (homely) and *heimisch* (native). Surprisingly enough, however, he also finds that the principle of uncanniness is implicated in the very definition of the *heimlich*, a word bearing among its connotations a sense of that which not only belongs to but is hidden within the house, secreted away from the prying scrutiny of strangers[16] in as much as it is deliberately denied public view, moreover, the *heimlich* becomes not so much domestic as strange and thus *unheimlich*. As Freud explains, 'Thus *heimlich* is a word the meaning of which develops in the direction of ambivalence, until it finally coincides with its opposite, *unheimlich*'.[17] The *heimlich* is always already charged, therefore, with incipient anxiety that its secrets will be brought to light and that in the process it will cease to *be* itself. For Freud, this movement of the uncanny within the *heimlich* itself is exemplified in Friedrich Schelling's assertion that ' "[*u*]*nheimlich*" is the name for everything that ought to have remained ... secret and hidden but has come to light'.[18]

As we consider 'Circe' in light of Freud's rather painstaking archaeology of the connotations of the term *unheimlich*, it may begin to seem perfectly fitting that the ungainly spectral forms of Virag and Gerty provoke more mirth than alarm. The uncanniness of such figures stems, however, not so much from their sheer apparition – from the sudden appearances so comic in their own right – as from the fact that their secret guises have been *allowed* to come to light in the first place. In this regard, it becomes especially important to notice how the mirthful response collapses – before such gross exaggerations of the transformative potential of revealed secrets – into an uneasiness marked by the virtual smirk heralding humour's discomfort with itself.

This is to say that, while the affective force of the apparitions themselves can be kept at bay through laughter, the rather disturbing nature of the *dynamic* whereby their intimate secrets are revealed hits rather close to home. For who lacks some secret that – were it subjected to Nighttown's uncanny logic – would not reveal one's kinship to the spectral beings haunting the episode? In this regard, it is nothing less than a conceptual error merely to revel in the uncanny comedy of 'Circe'. We might better reflect on the circumstances that have exposed the *unheimlich* aspects of Bloom's private life in the first place, the conditions that have brought to light that which would *ordinarily* remain hidden within psychic recesses inacessible to characterisation. Crucially in this regard, the dynamic that underlies – and prompts – the eruptions of the uncanny in 'Circe' is proleptically grounded in the themes and textual practices that Joyce inscribes in 'Oxen of the Sun'.

Here, Bloom's very concern for Mina Purefoy offers a clue to the inherent inability of the *heimlich* to keep its own secret *unheimlich* principle hidden away. In previous episodes, we have witnessed Bloom clucking over Mrs Purefoy's shockingly, indeed uncannily, protracted labour, but he keeps the actual degree of his concern to himself. Bloom's outward expressions of compassion, if always genuine, are characteristically muted, for in their *heimlich*, domestic character, they can be made known to others only in a relatively superficial manner; it follows that Bloom *must* keep the sheer, poignant degree of his concern to himself. It is particularly apt, therefore, that the hospital in which Mina Purefoy so desperately labours should be transposed – by means of the antiquated logic articulated in this episode – into the *House* of Horne; in its *heimisch* character, Horne's becomes a place where both Mina's suffering and Bloom's compassion can be kept hidden from the world, secreted away under the comforting *guise* of domesticity.

Significantly, while Bloom's compassion for Mina is utterly genuine, the sheer, unthinkable degree of her suffering profoundly irritates his sensibility; her three days' agony presents an *irreducible* uncanniness for Bloom, a species of the *unheimlich* that cannot be reconciled with the imperatives of domesticity, no matter how congenial or neighbourly the House of Horne or his concern may be. Bloom's resistance to that which is irreducibly uncanny in Mina's labour is evinced in his efforts to calm Stephen, who quails, waxing wan, at the 'black crack of noise' (p. 376) heard in the street as a storm thunders above Horne's Hospital:

> Master Bloom, at the braggart' side spoke to him calming words to slumber his great fear, advertising how it was no other thing but a hubbub noise that he heard, the discharge of fluid from the thunderhead, look you, having taken place, and all of the order of a natural phenomenon.
>
> (p. 377)

The mild diction of this passage belies the underlying sombreness of its concerns. Bloom's compassionate ethos can only temporise in the face of Stephen's terrified reaction to thunder, which, in its awe-inspiring, irreducible noisiness, alone adequately bespeaks the distressing nature of Mina Purefoy's condition.

Stephen – sensing that thunder may be anything but a merely natural phenomenon and fearing that thunder may, as Lynch suggests, be the anger of the 'god self' at Stephen's 'hellprate and paganry' (p. 376) – better comprehends, in his callow way, the fearsome uncanniness of Mina's condition than does Bloom. Try as Bloom might to see her condition as 'all of the order of a natural phenomenon' (p. 377), her three days' labour challenges – and indeed mocks – his notion of the supreme orderliness of phenomenality itself. The sheer extremity of Mina's labour, by disrupting Bloom's notion of a harmonious natural order, displaces his conception with a species of dissonance, a discord that does not readily harmonise with any vision of cosmic orderliness, much less with Bloom's prosaic notions regarding the processes of procreation and birth. For all his quailing at thunder, Stephen's horror at the sheer implacability of phenomenality itself is the subjective correlative of Mina Purefoy's condition. Bloom – his wealth of compassion notwithstanding – remains essentially paralysed before this incarnation of natural suffering protracted to an unnatural degree.

Hearing in thunder the voice of a deity 'waxing wroth' (p. 178) at any disruption to the workings of the oddly mechanical fecundity that it relentlessly ordains – a deity thus appropriately named 'Bringforth' (p. 377) – Stephen hears, at the same time, a challenge to Bloom's ethos of unbridled compassion:

> But was young Boasthard's fear vanquished by Calmer's words? No, for he had in his bosom a spike named Bitterness which could not by words be done away. ... Heard he then in that clap the voice of the god Bringforth or, what Calmer said, a hubbub of Phenomenon? Heard? Why, he could not but hear unless he had plugged up the tube Understanding (which he had not done). For through that tube he saw that he was in the land of Phenomenon where he must for a certain one day die as he was like the rest too a passing show.
>
> (p. 377)

Stephen sees the danger in elevating the realm of Phenomenon to the detriment of the dream, at least, of transcendence. From Stephen's perspective, Bloom's elevation of sheer order as a kind of supreme cosmic principle is in *itself* terrifying, eliding as it does the frightful randomness of a cosmos reduced to mere explainability, a cosmos whose uncannily familiar strangeness Bloom would erase under the rubric of a comfortable – and comforting – phenomenality.

The 'land of Phenomenon', an ultimately comic realm for Bloom, is indeed terrible for Stephen, for Stephen sees that, without hope of transcendence, this realm *can* be reduced to a mere 'passing show'. Anticipating the dramatic form of 'Circe', Stephen apprehends the 'land of Phenomenon' as a theatre, however hilarious, in which melancholy players briefly strut their stuff, only to be replaced, through a spirit of shockingly facile interchangeability, with other players fated to do the same. Crucially, the very quality enabling the 'land of Phenomenon' to be reduced to the foreshortened, emotionally dissipated status of 'passing show' is the *unheimlich* principle – the incipient terror at the prospect of an irreducible cosmic unexplainability – lurking within the *heimlich* phenomenology that Bloom articulates here. It is therefore most appropriate that this lurking movement of the uncanny within the *heimlich* – of that which is always already irreducibly *there* to trouble Bloom's sojourn in the House of Horne – should become the very principle animating the dramatic form of 'Circe'.

The Nighttown world into which Bloom and Stephen stumble is one wherein the slightest causes accomplish terrible effects, where the stuff of prosaic, everyday life has been so grossly magnified that everything that is terribly and poetically epic in Irish life has, for once, been quite occluded. In Nighttown, the great causes that have historically occupied – and haunted – the Irish are given little or no credence at all. Given the ubiquity of a certain logic in the episode – a logic wherein monstrous effects follow from seemingly incidental causes – it is perfectly fitting that Gerty's merely coquettish behaviour in 'Nausicaa' should be realised as utter degradation *here*:

> (*Leering, Gerty MacDowell limps forward ... and shows coyly her bloodied clout.*) ... With all my worldly goods I thee and thou. ... You did that. ... [w]hen you saw all the secrets of my bottom drawer. ... Dirty married man! I love you for doing that to me.
>
> (p. 420)

Merely pathetic in 'Nausicaa',[19] Gerty is now so degraded that her character would *seem* to embody the more unnerving aspects of the uncanny to an extraordinary degree. Even so, only the utterly humorless reader could fail to spare a chuckle for her depiction here. But if her condition is primarily humorous for the reader, it is because the affect implicit in her state is not directed *toward* the reader but at Bloom alone. Bloom alone bears the brunt of the uncanniness erupting in her sudden apparition, for the psychic problem here is so idiomatically his own that the reader is necessarily excluded from experiencing Gerty's plight *as* affect. After all, Bloom has already *made* Gerty a whore in 'Nausicaa', if only in the febrile sweatshop of his imagination. Bloom must find ways, of course, to suppress this fact, for such an admission would alienate him from his cherished self-image as a most compassionate being. In this regard, Gerty's reappearance in Nighttown enacts nothing less than a stunning return of the repressed, of that which can only manifest itself as a grotesque monstrosity precisely because its affective energy has been so effectively elided.

In Nighttown, a realm that is *nothing but* a passing show, the potential emotional force of Gerty's whorish manifestation is further leached of affect – and indeed becomes downright ludicrous – through Joyce's idiomatic use of synecdoche. In 'Circe', synecdoche is remarkably removed from the mere trope wherein a word otherwise denoting a part comes to stand for the whole. In Nighttown, there *is* no referent – and barely a trace of what Derrida calls the transcendental signified – stable enough to support the hierarchy of signifiers enabling the dynamic process of substitutionality fundamental to the traditional uses of synecdoche. Rather, sheer figuration has now become substance, and synecdoche, no longer constrained to substitutionality alone, comes to embody identity itself. Thus, Gerty's unveiling of her 'bloodied clout' marks no mere lurid display of *parts* but rather an eruption of the *unheimlich* in a crazed synecdoche that reveals Gerty simply to *be*, on the whole, the psychic clout, the unsuturable wound, that Bloom has himself bloodied: 'I thee and thou', as Gerty aptly puts it.

The principle whereby the synecdochic subject actually becomes the phenomenon that it would ordinarily merely suggest is strikingly embodied, furthermore, in the way that Bella's fan – suddenly *all* we see of her – voices its disapproval of Bloom: 'Married, I see. ... And the missus is master. Petticoat government' (p. 495). Bella's fan, veiling her, becomes, through an odd species of transformation, the very principle whereby Bloom's carefully veiled persona is torn away; the fan, made to shield and cool, becomes that which exposes his hot domestic secrets for all to see. Crucially, once the veil of Bloom's comfortable facade has been rent in such decisive fashion, his otherwise carefully guarded domestic secrets can become part of the passing show. His confusion and hurt over the state of his marriage – emotions that he usually suppresses – now become part of a ribald parade of wanton signifiers simply because they *have* been exposed to the general view. In the weird logic of Nighttown, simply to become fully apparent to another is, unnervingly enough, to be degraded as the unwelcome other, to be repudiated as a form of that which – in the logic of a milieu where identity is indistinguishable from otherness – ought to have been kept hidden away at home.

This creates a complex – and quite paradoxical – series of resonances for my argument: Bella, as whoremistress, would ordinarily signify the unacceptable other but becomes a figure of acceptable domesticity through the synecdochic intervention of her fan, which truly *becomes* her in this regard. Bloom, in contradistinction – though already known to us as a thoroughly domesticated 'womanly man' – is suddenly transformed into an uncanny and indeed unwelcome guest by means of a synecdochic logic of negation. In a milieu where even signifiers that have been decisively cut off from the signified can become new, psychically overdetermined signifieds, Bloom signifies nothing in himself. Indeed, his pretension simply to *be* a self – to be a good quotidian Dubliner – marks him as the sort of utterly unwanted harmony that the Nighttown milieu must seek to exclude. In Nighttown, the illusory harmonies of daily life give way to a riot of the very dissonances that such existence seeks to suppress. Thus, the *otherwise* unwelcome dissonances of everyday Dublin come to enjoy an unaccustomed predominance in 'Circe', where the oddly congenial – and improbably harmonised – manifestations of the uncanny become, through sheer proliferation, *heimlich* once again.

This domestication of the dissonance of the uncanny is superbly enacted as Bloom bends to tie Bello's bootlace, his submissive posture instantly gendering him female – again through a synecdoche that is not substitution but identity itself – even as Bella, shouting 'Down!' (p. 498), becomes the martinet Bello: 'Feel my entire weight. Bow, bondslave, before the throne of your despot's glorious heels, so glistening in their proud erectness' (p. 498). Here, a stark principle of *interchangeability* proves itself – and at the very moment when the circus sideshow is forever wedded to the petty perversions of the bordello – a more ludicrous than poignant conjuror of the uncanny. Amidst the passing show that *is* substance in

'Circe', perversion derives not so much from the simple proliferation of sexual roles or practices as from the sheer ease with which gender positions *become* interchangeable and thus essentially meaningless. From this perspective, the episode's frenzied instability of signification follows not from confused sexual identities alone but from the threat posed to the linguistic status quo by the principle of interchangeability itself. Taken to extremity – to the extremity embodied nowhere better than in the incarnate miasmas of Nighttown – this principle abrogates whatever stability remains in definitions, in the very meanings upon which status quo discursivity is founded and upon which it ideologically relies.

Colin MacCabe argues that the thematics of sexual perversion in Joyce herald a more profound deviance still, that whereby writing itself betrays the supposedly harmonious self-sufficiency of the signified, through a nearly wanton proliferation of dissonant signifiers.[20] The sort of discursivity which Mikhail Bakhtin terms 'unitary' or 'official'[21] – and which I have here called status quo – is inherently threatened, MacCabe argues, by the heterogeneity embodied in novelistic freedom, especially in the unprecedented latitude of Joyce's Odyssean prose. In *Ulysses*, moreover, the theme of sexual deviance is the very harbinger of novelistic freedom, a freedom thus inextricably bound up with the subversive liberation implicit in sexual perversion itself:

> submission to the signifier is a submission to writing and writing functions, throughout Joyce's work, as the very exemplar of perversion. The crucial feature of perversion, as Circe demonstrates, is the instability of sexual position. As writing commences and sends back novel messages to hitherto unnoticed receivers, the unitary subject dissolves into a play of many voices. In the reciprocity which founds desire – my desire is the desire for the other but it is also the other's desire (the place I am allocated by the other) – gender alternates with voice. Active and passive, male and female, every speaker is articulated as both subject and object. It is this fact that the pervert acknowledges in fantasy but it is the moment at which the fantasy is arrested, fixed, that the pervert can save his identity ... and enter the realm of communication and knowledge.[22]

MacCabe's remarks can be usefully extended to encompass the relationship, not only between Bloom and Dublin but between 'Circe' and *Ulysses* as a whole. The uncanny permutations to which Bloom is at first merely a witness in 'Circe'—and to which he is subsequently vengefully *subjected*—undermine the centrality of the subjective viewpoint established for him in prior episodes. The uncanny particulars of the episode give way, in other words, to a greater uncanniness still, as we are led to see that even a subjectivity so superbly rendered as Bloom's *can* be reduced through an abrupt shift in perspective to a state of utter abjection. That abjection is intimated as Bloom becomes the mere object, in Lacanian terms, of 'the desire of the Other'.[23] Bloom's supremacy as the subject of prior episodes decisively gives way, that is, to a minimalised perspectival position from which and *in* which he seems the mere object of an other's desire.[24] Indeed, Bloom becomes an object as surely as Bella becomes her fan, thus revealing the dynamic – banal nowhere but in Nighttown – whereby heretofore negligible concerns become fraught with the psychic value enjoined by the principle of overdetermination always already attending the *unheimlich*.[25]

This logic of overdetermination, a logic inherently linked to a more than facile principle of interchangeability, is at work *in* the subject too, transforming the relatively complaisant Bella into the frightfully hostile Bello, a creature whose frustrations are wholly entwined with Dublin's ubiquitously widespread mercantile ethos. Indeed, this transformation very precisely enacts the dynamic whereby Dublin becomes the great, even constitutive nexus of perversion not only in *Ulysses* but for Joyce himself. In other words, Joyce's Dublin becomes a determinant centre not only of paralysis, of 'haemiplegia of the will', but of an everyday life so skewed that its distortions can be adequately figured only in the sideshow mirrors and deranged perceptual confusions of Nighttown.

But Joyce's Dublin is a nexus of distorted – and distorting – perceptions not merely in the psychoanalytic but in the resolutely Marxian sense addressed in the work of Adorno and Slavoj Žižek. For Adorno, the post-Enlightenment yet wholly enlightened rise of capitalism places the earth itself in a crisis of disenchantment – the very spirit animating the listless spectres of Nighttown – a disenchantment so pervasive that it 'radiates disaster triumphant'.[26] This view invites a reading of Nighttown as a place *in* and uniquely charged with the psyche, a place whose material configurations are everywhere psychically rendered, psychically determined. This distortedly ordered place, this little disenchanted earth called Nighttown, is no mere sign but rather the veritable consequence of the dominant modes of being-in-the-world attending the rise of capitalism. For Žižek too, as we shall see, the disenchanted earth becomes the veritable excrescence of a human symptom, the symptom of a diseased relationship with material reality itself.

Curiously, relatively few Marxian critics have offered to struggle with the complex ideological modalities informing Joyce's Nighttown, much less with those of *Ulysses* as a whole.[27] Thus, an essay like Fredric Jameson's ' "Ulysses" in History' can be and often has been construed as a definitive Marxian reading of Joyce, particularly with respect to Jameson's unique understanding of the conditions melding the ideological strata of turn-of-the-century Dublin:

> Joyce's is the epic of the metropolis under imperialism, in which the development of bourgeoisie and proletariat alike is stunted to the benefit of a national petty-bourgeoisie ... [the] rigid constraints imposed by imperialism on the development of human energies account for the symbolic displacement and flowering of the latter in eloquence, rhetoric and oratorical language of all kinds[,] symbolic practices ... highly prized in precapitalist societies and preserved, as in a time capsule, in *Ulysses* itself. ... Dublin is not exactly the full-blown capitalist metropolis, but like the Paris of Flaubert, still regressive, still distantly akin to the village, still un- or under-developed enough to be representable, thanks to the domination of its foreign masters.[28]

To see this passage as confirmation that Joyce's Dublin is a non- or even precapitalist metropolis mistakes the meaning of the key words here: 'not *exactly* the full-blown capitalist metropolis' (my italics). Joyce's Dublin, though not exactly full-blown as such and certainly no mere 'time capsule', is a burgeoning capitalist metropolis all the same. This Dublin – *perhaps* unlike the modern or even postmodern metropolis – may indeed be regressively precapitalist enough still to 'be representable', in Jameson's terms, but the interactions portrayed in 'Circe' effectively embody the sort of collective dreamwork whereby capitalist ideologies gradually come to dominate a newly modern city's psychic life. Jameson's sense that Joyce's Dublin is caught, to revise Matthew Arnold, wandering between two worlds, one all but dead save in the richness of its speech, the other verbally powerless yet clamouring to be born, suggests the tension fuelling Nighttown's uncanny eruptions. So fraught, Nighttown symptomatically embodies the very sort of neurosis that, for Žižek as for Marx himself, everywhere attends the rise of modern capitalism.

In *The Sublime Object of Ideology*, Žižek elaborates an important aspect of Marx's thought that has, curiously, heretofore been largely slighted. This surprisingly overlooked notion identifies the uncanny as inextricably bound up with the effects of a particular neurosis not just attending but embodying capitalism itself.[29] Žižek readily acknowledges, however, that this idea is nothing new: Marx, he reminds us, saw capitalism as but the *symptom* of a great collective neurosis, a neurosis revealed in the exquisitely contradictory action of

> a certain ideological Universal, that of equivalent and equitable exchange, and a particular paradoxical exchange – that of the labour force for its wages – which, precisely as an equivalent, functions as the very form of exploitation. ... [with] the universalisation of the production of commodities ... [there emerges] a new commodity representing the internal negation of the universal principle of equivalent exchange of commodities; in other words, *it brings about a symptom*.[30]

The principle of equivalent interchangeability enabling capitalist exchange is symptomatic, in other words, of the constitutive perversity of a milieu where money itself comes to hold more worth than the things whose value it *nominally* only signifies. The symptomaticity attending such displacement is intensified, moreover, by the resolute suppression, under capitalism, of the mere recognition of this dynamic at work. Thus use value – the signified that money ostensibly signifies but to which money is nowhere subordinate – is superseded by a conception of capital so bloated that capital itself no longer appears valueless in its own right. Rather, the very fact that we have to be reminded that money has no use *save* in exchange signals a pernicious habituation to exchange itself, to a state in which the principle of facile interchangeability has become much more than a *symptom* of neurosis.

Žižek reasserts the indispensability of Marx's own materialist vision of the *unheimlich* in this regard. For Marx, simply to *recognise* the conditions underlying capitalist exchange bears all the force of an encounter with the uncanny, so alienated have the processes of exchange become, under the general fetishism of commodities, from the irreducible fact of materiality itself:

> There is a physical relation between physical things. But it is different with commodities. There, the existence of the things *qua* commodities ... has absolutely no connexion with their physical properties

> and with the material relations arising therefrom. There it is a definite social relation between [people], that assumes, in their eyes, the fantastic form of a relation between things. ... to find an analogy, we must have recourse to the mist-enveloped regions of the religious world. In that world the productions of the human brain appear as independent beings endowed with life. ... So it is in the world of commodities [where] Fetishism attaches itself to the products of labour, so soon as they are produced as commodities, and [is] therefore inseparable from the production of commodities.[31]

Little wonder, then, that in Nighttown the principle of exchangeability is precisely so confused with the value of things in themselves, the value that makes exchange possible, yet that exchange itself tends to occlude. Here, psychic over-determination is enacted not only in the *language* of the marketplace but as its secret, informing drama. In other words, exchangeability becomes not just the central principle of economic but of psychic value, and objects like Bella's fan are willy-nilly accorded an immense and wholly unwarranted worth. The confused principle of exchangeability attending the rise of capitalism itself thus comes to be enacted in the *perceptual* disorders haunting even that most incipiently modern of cities, Joyce's Dublin. Joyce's lifelong effort to portray a milieu fraught with a certain psychic perversity – a perversity born of the symptomatically facile equivalences endemic to a burgeoning capitalist modernity – hereby comes to fruition in 'Circe'. Nighttown finally embodies an uncannily exaggerated, however phantasmal, version of the neurotic aura clinging to diurnal Dublin and thus rightly assumes the guise of *that* Dublin's uncannily ubiquitous Doppelgänger.

The symptomatically crass mercantilism of everyday Dublin is embodied, as Sheldon Brivic has shown, in the composite figure of Bella/Bello, a figure embodying nothing less than the entire 'capitalist Establishment in an episode built on the metaphor of modern civilisation as a whorehouse'.[32] Indeed, the implicit connection between capitalism, modern civilisation, and Bella/o's status as whoremistress is made quite explicit in the following passage, where s/he

> (*Squats, with a grunt on Bloom's upturned face, puffing cigarsmoke, nursing a fat leg.*) ... Guinness's preference shares are at sixteen three quarters. Curse me for a fool that didn't buy that lot. ... And that Goddamned outsider *Throwaway* at twenty to one. (*He quenches his cigar angrily on Bloom's ear.*)
>
> (pp. 500–1)

The impressive virulence of this scene stems from Bella/o's frustration with a mercantile Dublin that everywhere promises – and resists – the subject's fulfilment. For those who are blind, like Bella/o, to the systemic contingency undermining the putative stability of this milieu, even a failure in enterprise can only signify a sort of primal perversion in the cosmos itself. Bella/o's petty mistreatment of Bloom is tacitly given as a simple consequence, therefore, of the constitutive perversion informing existence itself, at least according to Bella/o's reckoning of what existence *is*. In this light, it is particularly apt that Bloom should be not just initiated but 'nurse[d]' in the 'proper fashion' of perversity at the hands of Bella/o (p. 501). The petty acts of perversion depicted here, far from figuring a simple modality of pleasure and violence, are aimed at *subjecting* the suddenly infantile Bloom to the imperatives of being itself; by thus subjecting Bloom, Bella/o confirms – and insists upon – a frustrated vision of what being is and can be.

For Bella/o, just being entails teeming with hatred for a Dublin that – like any modern metropolis – everywhere both evokes and frustrates desire for all sorts of boons that it finally cannot bestow. As intensified through the synecdochic logic of Nighttown, desire reaches its logical representational terminus in acts of the most frightful frustration. In the images limned in the inverted lens of Nighttown, no freedom can lurk, moreover, in desire for the other. Such desire is thus aptly displaced onto the sort of *inadvertent* object – Bloom! – that Jacques Lacan identifies as the *object petit à*:

> The *object à* is something from which the subject, in order to constitute itself, has separated itself off as organ. This serves as a symbol of the lack ... of the phallus, not as such, but in so far as it is lacking.[33]

Even in a state of utter abjection, wallowing masochistically in subjection to the tawdriest sorts of *things*, Bloom helps uncover Bell/o's constitutive lack. This lack is not that of the phallus – though it is interesting to note that, in a poignant sense, Bello *is* a sort of excrescent embodiment of Bella's 'missing' phallus – so much as it figures the missing plenitude of well-being that nominally attends a wealth of material bounty. To his angry sorrow, that is, Bella/o lacks nothing less than the phallic plenitude of capitalist fulfilment.

Moreover, Joyce's unrelenting depiction, however feverish, of precisely *this* milieu gainsays MacCabe's contention that writing itself is the ultimate site and sign of perversion in Joyce. While Joyce certainly enacts a kind of writerly perversion by skirting the putative harmony of the signified in favour of a dissonant proliferation of signifiers, it is absolutely crucial that this happens as he writes *about* turn-of-the-century Dublin; the great arbiter of perversion in 'Circe' is not writing as such but rather the inscription of the crass mercantilism already pervading the episode's milieu. If the acts of perversion depicted in 'Circe' are symptomatic of a psychic unrest intrinsic to Dublin's burgeoning mercantilism, then Bloom himself – inasmuch as he serves as a sort of exemplary shill for the illusory delights of his age – is the great, natural *sign* of the abject humiliation attending not just certain acts of sexual and even ideological perversion but of that great constitutive perversity itself.

As Bloom's eerily knowing desire to be forced into submission, not just to Bella/o but to the very spirit of his age, becomes plainly evident, he does not simply change his dress from that of a comfortably bourgeois male to that of a socially degraded female; rather, Bella/o makes sure that Bloom's very identity is not just feminine but degradingly so:

> What you longed for has come to pass. Henceforth you are unmanned and mine in earnest, a thing under the yoke. Now for your punishment frock. ... BLOOM. ... O crinkly! scrapy! Must I tiptouch it with my nails? BELLO (*Points to his whores.*) As they are now, so will you be ... laced with cruel force into vicelike corsets ... restrained in nettight frocks.
>
> (pp. 501–2)

In the logic of perversion acted out in 'Circe', to assume female dress is to wear, as the very sign of identity itself, a 'punishment frock': not merely to be *dressed* in the guise of a Bella/o whore but to be subject to – even to the point to having to *wear* – the punishments meted out within the repressive 'family' embodied with such strange, pressing poignancy here.

Such punishments surely need not be portrayed merely by recourse to the classic signs of perversion, need not be represented by flagellation and petty torture alone. Rather, the stark manner whereby Joyce's Dublin reduces the excess of desire to banal yet latently hostile mercantile concerns heralds an age where sexual perversion is itself but symptomatic of a greater, more ubiquitous, and indeed *constitutive* perversity still. This is the very condition embodied, strangely enough, in Bloom's apparition as 'charming soubrette', replete with

> [...] *dauby cheeks, mustard hair and large male hands and nose, leering mouth.*) I tried her things on only once ... When we were hardup I washed them to save the laundry bill. ... It was the purest thrift. BELLO (*Jeers.*) Little jobs that make mother pleased, eh? and showed off ... behind closedrawn blinds your unskirted thighs and hegoat's udders, in various poses of surrender, eh?
>
> (p. 502)

The reader may well have difficulty discerning what earns Bloom Bella/o's jeers the most, the fact that he has tried on Molly's 'things' *only* once or that he lies in saying that the handling of those garments was inspired *not* by perversity but by the 'purest thrift' alone.

The act whereby the inherent excess, the unharmonisable dissonance of desire is reduced to a rationale of 'purest thrift' is itself a sign of the great perversity overdetermining all the petty perversions enacted in the distorting mirrors of Nighttown. To witness this is to witness the uncanniness of capitalism itself, of the great capitalist secret come to light. We witness the unveiling, no less, of the furtive dynamic whereby the fetishism of commodities comes to undermine the *relatively* incidental fetishes of spirit. This is the secret carefully concealed within the ethos of capitalism, the secret that ought not come to light. In the weird logic of Nighttown, however, such secrets virtually *must* come to light, a dynamic heralding the most poignant manifestation of the uncanny in 'Circe': not the mere apparitions, the interchangeably spectral embodiments of exchange, but the collective psychosis embodied in facile interchangeability itself. In bringing the uncanniness of this dynamic to light, Joyce has proffered us an extraordinary glimpse of a crucial yet too often unlooked-for link between the Freudian and Marxian notions of the *unheimlich*. By enacting the retrograde motion – the very homecoming – of the uncanny itself, Joyce leads us inexorably back from Freud to Marx.

From *James Joyce Quarterly*, 33:1 (Autumn 1996), 49–68.

Notes

[Michael Bruce McDonald's essay emphasises the significance of the uncanny, Freud's *unheimlich*, in the 'Circe' episode of *Ulysses*. In concentrating on Bloom, he argues against humanist attempts to find in *Ulysses* reconciliatory gestures that promise harmony while ignoring dissonance and ruptures. When the uncanny encounters in this episode are taken seriously – rather than read as slapstick – they point towards existential anxieties, but also towards basic problems of textuality. This becomes evident when 'Circe' is paralleled with 'Oxen of the Sun' and the painful labour of childbirth and text production depicted in the latter. When this suppressed work that goes into writing resurfaces with a vengeance in 'Circe', it opens up a vantage point for a critique of an even more pervasive production, that of profit in a capitalist economy. The seemingly psychological manifestations of abandon and trauma in 'Circe', when read through Marx, become evidence of the traumatic impact of the capitalist logic of inverting use and exchange values. All page references to *Ulysses* are to the Oxford World's Classics edition, ed. Jeri Johnson (1993). Ed.]

1. Richard Ellmann, *James Joyce*, revd edn (New York, 1982), p. 140.
2. For reasons that will become clear as my argument develops, I have chosen to focus exclusively on Joyce's depiction of Bloom in Nighttown. Stephen is also plagued, of course, by apparitions of the uncanny in 'Circe', as in his eery confrontation with his dead mother's ghost (pp. 539–42).
3. T. S. Eliot, '*Ulysses*, Order, and Myth', *Selected Prose*, ed. Frank Kermode (London and Boston, 1975), p. 177.
4. For an extended discussion of the interdependent roles played by harmony and dissonance in Joyce, see my dissertation 'James Joyce and the Aesthetics of Dissonance', University of Oregon, 1991.
5. Richard Ellmann, *'Ulysses' on the Liffey* (New York, 1972), p. 140.
6. Ibid., p. 149.
7. The exceptions to this assertion, while few, are most significant. See especially Sheldon Brivic's psychoanalytic reading of 'Circe' in *The Veil of Signs: Joyce, Lacan, and Perception* (Urbana, IL, 1991). Kimberley J. Devlin has convincingly shown that the *textual* uncanny of the *Wake* is embodied in Joyce's subtle reworking of elements of previous works there. See *Wandering and Return in 'Finnegans Wake': An Integrative Approach to Joyce's Fictions* (Princeton, NJ, 1991), pp. ix–xiv. Alse see Robert Spoo's provocatively groundbreaking 'Uncanny Returns in "The Dead": Ibsenian Intertexts and the Estranged Infant', in *Joyce: The Return of the Repressed*, ed. Susan Stanford Friedman (Ithaca, NY, 1993), pp. 89–113.
8. Daniel Ferrer, 'Circe, Regret, and Regression', in Derek Attridge and Daniel Ferrer (eds), *Post-structuralist Joyce: Essays from the French* (New York, 1984), p. 128. A sort of reactive smirk is also evident in Mark Shechner's commentary in *Joyce in Nighttown: A Psychoanalytic*

Inquiry into 'Ulysses' (Berkeley, CA, 1974): ' "Circe" is self-revelation as slapstick, and if we have hesitated to recognise it as such before, it is because we ourselves have been uncomfortable at seeing this fabulous artificer self-caricatured as fetishist, masochist, onanist, public enigma, and private buffoon' (p. 101). Shechner reduces the uncanny in Joyce to mere emanations of the author's 'psychosexual nature'. 'Circe' both embarrasses and secretly delights Shechner, inasmuch as it enables him to bear witness to the self-humbling of a 'fabulous artificer'. Even with its nominal concern for the intimacies of Joyce's inner, Shechner's reading, with its unflinching insistence that 'Circe' amounts to little more than Joyce's own psychosexual self-revelation, manages to ignore the important ways in which the episode's *uncanny* slapstick affects – or strangely fails to affect – the reader.

9. See the reading of *The Odyssey* in Max Horkheimer and Theodor W. Adorno, *Dialectic of Enlightenment*, trans. John Cummings (London and New York, 1979). Linking the problem of the Sirens' uncanniness to the question of art's status as a form of praxis, the authors argue that so long 'as art declines to pass as cognition and is thus separated from practice, social practice tolerates it as it tolerates pleasure. But the Sirens' song has not yet been rendered powerless by reduction to the condition of art' (pp. 32–3). Arguably, the sort of literary practices embodied in 'Circe' – and elaborated in the *Wake* – comprises a unique attempt to circumvent the burgeoning historical powerlessness of art in the West. Precisely by making art problematic for the powerless ethos implicit in conventionally-defined aesthetic enjoyment, Joyce has indeed raised art to 'the level of cognition'.

10. See Freud's discussion of 'The Sandman' in 'The "Uncanny" ' in *Art and Literature*, ed. Angela Richards and Andrew Dickson, The Pelican Freud Library, 14 (London, 1985). 'The Sandman' has been rendered into superb English in *Selected Writings of Hoffmann*, vol. 1, trans. Leonard J. Kent and Elizabeth C. Knight (Chicago, 1969).

11. Depictions of the uncanny are characteristically attended by a certain preoccupation with vision and with the very nature of the visual. Brivic has shown, for instance, that the uncanny series of events transpiring in Bella's bordello occurs while Bloom gazes not only fixedly but in an utterly *arrested* state at Bella herself. See *The Veil of Signs*, pp. 114–17.

12. See *Dialectic of Enlightenment*, especially pp. 3–42.

13. Theodor W. Adorno, *Aesthetic Theory*, trans. C. Lenhardt, ed. G. Adorno and R. Tiedemann, The International Library of Phenomenology and Moral Sciences (London, 1984). p. 118.

14. James Joyce, *A Portrait of the Artist as a Young Man* (London, 1977), p. 185.

15. Freud, 'The Uncanny', p. 340.

16. Ibid., p. 344.

17. Ibid., p. 347.

18. Friedrich Schelling is quoted in 'The Uncanny', p. 347.

19. For a much more mordant view of Gerty's status in 'Nausicaa', see Suzette A. Henke, 'A Speculum of the Other Molly: A Feminist/ Psychoanalytical Inquiry into James Joyce's Politics of Desire', *Mosaic*, 21:3 (1988), 108–9.

20. Colin MacCabe, *James Joyce and the Revolution of the Word* (London, 1979), pp. 121–3. Also see Jacques Derrida's remarks on the 'originary' perversion of writing in *Of Grammatology*, trans. Gayatri Spirak (Baltimore, 1974), pp. 18–26. Following Friedrich Nietzsche in this regard, Derrida extols the 'originary' operation whereby writing does not 'first have to transcribe or discover ... a truth signified in the original element and presence of the logos'. Writing 'is not originarily subordinate to the logos and to truth'; rather writing opens up the very 'history of the logos'. Moreover, Western metaphysics *must* suppress any recollection of this originary, 'opening up' operation of writing, since it insists on the subordination of writing to the logos itself. From this perspective, Nietzsche's claims for the originary function of writing, far from seeming to open up the discourse of historicity, can only *appear* to pervert it.

21. Mikhail Bakhtin, *The Dialogic Imagination*, ed. Michael Holquist, trans. Caryl Emerson and Michael Holquist (Austin, TX, 1981), pp. 270–5.

22. MacCabe, *Revolution of the Word*, p. 123.

23. However, just as Derrida argues that writing appears perverse and degrading only from a position that insists on its subordination to the logos, so Jacques Lacan asserts that even subjection to the desire of the other is potentially liberating. Thus the very trauma attending the psychoanalytic transference – far from being an undesirable state that must be remedied – bears profound transformative potential. See Jacques Lacan, *Four Fundamental Concepts of Psychoanalysis*, trans. Alan Sheridan, ed. Jacques-Alain Miller (New York, 1978), p. 129. Indeed, the very trauma to which Bloom is subjected in 'Circe' appears to leave him strangely refreshed, if not precisely rejuvenated, as the episode ends.

24. See Brivic, *Veil of Signs*, pp. 114–17.

25. See Sigmund Freud, *The Interpretation of Dreams* [1900], trans. James Strachey, ed. Angela Richards, Pelican Freud Library, 4 (London, 1976), pp. 388–9.

26. Adorno and Horkheimer, *Dialectic of Enlightenment*, p. 3.

27. While exceptions to this are few, they are well worth noting. See especially Franco Moretti's discussion of the limitations imposed on Bloom (and on Joyce himself) by bourgeois culture in 'The Long Goodbye: *Ulysses* and the End of Liberal Capitalism', in *Signs Taken for Wonders* (London, 1983), pp. 183–208. Also see Mary C. King, ' "Ulysses": The Dissolution of Identity and the Appropriation of the Human World', in Bernard Benstock (ed.), *James Joyce: The Augmented Ninth* (Syracuse, NY, 1988), pp. 337–45.

28. Fredric Jameson, '*Ulysses* in History', in *James Joyce*, ed. Harold Bloom (New York, 1986), p. 182.

29. The comparative scarcity of his sort of insight is suggested by the attention recently accorded Žižek, a phenomenon signalled by the panel devoted entirely to his work at the 1992 MLA convention.

30. Slavoj Žižek, *The Sublime Object of Ideology* (New York, 1989), pp. 22–3.

31. Karl Marx, *Capital*, vol. 1, *The Marx–Engels Reader*, second edition, ed. Robert C. Tucker (New York, 1978), p. 321.

32. Brivic, *Veil of Signs*, p. 115. Lest this remark seem hyperbolic, witness Ellmann, who points out that the Monto district of Dublin – the area after which Joyce modelled Nighttown – had been 'labelled about 1885 ... as the worst slum in Europe'; Ellmann, *Joyce*, p. 377.

33. Lacan, *Four Fundamental Concepts*, p. 103.

10

Molly Alone: Questioning Community and Closure in the 'Nostos'[1]

ENDA DUFFY

[...]

This chapter considers the closure of *Ulysses*. In postcolonial writing that operates as homology of the forces in conflict during the revolution, the struggle is represented as a new beginning. The past is, relatively, disregarded: in *Ulysses*, especially in the first two opening episodes of the text, the accepted version of nationalist history is ridiculed as a pastiche of a series of mythologies, most of them mere faked copies of imperial originals that had been developed in the first place to subjugate the peripheral peoples. Rather it is the future, and the possibility of imagining a newly independent national community that will take shape in that future, which preoccupies the work. For the postcolonial author working up the first tentative texts in the new voices of a national culture, it might appear that the beginning of a narrative would have been most difficult. In practice, however, the writer sustained the act of beginning as a concerted effort to displace those hackneyed discourses of 'history' that had already been set in place to narrate the potential new nation. Instead, it is the conclusion of the text, as the test case in the narrative for the successful imagining of a new community, that is difficult.

Closure in any text that is preoccupied with marking a new beginning will not be easy; in one with the sceptical political sensibilities marking *Ulysses*, it was almost impossible. Both Joyce and Yeats in their later work (*Finnegans Wake* and *A Vision*) would circumvent this demand for closure by invoking respectively notions of Viconian cycles and occult 'gyres'; in *Ulysses* the author is, as it were, caught unawares without such a commodious philosophy of history, and the issue of how the future might be envisaged must be dealt with in the face of the closure of the text. Hence the usefulness of the ploy of documenting only a single day: besides effectively devaluing the perspective of history or the past in the work, it meant that the book was forced to end, literally, once night fell. Still, the importance of closure in *Ulysses* for its author may be gleaned in the fact that, to effect it, he invoked a principle of radical difference. He turns around what he had up to now composed as a masculinist narrative, to close with a monologue by a woman. Joyce himself termed the 'Penelope' episode the 'indispensable countersign' to *Ulysses*;[2] when Molly Bloom, at the last moment, presents an other viewpoint in the text, she questions much more thoroughly than before the possibility of envisioning a national community, beyond masculinist fellowship or the lack of it in this novel.

Closure marks the success or otherwise of imagining a new national community; the text's utopian project is at stake. I suggest that *Ulysses*, given its author's distance (as modernist 'exile') from the events it encodes, rather than fretting over the imagining of such a community, instead poses the more radical question of whether in fact, at the moment of revolution, such an entity can be imagined at all. Consider the impulses toward an imaginary community in this novel; the full comic impetus in *Ulysses* to bring subjects together as empathetic groups. In the male-centred narrative occupying the greater part of the text, this is focused on the tentative relationship, developed through a series of coincidences, between Stephen and Bloom. Even if what we are given at this level is a figural, rather than an actual, father and son, and if their paths cross only by chance, by webs of coincidence rather than by a symbolic filiation in the way that Bloom himself would like to imagine (see 'Eumaeus'), here is still the pattern, however distant and faded by replication, of a key thematic of nineteenth-century realism. Because it is a very late copy, with much of its supporting sensation-text stripped away, we are allowed continually to see the underlying panoptic regime of surveillance. I have shown how this regime is exposed to us in the 'Cyclops', 'Sirens', and 'Circe' episodes of *Ulysses*. Because the panoptic regime is rendered visible, this form of late realism is highly effective as a late-colonial text: it uncovers again and again the brutally tight control exerted by the colonial government over the native subjects under its rule. The colonial police state mediates the intersubjective relations not only between colonist and native, but also among the natives themselves. If we take the 'Nostos', the final three episodes of *Ulysses*, as the strategic closure of the novel, then 'Eumaeus' clearly brings to a crisis both the father–son relationship and the regime of colonial surveillance portrayed in this aspect of the narrative. On the one hand, Bloom and Stephen at last sit opposite each other and talk; on the other, this takes place in an atmosphere of suspicion, rumour, and even pseudo-political intrigue that marks the apogee of the panopticist motif in the text.

Underlying this fundamentally male-centred, realist narrative, which is at its strongest in the opening episode of *Ulysses* but survives, despite a panoply of defamiliarising onslaughts in episode after episode, at least until the very end of 'Eumaeus' in the novel, there is threaded through the text the second narrative impulse, modernist in form, which identifies more thoroughly with the subaltern predicament and which, significantly, is centred on a series of images of women. If the male-centred realist-inspired narratives work (in the novel written at the moment of decolonisation) as critiques of colonialism's exercise of power and management of knowledge of the social sphere, then this second strand of the novel (that for which it is considered 'difficult' and for which it is truly notorious) works to give voice to versions of subaltern difference that tentatively but uncompromisingly enter the novel's field of vision.

From the moment the old milkwoman – less a pathetic and ignorant victim than a canny manipulator of clichéd realist expectations about what she represents – steps into the Martello tower in the opening 'Telemachus' episode, it is around images of women that the innovative modernist trajectories of the text adhere. 'Aeolus', the first episode in which the smooth face of the narrative is shattered (here by the jocoserious headlines), culminates in 'The Parable of the Plums', a murkily allegorical tale about two midwives who toss plumstones from atop the column commemorating Nelson, British seaman and 'onehandled adulterer' (p. 142), in O'Connell Street. 'Sirens', the first significantly obscure episode (as Ezra Pound noted) centres on the two barmaid-sirens, Miss Douce and Miss Kennedy. Note that all of these women in the first half of the novel are workers, in fact very clearly members of the working class. Most of the male characters who figure in the first half of the novel are either bohemians or petty bourgeois. Thus a gendered division of labour in the colony is implicitly posited early in the novel. 'Nausicaa', its style contorted into a pastiche of Victorian kitsch romance, eulogises Gerty MacDowell, while 'Oxen of the Sun', the novel's modernist tour-de-force exposition of successive literary styles, is meant to tell of Mrs Mina Purefoy giving birth. These women are not paid workers as are, for example, the barmaids; rather, they are shown as the bearers and minders of children. Seeing this portrayal against that of the earlier women, however, these bourgeois women who are wives and consumers seem all the more abject.[3]

Every one of these women are abjects, more thoroughly interpellated by the various hegemonic forces controlling the culture than are any of the men here: as such, the scenes of the women are the scenes of the most thoroughly delineated subalternity in *Ulysses*. And the text, facing this subalternity in all its vividness – from that of the milkwoman, whose own viewpoint we are barely allowed to glimpse, to that of Molly, whose viewpoint is directly her own – has invariably to cast about to find new and more appropriate ways to narrate this abjection.

I have worked to demonstrate how, in both realist and more markedly modernist episodes of the novel, the critique of oppression on the one hand (in, for example, the split subjectivity displayed in 'Cyclops') and the delineation of subalternity on the other (as in the regimes of surveillance shown in 'Circe') are both transformed through the novel's comic impetus by flashes of a vision of postcolonial subjectivity. As regards the utopian potential of the text to imagine many such subjectivities into a new community, the reader can hardly hope that the male-centred realist narrative, copied from models that celebrated an imperialist nationalist world, will prove an appropriate vehicle. Once 'Eumaeus', where that realist narrative reaches its climax, is over, it is dispersed; hence Stephen blithely walks away from Bloom in the stylistically uncompromising 'Ithaca' episode. The question that then remains about the women-centred moments of the text is this: to what extent do these representations of abject women go beyond delineating the grimness of abjection to foster notions of a novel community of those once downtrodden? *Ulysses* in its latter moments presents us with a portrait of a lone woman, Molly, rather than of a group of women together, and it never allows the abject women it represents (with the exception of the Nighttown prostitutes of 'Circe') to come together in the work. This is indicative, I suggest, of a text that does not ultimately present us with a readymade new community but rather poses the more difficult question of what such a community might imply.

The reader must seek the roots of the novel's reticence on this score in both the general difficulty (especially in leftist critiques) of ever imagining the Utopia that should follow a revolution, and, more specifically, in a strain of pessimism infusing any colonial subaltern political sensibility. This sensibility, although made famous by Joyce as his vaunted rejection of Ireland's political and cultural narrowness, was by no means specific to him alone. The issue of a utopian component in materialist thought has always been contentious; Marx's own writing is vague about what the world under the rule of the proletariat might resemble. Leftist critics have always looked with a certain envy upon the utopian appeal of such secular religions and galvanising forces as nineteenth-century nationalism. The argument about whether an avowal of utopian longings as a component of a materialist critique does not represent a shameful sliding into a discredited idealist liberalism has gained new urgency with the birth of the various structuralist and poststructuralist versions of Marxism, particularly in France and Britain, during the last two decades. Critics such as Fredric Jameson have argued cogently for a utopian dimension as a fitting acknowledgment of the component of desire in western materialist thought,[4] if only in the sense that any ideological trajectory must awaken utopian desires in order to critique them. (Stuart Hall, in similar vein, following Gramsci, has controversially urged that British leftists might learn from the appeals to popular longings manipulated by resurgent British conservatism.)[5] At the same time, an infusion of the radical philosophic spirit of what Gayatri Spivak characterises as Derrida's geo-deconstruction[6] into the newer leftist critiques has made many of these latter-day appeals for leftist utopianisms seem like last-ditch retrenchments; the new work has begun to question the grounds of any materialist assumption of a utopian future time. Thus the feminist historian of science Donna Haraway,[7] for example, attacks both Marxism and Freudianism, the nineteenth-century theories of the social and psychic body, as themselves thoroughgoing realisms that emphatically replicate the mirage of original unity of every imperial cultural formation, so that a hypothetical ultimately unified community must be suspected as merely a projection of what should have been abandoned. This is the point at which I wish to situate my own reading of the plot of closure in *Ulysses*. Against a nostalgia for such an original unity, as expressed in the realist tale of Bloom the would-be father encountering Stephen the figural son, *Ulysses* is well equipped to show the difference between this desire and the regime in which it exists, but, I suggest, it balks at the prospect of allowing its most obvious subaltern subjects, the women it portrays, any potential unity beyond colonial interpellation. As such it merely proposes to the reader the more stark and profound question of whether such a unity can be imagined in any real sense at the moment of anticolonial revolution.

In the second place we must consider the text's refusal to end by imagining a novel community as proof once again of the difficulty of overcoming the pessimism of subaltern politics in the late-colonial period. The perspective I have in mind is less the youthful Dedalus's '*Non serviam*', which personalises and psychologises one response to the national political dilemma, than the pervasive scepticism regarding anticolonial revolution suggested, for example, in such texts as the following epigram by Yeats, published in his *Last Poems* of 1939:

Parnell

Parnell came down the road, he said to a cheering man:
'Ireland shall get her freedom and you still break stone.'[8]

Joyce's youthful political pessimism, as the careful researches of Dominic Manganiello have shown,[9] was first evidenced in his interest in the socialist doctrine of his day; when he later discovered himself as an artist – if we are to take *A Portrait* as biographical manifesto – this pessimism reformulated itself as a late example of the alienation of the romantic artist. Both manifestations are similar even if, in conventional political terms, one seems the avowal of political involvement and the other its repudiation, in that they both represent a young colonial subject's pessimism in the face of rule, as Stephen himself puts it, by '[t]he imperial British state' (p. 20). As such they foreshadow the disillusion that Joyce as well as Yeats, whose politics noticeably evolved over the decades, came to feel for the 'New' (i.e., independent) Ireland. (Yeats's cheering man is the poet's counterpart to Molly Bloom, because here too, close to the end of his poetic-political testament, he focuses his gaze upon a lone and abject figure rather than the cheering crowd or community one expects to find standing before the pontificating politician. Molly, however, might well have sneered where Yeats's old man cheered.) As such also we might infer that Joyce's refusal at the end of *Ulysses* to postulate a new community in solidarity was prescient about the actual conditions of the independent postcolonial state that was founded after the treaty of 1921. Neither Saorstát Eireann, the new Irish Free State, nor Northern Ireland – the two political entities into which the island of Ireland was split by the treaty – lived up to the utopian ideals of the revolutionaries. The Free State itself was immediately torn in a civil war over whether the territorial split agreed on in the treaty was acceptable; this was the first legacy of the treaty that was negotiated in London while Joyce was finishing his novel across the Channel.

Still, it would require an undue pessimism on our own part to read Joyce's refusal to imagine a real community outside abjection as a failure of the novel's political project; rather, it aptly represents the mixed idealism and limitations of the new Irish Free State itself. In this sense Molly Bloom as representative Irish subject acts to taunt – as *Ulysses* has taunted from its first moments – nationalist stereotypes of Irish identity, while still retaining, as did the new state, a consciousness of her continuing subalternity. With the novel ending, however, just as the new state was about to come into being, the text effectively replaces the issue of difference based on colonial power versus native abjection, which the novel, like the treaty itself, has resolved in favour of a limited new national subjecthood for most of the inhabitants of the island, with the issue of difference among the native subjects themselves, which it epitomises through difference based on gender. In this sense, if *Ulysses* is read as 'national allegory',[10] then Molly, in the 'Nostos' of *Ulysses*, is a mirror image, in the text's depiction of home, of Deasy, the schoolmaster of the opening 'Telemachiad'. For Deasy is the Protestant and Orangeman in the largely Catholic Dublin of *Ulysses*, and it was unresolvable differences between the mostly Protestant unionists who wished to remain with Britain and Catholic nationalists who wished for an independent Ireland that led to the civil war between different nationalist factions in 1922, as it has led to much strife between nationalists and unionists in Northern Ireland since. Molly's insistence on her difference based on gender may be paralleled with Deasy's avowal of his difference based on politics and creed. What we are presented with at the end of the novel is its focus on the continuing oppression of the figures of the most abject subalternity here, and the fact that this abjection is based on difference in gender is accentuated. With Molly as the 'indispensable countersign', 'Penelope' is the most challenging, the most radically interrogative, moment of the text. With this in mind, let us now turn to a more particular reading of the 'Nostos' episodes.

Suspicion and difference

At the outset I stressed the radical interrogativity of *Ulysses* as a whole: its determination to question every implication of representation. This turns the text in the first instance toward a paranoid mimeticism, an eagerness to be correct with every timetable and house number on the one hand, and a desire to undermine every protocol of realist narrative on the other. Interrogativity, relentless questioning, takes over as the very engine of the text in the final three episodes comprising the 'Nostos'; it is most evident in the central set-piece, 'Ithaca', where stark question-and-answer is posited explicitly as the episode's form, but it is none the less pervasive in 'Eumaeus' and 'Penelope'. In 'Eumaeus', set in the murky cabman's shelter on the Dublin quays between 12:40 and 1:00 A.M., this questioning takes the form of suspicion regarding identity. It is also the questioning through which Bloom and Stephen come to know each other (to the extent that they do). Theirs is a vestigial community of two, the only community engineered by the realist strand of the novel, which is inaugurated against a fitting background of an intense police and judicial presence reflecting the pervasiveness of colonial state power. What 'Eumaeus' proves is that their gesture of coming to know one another is acted out against a background of politically charged suspicion which is in turn depicted as a microcosm of the pervasive suspicion of the colonial regime.

The cabman's shelter is a new kind of setting in the successive urban locales of *Ulysses*, and one that effects an important strategic compromise between what was alien and familiar in a turn-of-the-century city like the Dublin Joyce describes. Up to now the novel in this regard has had it both ways: appearing to be a modernist metro-text that describes life in the increasingly crowded city, we might have expected it to show a world of strangers and alienated inhabitants. On the contrary, *Ulysses* has delineated a milieu in which almost every major character turns out to be familiar with the others, either through acquaintance or family relationship – the kind of world we expect to encounter in a nineteenth-century realist novel. Bloom, for example, is troubled, as we discover in 'Ithaca', by one question: 'Who was M'Intosh?' (p. 681), the only person whom he did not know at the funeral of Paddy Dignam; Richie Goulding, with whom Bloom ate dinner earlier in the Ormond Hotel, is, we realise in the same episode, the husband of Stephen's Aunt Sara (p. 623).

The cabman's shelter as setting, however, effects a compromise between the alienated urban scene and the typical realist locale of familiar characters, for it is a small room in which strangers are expected to be familiar with each other. The shelter is late-colonial Dublin's grim version of cafe culture, the setting for encounters between strangers appropriate to the great imperial metropolises. (In such late nineteenth-century metropolitan realist fictions as the detective story, settings such as 'the club' and the railway carriage were likewise used as locales that sustained strands of a parlour familiarity and a street anonymity at once.) Thus a group of strangers are brought together to speak to one another, but the kind of forced community thus created is a highly uneasy one, charged with the kind of suspicion often bred of a fear of violence.

This suspicion is generated against a background sense, strongly suggested especially in the opening pages of 'Eumaeus', of a heavy police presence. Approaching the shelter, Stephen and Bloom wander through 'Store Street, famous for its C division police station' and moments later Bloom is 'recalling a case or two in the A Division in Clanbrassil Street' where a policeman 'admittedly unscrupulous in the service of the Crown ... [was] prepared to swear a hole through a ten gallon pot' (pp. 570–1). Not only do these passages give a strong sense of the police network in the city, but, as in the above lines, they associate this official surveillance with untrustworthy tellings and false knowledge. Further suspicion and efforts to guard against it are suggested by the presence of the corporation watchman under the dark Loop Line Bridge, who turns out to be 'the eldest son of Inspector Corley of the G Division' (p. 572) – the G Division was the police undercover detective agency. By now the episode has mentioned each of the best-known police divisions in central Dublin. The police presence, heavy throughout *Ulysses* – in 'Lestrygonians' Bloom had watched a phalanx of Dublin Metropolitan policemen march out of College Street police station (p. 154) – is accentuated here, as it was in 'Cyclops'. This underlines the real stakes, for the society, of the suspicion soon to be generated among the characters in the shelter.

What these stakes might be is suggested by the discourse of conventional politics infiltrating this episode. The way in which strangers are forced to be familiars in the cabman's shelter acts as a licence for political figures to be discussed as familiars also. Hence Charles Stewart Parnell is the subject of more explicit extended discussion here than in virtually any other episode.[11] Also, the immediacy of insurgent political action is brought home to us here through Bloom's suspicion that the keeper of the shelter is none other than 'Skin-the-Goat', once a member of a secret terrorist group of the 1880s, the Invincibles. 'Skin-the-Goat' was said to have driven the horse and cart of the assassins who killed Lord Cavendish and T. H. Burke, the chief secretary for Ireland and his undersecretary, in the infamous 'Phoenix Park Murders' of May 6, 1882.[12] (Remember that this episode was being written at a time when the guerrilla War of Independence in Ireland had grown so intense that the British army and authorities were forced to sue for a cease-fire, at a time when assassinations and attempted shootings in Dublin were daily occurrences.) When the supposed ex-Invincible, who still harbours patriotic views, and the drunken sailor D. B. Murphy, who has just been discharged from the British merchant marine and who speaks of 'our empire' (p. 596), begin to argue, the level of political discourse that is given an airing is merely the stereotyped sloganeering which we have already heard from the Citizen in 'Cyclops' or at moments in Joyce's *Dubliners* story 'Ivy Day in the Committee Room'; it is quickly dismissed by Bloom's private thoughts in the narrative. Rather, the flashpoint occurs when the ordinary suspicions harboured by the various strangers in the shelter regarding one another unwittingly touch upon the notoriety of Skin-the-Goat's terrorist past. This, as we will see, also turns out to be the first empathetic moment between Stephen and Bloom.

The sailor is telling of a murder he witnessed; this leads to a discussion about knives. Someone notes that '[t]hat was why they thought the park murders of the invincibles was done by foreigners on account of them using knives' (p. 584). Up to now, Bloom has encouraged Stephen to speak, but the younger man has responded without spirit. At this point, however, the text draws back to record one of their first mutually empathetic moments:

> At this remark, passed obviously in the spirit of *where ignorance is bliss*, Mr Bloom and Stephen, each in his own particular way, both instinctively exchanged meaning glances, in a religious silence of the strictly *entre nous* variety however, towards ... Skin-the-Goat
>
> (p. 584)

Here is the first and indeed one of the very few points at which Bloom and Stephen appear to agree; less forceful than the tableau of father and fallen son at the end of 'Circe', it is nevertheless perhaps the most touching moment in the strand of the narrative that celebrates the meeting of these two. What is striking about this throwaway mutual glance, however, is that it shows the two agreeing only on an issue drawn from the conventional discourse of Irish political and insurgent affairs.

This is appropriate, since the realism that has fostered Bloom and Stephen as characters is also most at home with the hackneyed versions of Irish political discourse. This nevertheless marked a failure of the realist masculinist plot to bring the two together on (in its own terms) a more 'meaningful' level; their only opening to empathy takes place at the most conventional plane of Irish politics, and furthermore, one that has been denigrated by the realist strand of the novel itself from its opening pages. This is borne out in 'Ithaca', where the most profound material the two find to discuss as they drink Epps cocoa in the kitchen of 7 Eccles Street is the characteristics of the race to which each professes to belong: the discourse of racial character, as 'Cyclops' has proven, being closely related to that of jingoist nationalist politics. It is fitting therefore that Stephen does not spend the night under Bloom's roof, and that the spell of the realist pseudo-family romance is finally broken. Bloom succumbs to a yearning to simulate the fundamentally *Gemeinschaft*[13] world of the realist novel within this text, but Stephen is too ferociously modern to accept this. He pushes nastily at the borders of tolerance while Bloom and he, seated in Eccles Street, discuss their respective races: he sings a song about a Jewish girl who kills a neighbouring boy (pp. 643–4), and plays the Jew's harp, apparently as a kind of taunt when, having left Bloom, he walks away down the dark alley (p. 657). Stephen's departure and implicit disavowal of the possibility of any real connection with Bloom clearly came none too soon; the implication of the postcolonial text is that no new national community will be envisioned within the terms of the realist narrative of relationships invented and perfected by the imperial culture.

Apart from documenting Bloom's and Stephen's failure to empathise, moreover, the text of 'Eumaeus' had been preparing us for this split by thematising the doubtfulness of the identity of virtually everyone mentioned in the episode. Old versions of identity, devastated as early in the novel as 'Cyclops', are now in full rout in the masculinist strand of the text. Already in 'Cyclops', identity based on nation per se is reviled; here in 'Eumaeus', the garrulous narrative becomes entangled in continuously repeating its doubts about the identity of all the strangers who are brought together in the dank shelter and asked to be familiar with each other. Often this makes for comedy: the drunken sailor, for example, tells Stephen that he knows Simon Dedalus, but his Simon turns out to have 'toured the wide world with Hengler's Royal Circus' (p. 579), and was seen by the sailor in Stockholm. Later, when Bloom notices that the postcard the sailor displays was addressed to one '*A. Boudin*' (p. 581), he begins to doubt that the drunkard's name is Murphy, although the latter has just shown off his discharge papers to prove it. Bloom himself is referred to as L. Boom (p. 602) in the *Evening Telegraph* report on Dignam's funeral, while 'Skin-the-Goat' is seldom mentioned here without the addition of the phrase 'assuming he was he' (p. 595). All in all, every male identity is undermined, especially in this self-conscious narrative, so that by the end we can easily agree with Bloom's proposition that 'when all was said and done, the lies a fellow told about himself couldn't probably hold a proverbial candle to the wholesale whoppers other fellows coined about him' (p. 591). When we remember that a stable sense of identity (i.e., an identity based on norms that a particular community implicitly agrees to accept) whether personal, national, or 'racial', is integral to sustained realist narration, we can appreciate how the suspicions generated by the conflation of a *gemeinschaftlich* easy familiarity and the *gesellschaftlich* alienation of a modernist metro-text here effectively forestall the attainment of a sense of community acceptable within the realist tradition.[14]

It is appropriate, given the nostalgia in 'Eumaeus' for a community recognisable within realist expectations, that most of the questions asked in the episode should be part of an effort to get to know the strangers present; even more appropriately, given the fact that such a community does not materialise, most of these questions are either sidestepped or ignored. Characteristic is Stephen's laconic reply to the sailor on being asked if he knows Simon Dedalus: 'I've heard of him', Stephen says (p. 578). Later the sailor refuses to answer Bloom's repeated inquiries about whether he has seen the Rock of Gibraltar. Conversely, given the episode's impulse to document an alienated world of passing strangers, it fits that most of the thoroughgoing discussions regarding identity concern not any of the individuals present but rather celebrity court cases, of which those in the shelter might have read in a newspaper. We hear of the 'Cornwall case' (p. 600) and the 'Tichborne case' (p. 604) – the second of which involved the issue of a claimant's real identity – and above all of the divorce case of Kitty O'Shea, Parnell's lover.

Parnell here is the heroic identity whose fall might be said to have presaged the fragility of all the identities on display in nighttime Dublin. To preserve his reputation, he had, we are told, started 'to go under several aliases such as Fox and Stewart' (p. 603). What is done systematically to the memory of his reputation here is that it is removed from the public, political sphere and, processed in Bloom's mind, is transformed into a clichéd love story from the genre of realist romance: the kind of tale that Gerty MacDowell might have enjoyed reading. When Bloom extracts from Parnell's fall the moral that here was 'The eternal question of the life connubial ... Can real love, supposing there happens to be another chap in the case, exist between married folk?' (p. 605) he has posed the last question in 'Eumaeus' from the realist plot that seeks closure in a conforming marital relationship. The effect is extraordinarily comic not merely because the question is hackneyed in the extreme, but because it confronts us in a text that also portrays a twentieth-century alienated world. Conversely, the last memorable question in 'Eumaeus' comes out of that urban milieu of alienated *flânerie:* Stephen's query as to 'why they put tables upside down at night, I mean chairs upside down on the tables in cafés' (p. 613). This is mordantly comic here (it might have rung somewhat differently, for example, in a French existentialist novel of thirty years later) simply because it is a flâneur's question in what still appears a family-romance text, the sort of novel in which the work of the servants (sweeping the floors in the morning) is taken for granted. The fact that the furniture is upside-down, however, and the fact that it is not disposed in a drawing-room but in the new urban world of the streets, is an apt image of the confusion of realist narrative regarding its function at this stage in the novel.

It is in this context that we can begin to understand why the novel undertook the 'Ithaca' episode in the form of a stark series of questions and answers. The function of 'Ithaca' may be grasped as an effort to bridge the different literary trajectories of 'Eumaeus' and the closing episode 'Penelope', which are, respectively, the male- and female-centred worlds of the 'Nostos'. In the masculinist 'Eumaeus' as we have seen, the realist world of a web of relations based on familiarity is not, despite a stitching of questions, reconciled with the modernist metro-text that documents the alienating city. The realist narrative, telling centrally the story of Bloom as father and Stephen as son, proves incapable of creating a satisfying community of father and son in this context; the modernist city-text that defeats it, on the other hand, is more appropriate for describing a grand European capital than a backward late-colonial metropolis. In 'Penelope', as I will show, there is staged on the contrary an altogether more novel strategy, which poses the possibility of community as an issue rather than hankering after it nostalgically as a utopian possibility. 'Penelope' too might seem a realist parlour-romance, set in the boudoir and bedroom of its seductress, but Bloom discovers that the furniture of that boudoir has been moved about by Molly, and, comfortable in the dark with his old expectations, he bangs his head in finding this out (p. 658). The bridge episode of 'Ithaca' is devoted primarily to making a last-ditch effort to complete the novel's realist project, and latterly, to setting the conditions for the unique narrative of 'Penelope'. In pursuing these objectives, 'Ithaca' exposes the regimes of surveillance that are the political unconscious of the realist tale of 'Eumaeus' and, in uncovering the materials of this realism in its final phase, it shows off the material bases on which Molly's monologue is built. In a sense 'Eumaeus' poses the question of the possibility of community under the old realist rubric, to which 'Ithaca' responds with a negative answer; it implies that for the subaltern, strict realism (here pared down to the question-and-answer of the police interrogator and suspect) will never escape the panoptic intent of those in power who invented it. 'Penelope' then reformulates the question and the terms under which the utopian project of subsequent postcolonial narratives should operate.

The marshalled questions of 'Ithaca' let us know that Stephen and Bloom found little to discuss beyond the defunct prestige of racial characteristics. They allow us to contemplate Stephen's refusal of Bloom's hospitality without having to dwell on the rejection of a comfortable realist close that this gesture represents. More importantly, they allow us to glimpse in its thoroughness the collection of information on which realist narrative is built. 'Ithaca' is generally termed a catechism, and is taken to mimic both collections of Catholic doctrine (the Maynooth Catechism, for example) and nineteenth-century popular compendiums of scientific information. But the first half of 'Ithaca' while it appears to be presenting lists, dicta, and accounts of sins or experiments (as in the church and scientific catechisms), instead described what two men, both clad in black, were doing on the streets of Dublin and in an Eccles Street basement between one and two o'clock in the morning. As such, it is more accurately the account of a police investigation with model answers – the transcript of an inquiry that might have taken place, let us imagine, in the interrogation room of Store Street divisional police station, which Bloom and Stephen passed on their way to the cabman's shelter.

The questions about how Bloom entered his own home (he climbed over the railings, let himself fall into the area, and entered through the area door), for example, have all the eagerness of a police detective investigation of suspicious movements: 'Bloom's decision?' 'Did he fall?' 'Did he rise uninjured by concussion?' 'Did the man reappear elsewhere?' (pp. 621–2). Hence it is in 'Ithaca' that the massive regime of surveillance of the colonial state is made explicit in the form; we are confronted with a series of questions and answers that is at once a catechism (implying a compendium of the important knowledge of the culture) and a police interrogation (implying the grip of the panoptic regime upon the dispersal and even the very existence of the culture's pool of knowledge). As is fitting in this *envoi* to the novel's realist narrative, the apparently 'obscure' (modernist) text has seldom, throughout the whole book, been so literally transparent. A keyword in 'Eumaeus' had been 'Sherlockholmesing' (p. 590); this is made the operative principle of 'Ithaca' itself. Note too that this police-interrogation continually suggests a threat of violence that contrasts painfully with the cosiness of the cocoa-drinking scene being described.

It is in the second part of 'Ithaca' that we realise what its role as *envoi* of realism in the novel entails. When we are shown Bloom alone here, we are forcefully reminded of the utterly interpellated subjectivities to which the regime of surveillance encoding the whole episode gives rise.[15] We are given a list of Bloom's books (pp. 660–2), his budget for the day with debits and credits noted in the best accounting order (p. 664), and his ambition – to own a suburban villa ('Bloom Cottage. Saint Leopold's. Flowerville' [p. 667]) complete with water closet, tennis court, shrubbery, and facilities for 'Snapshot photography' and the 'comparative study of religions' (p. 667): the chosen field of many an enlightened retired colonial official. The wedding presents, pieces of furniture, papers, and *bibelots* of the Bloom household are all catalogued. What the novel returns to at this finishing-point of realist narration – perhaps a closing point in high literature for the genre itself – is the spirit informing its beginning in Britain almost two hundred years earlier in the early days of Britain's colonial expansion, in the fictions of one of Joyce's favourite authors, Daniel Defoe.

Molly Bloom, cleverly placing herself inside and outside her own text at once, both an admirer and a critic, tells us that she doesn't 'like books with a Molly in them' and refers us to Defoe's *Moll Flanders*, whose heroine she remembers 'always shoplifting anything she could cloth and stuff and yards of it' (p. 707). (Molly remembers Moll as a deviant consumer rather than as an aggressive businesswoman – or she may imply a comic conflation of both roles.) She had earlier folded the form of 'Ithaca' back upon itself and ensured that it ended as a remarkably self-reflexive text, by posing to Bloom a succession of questions about his day. Molly's inquisitiveness means that the last part of 'Ithaca' becomes a series of questions about a series of questions. Its realist relentlessness is enervated by a spiral of conditional tenses supplanting interrogative forms, as in the wistful late question, 'If he had smiled why would he have smiled?' (p. 683). Through flashes of extra-textuality of this sort – at another point, squatting on the chamber pot, Molly calls on 'Jamesey' (i.e., Joyce as author, perhaps) to 'let me up out of this' (p. 719) – Molly as subject is granted a mercurial, shifting position both inside and at once outside the text she is destined to carry to its conclusion.

What is striking, however, is the extraordinary particularity of the material base on which such a mercurial subjectivity is constructed. Interpellated by the pleasures of middle-class commodity culture quite as thoroughly as is her husband, Molly too thinks of the furniture (the jingly old bed, for example), bibelots, and advertised clothing, as in 'one of those kidfitting corsets Id want advertised cheap in the Gentlewoman with elastic gores on the hips ... what did they say they give a delightful figure line 11/6 obviating that unsightly broad appearance across the lower back ...' (p. 702).

(Like Bloom, she too has an eye for advertisements.) Her speech is a palimpsest of middle-class clichés ('sure you cant get on in this world without style' [p. 702]), so that her voice never sounds less than directly derived from that of others ('of course hed never find another woman like me to put up with him the way I do' [p. 696]). Molly Bloom is, therefore, both the image of the wholly interpellated subject, a type of the ideal colonial native, and simultaneously a shifting signifier that is at flash-moments deployed at a distance from the text altogether. It is in the space between these two roles that the voice of Molly as interrogator of postcolonial community operates.

Molly Bloom is an ideal colonial subject to such a degree that she may be compared to Kimball O'Hara, the 'Kim' of Kipling's novel of the same title.[16] Like Kim, she is the daughter of an Irish colonial soldier in the British army. As offspring of colonial soldiers and, apparently, 'native' women (in both cases the identities of their mothers are kept vague), Kim and Molly are curiously both members of the colonist and native cultures at once. This is underlined in both cases by the darkness of their skin: Kim seems to be 'a young heathen' to the British officers who offer to educate him, while Leopold Bloom is proud that Molly, from Gibraltar, is a Spanish type (p. 606). Both Kim and Molly represent on the one hand a utopian ideal of assimilation of the colonist masters and native colonial subjects; on the other, they transgress a boundary that, because the rigid division between colonists and natives sustaining the empire had to be kept up, was the greatest taboo of all to cross.

Further, Molly as a native of Gibraltar who now lives in Ireland – that is, a person from one colony or outpost of empire who now lives in another – has also successfully transgressed the unspoken rule that the natives of that colony will keep to their own territory. Benedict Anderson, in *Imagined Communities*,[17] his study of the relation of nationalism and imperialism, points out that a key way in which the imperial power reinforced local chauvinisms, as well as its own tacit belief in the particular inferiority of each colony compared to the centre, was to forestall any mixing among the colonial peoples: an Indian functionary, for example, even after a standard 'British' education, would never have been encouraged to go to work in Hong Kong. Molly Bloom, however, has evaded this stricture. Thus just as Bloom, in 'Cyclops', stands for the principle of oppressed peoples who must, he implies, be in solidarity with each other ('And I belong to a race too ... that is hated and persecuted' [p. 318]), Molly signifies the principle of native oppression rather than the ideological narrowness of any particular national chauvinism. Unlike Bloom, however, she does not focus on this oppression as the enabling integer of her subjectivity.

Further, with her father as Irish soldier in the British colonial service and her mother possibly a Jewish Spaniard, her family history marks her at once as a figure who will never be allowed, even if she had wished, to represent herself as an 'authentic' nationalist. Earlier we saw how Bloom, as a politically conscious Jew ('though in reality I'm not' [p. 597] he tells Stephen in 'Eumaeus') and an Irish person, stands not for a single chauvinist nationalism but, in his interest in the future of a Jewish state as well as an Irish one, rather for the more magnanimous principle of national independence for all oppressed peoples. Now we see that Molly is not a native of one colonial territory, but rather, with her heritage of Ireland and Gibraltar, is a subaltern native of the empire itself: she becomes a signifier of colonial subalternity in general.

Moreover, as a woman in a male-dominated colonial system that almost always assigned women the lowest rung in the hierarchy of power, Molly is the last of a line of women in *Ulysses* who are the text's most abject subaltern subjects. This series began with Stephen's sick mother, whose grim degrading death is reported in the opening pages of the text, and continued with such figures as the poor milkwoman, who is merely interested in being paid; Mrs Breen, the harried 'melancholily' (p. 150) wife of Denis, the victim of the 'U.P.: up' postcard; Gerty MacDowell, wistful, limping, poorly educated and dreamy on Sandymount strand in contrast to Stephen's well-read cockiness on the same beach earlier; Mina Purefoy, who is giving birth to her ninth child in Holles Street Hospital; Mrs Keogh, the brothel cook in 'Circe'; and 'the partially idiotic female', a prostitute whom Bloom encounters along the quays in 'Sirens' and who, 'glazed and haggard under a black straw hat, peered askew round the door of the shelter' (p. 587) in 'Eumaeus'.

The degree of abjection under which these women suffer at the hands of the patriarchal colonial culture is perhaps most ferociously suggested by the 'Oxen of the Sun' episode of *Ulysses*. The important event reported in this stretch of narrative is the birth of a boy to Mina Purefoy after a long labour; the great bulk of the episode, however, is given over to an account of a bawdy group of medical students in the hospital dayroom, whose jokes are related in a compendium of pastiche styles that represent key stylistic turns in the history of the English literary canon. It is as if such styles, the styles of England's literary history, could not be brought to bear on a description of a woman in labour in one of England's colonies, so that they can only refer to the lives of women as fleetingly glimpsed background figures in a world of men.

Molly Bloom, as the first woman in the text to be allowed to think for an extended period in her own voice, is as interpellated by the colonial patriarchal culture as these women, but she exceeds it as well. She too is an abject; in contrast to Poldy, she is limited in her movement to the grim Eccles Street house, so that her night thoughts often turn to escape into the city streets in a *flânerie* similar to that her husband has practised all day – she thinks of setting out for the market in the morning, for example. She has few friends, and if loneliness is to be considered the pervading sensation of this text, she has surely much more reason to be lonely than Bloom. ('they have friends they can talk to weve none either' [p. 728]). On the other hand, she has been successfully interpellated as an ideal colonial subject from the coloniser's viewpoint: she is struck, for example, by the pageantry of 'the prince of Wales own or the lancers O the lancers theyre grand or the Dublins that won Tugela' – referring to different regiments in the British army (p. 700) – and, more important, she fulfils the role of the eager native consumer of colonial commodities: she and Boylan ate the jar of Plumtree's Potted Meat together, and she wishes that Bloom would allow her more money for clothes (p. 702). In other words she may strike us as an extraordinarily acquiescent, even eager, late-colonial native subject.

Further, she is a woman alone, not part of any group that might suggest the solidarity of resistance. She is markedly apolitical in any conventional sense, jeering at Bloom's suggestion that Arthur Griffith, the Sinn Fein leader, is the coming man ('well he doesnt look it thats all I can say' [p. 700]). (Events that occurred before Joyce wrote this episode proved Bloom right here; Griffith, a marginal figure in Irish politics in 1904, had become a central figure in the founding of the Irish Free State.) This, taken together with her unrepressed thoughts on sexuality as well as her unpunctuated flow of language, seems to imply a rejection of the public and the communal in favour of the personal or the erotic. Yet just as Stephen's corresponding 'Proteus' monologue is not as introverted as it might have seemed, what is striking about Molly's thoughts is that she reconnoitres her aloneness, her apoliticality, her sexuality, and even her self-presentation as a matter of information and its control by those who have power to manipulate it. Against regimes of information she uses interrogativity as a striking rhetorical feature of her thought, in order to present us, at the end of the novel, with a fully subaltern perspective on the opinions, prejudices, and beliefs of the Dublin of her day. In the first place, she recounts a series of scenarios in which men are tiresome questioners. She remembers Bloom 'drawing out the thing by the hour question and answer would you do this that and the other with the coalman yes with a bishop yes' (p. 692), and on Breen's mystery postcard she opines 'wouldnt a thing like that simply bore you stiff to extinction' (p. 696). She knows much about the skilful use of information: she laughs at Josie Powell 'because I used to tell her a good bit of what went on between us but not all just enough to make her mouth water' (p. 695). At the next level, she remembers throughout the episode scenes where men holding officially sanctioned positions questioned her. Molly represents these as occasions on which she either kept her distaste to herself, or cleverly acted as an innocent to enjoy a joke of her own at the questioner's expense. Thus she thinks of the gynaecologist on the Pembroke Road (p. 720), and of Catholic confession:

> when I used to go to father Corrigan he touched me father and what harm if he did where and I said on the canal bank like a fool but whereabouts on your person my child on the leg behind high up was it yes rather high up was it where you sit down yes O Lord couldnt he say bottom right out and have done with it
>
> (p. 693)

Lines like this ('and I said on the canal bank') are probably the best uses of subaltern carnival discourse in either western or postcolonial modernism. They aptly represent the strategies that the abject colonial native, denied direct access to her own speech and language which is instead mediated to her through the searching interrogations of those in power, brings to bear to subvert the oppressor's words. The comedy of 'Penelope' (and it is by far the most humorous episode in this intensely comic work) is again and again derived from the kind of knowing yet apparently innocent subversion of the words and actions of those in power: if Molly could not find an appropriate muttered line at the time to respond to a condescending interrogator, she invents such lines now, describing the solicitor Menton 'and his boiled eyes of all the big stupoes I ever met and thats called a solicitor' (p. 691), and observing of Bloom himself 'somebody ought to put him in the budget' (p. 705). The 'Penelope' episode, then, points us to the very principle of difference that will undermine any postcolonial imagined utopian community by granting the last word in what has been a resolutely male-centred text to a woman; further, it shows this woman as a more profoundly interpellated subaltern subject who actively works in her use of language to subvert the tropes that would either create a colonial pseudo-community (the 'Commonwealth of Nations' or 'Family of Man') or imagine its postcolonial mirror image ('the Irish Free State').

It is with the depth of Molly's abjection as a colonial native woman in mind that we can appreciate the effect of her controversial 'Yes', which rings through her narrative and eventually closes her text. Remember the scene this episode depicts: it is of a woman lying in bed, near sleep, between 1:45 and 2:20 A.M. on June 17, 1904. In fact not one word is uttered aloud during this episode. Here is interior monologue brought to its logical conclusion – the utter silence of the thinking subject – and it makes us realise the peculiar appropriateness of this form of narration for colonial subjects – the subaltern whom the colonial master would ideally render silent and of fixed abode. As in the culture of slavery, the only word the native is expected to utter is the token of acquiescence in response to an order – a servile 'yes' Molly, at the end of *Ulysses*, renders the very act of accepting Bloom in marriage a part of this colonial question-response when she utters her 'yes' in answer to his question. Yet she also toys with the question, tosses it back at him, using the subversive ruse of the subaltern to turn the voicing of that 'yes' into an effect suggesting equality. She herself *also* asks – if silently – and they first utter the yes together:

> yes he said I was a flower of the mountain yes ... that was one true thing he said in his life and ... I gave him all the pleasure I could leading him on till he asked me to say yes and I wouldnt answer first only looked out over the sea and the sky I was thinking of so many things he didnt know of ... and I thought well as well him as another and then I asked him with my eyes to ask again yes and then he asked me would I yes to say yes ... and his heart was going like mad and yes I said yes I will Yes.
>
> (pp. 731–2)

The truth is that we can never know whether the 'Yes' that marks the end of the book is the *last* acquiescence of the most deeply interpellated colonial abject, marking a new equality that will now mean that the freed subjects can henceforth pose questions to each other, or whether it is merely one more acquiescence that marks another turn in the repetitive cycle of oppression. Yet, with the necessity to accept difference among the native group, through the force of this episode, now thoroughly in place, a community, if it is to be created, will be built on the acceptance of equality between different but equal groups and subjects rather than on any ill-defined utopianism that would likely replicate the fake community of the empire itself. That such a state will come about is augured by Molly Bloom's spirited deployment of the carnival of subaltern language. Hers is not some lapse into the 'flow' of the personal and the apolitical, but rather the subaltern's deft redistribution of forces in the language-economy of late-colonial power.

From Enda Duffy, *The Subaltern Ulysses* (Minneapolis, 1994), pp. 165–88.

Notes

[In the final chapter of his postcolonial study of *Ulysses*, Enda Duffy argues that the touchstone for inventing an alternative history (or indeed an alternative to history) is not the opening, but the closure of a text. In *Ulysses*' manifold (and often unsuccessful) attempts to envisage communities, the fact that a gender switch happens between its penultimate and final chapter is highly significant. This and other stylistic ruptures in the final three episodes serve to undermine the controlling gaze of male-centred realist perspective in the novel that is identical with the colonial superiority of English culture. Colonial and class struggle meet gender in the abjection of women in the text (most of whom are working class). This break from the dominance of realism enables *Ulysses* to become a truly modernist text in the first place. It also produces a text that asks about the possibility of community rather than simply presenting its own utopian version. This possibility is encapsuled in Molly's final 'yes', which can be read as an assertion of identity, but also as a surrender. All page references to *Ulysses* are to the Oxford World's Classics edition, ed. Jeri Johnson (1993). Ed.]

1. ['*Nostos*' is Greek for 'return' and refers to the last three sections of *Ulysses*: 'Eumaeus', 'Ithaca', and 'Penelope' – Ed.]
2. Quoted in Bonnie Kime Scott, *Joyce and Feminism* (Bloomington, IN, 1984), p. 156.

3. On how the culture of consumption shapes women in *Ulysses*, see Thomas Richards, *The Commodity Culture of Victorian England: Advertising and Spectacle 1851–1914* (Stanford, CA, 1990).

4. See especially chapter 6, 'Conclusion: The Dialectic of Utopia and Ideology', in Fredric Jameson, *The Political Unconscious: Narrative as a Socially Symbolic Act* (Ithaca, NY, 1981), pp. 281–99.

5. Stewart Hall, 'The Toad in the Garden: Thatcherism among the Theorists' in *Marxism and the Interpretation of Culture*, ed. Cary Nelson and Lawrence Grossberg (Urbana, IL, 1988), pp. 35–57.

6. Gayatri Chakravorty Spivak, 'The Political Economy of Women as Seen by a Literary Critic', in *Coming to Terms: Feminism, Theory, Politics*, ed. Elizabeth Weed (New York, 1989), pp. 218–29.

7. Donna Haraway, 'A Manifesto for Cyborgs: Science, Technology and Socialist Feminism in the 1980s', in Weed, *Coming to Terms*, pp. 173–204. See p. 175.

8. William Butler Yeats, *Collected Poems* (London and Basingstoke, 1982), p. 359.

9. Dominic Manganiello, *Joyce's Politics* (London, 1980), pp. 67–114.

10. Fredric Jameson, 'Third World Literature in the Era of Multinational Capitalism', *Social Text*, 15 (Autumn 1986), 65–88.

11. On the significance of the changing attitudes to Parnell represented in *Ulysses*, see my 'Parnellism and Rebellion: The Irish War of Independence and Revisions of the Heroic in Ulysses', *James Joyce Quarterly*, 28:1 (Autumn 1990), 179–95.

12. Mark Tierney, *Modern Ireland: 1850–1950* (Dublin, 1972), p. 32.

13. ['*Gemeinschaft*' is German for 'community' – Ed.]

14. ['*gemeinschaftlich*' means 'related to community', '*gesellschaftlich*' 'related to society'. Duffy borrows the German terms from Ferdinand Tönnies, *Community and Society*, trans. Charles P. Loomis (New York, 1963) – Ed.]

15. [That subjectivity is 'interpellated', i.e. called into being by the address of ideology, is a central claim of the French Marxist theorist Louis Althusser. See his 'Ideology and Ideological State Apparatuses', *Lenin and Philosophy*, trans. Ben Brewster (New York, 1971), pp. 127–86 – Ed.].

16. Rudyard Kipling, *Kim*, ed. Edward Said (London, 1987).

17. Benedict Anderson, *Imagined Communities: Reflections on the Origin and Spread of Nationalism* (London, 1983), p. 105.

Further Reading

These suggestions reiterate the critical outlooks and topics of each chapter. Further reading is also suggested for aspects of theory.

Introduction

Perhaps the most convincing attempt to outline the structure of modernism, including its ambivalence towards universalism and particularity, is Astradur Eysteinsson, *The Concept of Modernism* (Ithaca and London, 1990). A recent collection of essays dedicated to the problematic foundations of modernist writing is Michael Bell and Peter Poellner (eds), *Myth and the Making of Modernity: The Problem of Grounding in Twentieth-Century Literature*, Studies in Comparative Literature, 16 (Amsterdam and Atlanta, 1998). The starting point for many of the debates covered in the above books remains Max Horkheimer and Theodor W. Adorno, *Dialectic of Enlightenment*, trans. John Cummings (London and New York, 1979). On objects in modernism see Douglas Mao, *Solid Objects: Modernism and the Test of Production* (Princeton, NJ, 1998). On death see Simon Critchley, *Very little ... almost nothing: Death, Philosophy, Literature*, Warwick Studies in Contemporary Philosophy (London, 1997) and Jacques Derrida, *Aporias: Dying – Awaiting (One Another at) the 'Limits of Truth'*, trans. Thomas Dutoit (Stanford, CA, 1993) and *The Gift of Death*, trans. David Wills, Religion and Postmodernism (Chicago, 1995). On desire see Jean Baudrillard, *Seduction*, trans. Brian Singer, Culture Texts (Basingstoke and London, 1990), and Catherine Belsey, *Desire: Love Stories in Western Culture* (Oxford and Cambridge, MA, 1994).

1. Lehan

Geert Lernout, *The French Joyce* (Ann Arbor, MI, 1990) is the study that summarises and criticises poststructuralist approaches to Joyce. Some of the criticised positions are assembled in Bernard Benstock (ed.), *James Joyce – The Augmented Ninth: Proceedings of the Ninth International James Joyce Symposium, Frankfurt, 1984* (Syracuse, NY, 1988), a book which contains papers given at a crucial event in the establishment of deconstructionist Joyce criticism. Others can be inspected in Derek Attridge and Daniel Ferrer (eds), *Post-Structuralist Joyce: Essays from the French* (New York, 1984). A useful overview of the changing critical trends in relation to Joyce is John Coyle (ed.), *James Joyce*, Icon Critical Guides (Cambridge, 1997).

2. Murphy

Murphy acknowledges the influence of Morris Beja, 'The Mystical Estate or the Legal Fiction: Paternity in *Ulysses*', in Benstock, *The Augmented Ninth*, pp. 215–18, and Jean-Michel Rabaté, 'Paternity, Thy Name is Joy', ibid., pp. 219–25 on his ideas concerning Stephen's (and *Ulysses*') struggle with creativity. I have discussed the problem in relation to poetry in 'Macro-Myths and Micro-Myths: Modernist Poetry and the Problem of Artistic Creation' in Bell, *Myth and the Making of Modernity*, pp. 181–96. Gerald Siegmund approaches the issue from the perspective of memory and psychoanalysis in 'Freud's Myths: Memory, Culture and the Subject', ibid., pp. 197–211. The other side of protean creation is addressed in Henry Staten, 'The Decomposing Form of Joyce's *Ulysses*', *PMLA*, 112:3 (May 1997), 380–92.

3. Weinstock

The seminal reassessment of the significance of ghosts in literature is Marjorie Garber, *Shakespeare's Ghost Writers: Literature as Uncanny Causality* (New York, 1987). Specific essays on Ulysses's ghosts are Maud Ellmann, 'The Ghosts of Ulysses', in *James Joyce: The Artist and the Labyrinth*, ed. Augustine Martin (London, 1990), pp. 193–227, and Shari Benstock, '*Ulysses* as Ghoststory', *James Joyce Quarterly*, 12 (Summer 1975), 396–413. An essay that outlines the significance of the uncanny in modernism is Steven Connor, 'Echo's Bones: Myth, Modernity and the Vocalic Uncanny', in Bell, *Myth and the Making of Modernity*, pp. 213–35. The most daring attempt to bridge the gap between psychoanalysis and deconstruction via the concept of haunting is Jacques Derrida, *Specters of Marx: The State of the Debt, the Work of Mourning, and the New International*, trans. Peggy Kamuf (New York and London, 1994). An interesting new collection of essays dealing with literary, cultural, and theoretical hauntings is Peter Buse and Andrew Stott (eds), *Ghosts: Deconstruction, Psychoanalysis, History* (London and Basingstoke, 1999).

4. Woodruff

One of the earlier essays dealing with Joyce's position towards nationalism is Seamus Deane, 'Joyce and Nationalism', in Colin MacCabe (ed.), *James Joyce: New Perspectives* (London, 1982), pp. 168–83. David Cairns and Shaun Richards, *Writing Ireland: Colonialism, Nationalism and Culture* (Manchester, 1988) provides a larger framework. Robert Spoo, ' "Nestor" and the Nightmare: The Presence of the Great War in Ulysses' and Daniel Moshenberg, 'What Shouts in the Street: 1904, 1922, 1990–93', in Wollaeger, *Joyce and the Subject of History*, pp. 105–24 and 125–40 broaden the picture to include world history and continuing social conflicts. Joyce's debunking of nationalism is discussed in Theresa O'Connor, 'Demythologizing Nationalism: Joyce's Dialogized Grail Myth', in *Joyce in Context*, ed. Vincent J. Cheng and Timothy Martin (Cambridge, 1992), pp. 100–21. A comprehensive, if rather pedestrian, study is Emer Nolan, *James Joyce and Nationalism* (London and New York, 1995).

Slavoj Žižek ultimately provides the link between ideological and psychoanalytic criticism in *The Sublime Object of Ideology* (London, 1989); 'From Joyce-the-Symptom to the Symptom of Power', *Lacanian Ink*, 11 (1997), 13–25; *For They Know Not What They Do: Enjoyment as a Political Factor* (London, 1991); and *The Plague of Fantasies* (London, 1997).

5. Stanier

Derek Attridge's 'Molly's Flow: The Writing of "Penelope" and the Question of Woman's Language', *Modern Fiction Studies*, 35:3 (1989), 543–65 was one of the first essays to question the simple split between masculine and feminine voice in *Ulysses*. Luce Irigaray's 'When Our Lips Speak Together', trans. Carolyn Burke, *Signs: Journal of Women in Culture and Society*, 6:1 (1980), 69–79, and *This Sex Which Is Not One*, trans. Catherine Porter (Ithaca, NY, 1985) are interventions that claim that Molly's monologue embodies *écriture féminine*. In the meantime, countless essays on gender in *Ulysses* have appeared. Some of those that focus on its final section are collected in Richard Pearce (ed.), *Molly Blooms: A Polylogue on 'Penelope' and Cultural Studies* (Madison, WI, 1994).

6. McLean

McLean's most prominent reference point is Julia Kristeva, whose ideas on abjection combine psychoanalytic with feminist and poststructuralist positions. See Julia Kristeva, *Powers of Horror: An Essay on Abjection*, trans. Leon S. Roudiez (New York, 1982). Shari Benstock, *Textualizing the Feminine: On the Limits of Genre* (Norman, OK, 1991) offers another linking of gender analysis and literary studies. McLean also employs feminist assessments of pornography to address masculine ambivalence towards female (and male) bodies. An example is Linda Williams, *Hard Core: Power, Pleasure, and the 'Frenzy of the Visible'* (Berkeley, CA, 1989). Judith Butler, *Bodies That Matter: On the Discursive Limits of 'Sex'* (New York, 1993) is the most prominent recent intervention in the field.

7. Osteen

Osteen uses a mixture of traditional economic criticism and ideas on population control and combines them with recent theories of textual economy, taking plagiarism as his starting point. See Thomas Mallon, *Stolen Words: Forays into the Origins and Ravages of Plagiarism* (New York, 1989); Kurt Heinzelmann, *The Economics of the Imagination* (Amherst, MA, 1980); and (with regard to modernism in poetry) 'Towards an Economy of the Modernist Poem' in my *Modernism in Poetry: Motivations, Structures and Limits*, Studies in Twentieth-Century Literature (London and New York, 1995), pp. 172–206. On ideas of population control and traditional economics that influenced Joyce, see Mary Lowe-Evans, *Crimes against Fecundity: Joyce and Population Control* (Syracuse, NY, 1989) and P. D. Anthony, *John Ruskin's Labour* (Cambridge, 1983).

8. Ziarek

Ziarek lists, among others, the following studies on women and modernism as her influences: Alice A. Jardine, *Gynesis: Configurations of Woman and Modernity* (Ithaca, NY, 1985); Marianne DeKoven, *Rich and Strange: Gender, History, Modernism* (Princeton, NJ, 1991); Bonnie Kime Scott (ed.), *The Gender of Modernism: A Critical Anthology* (Bloomington, IN, 1991); and Bonnie Kime Scott, *Refiguring Modernism*, vol. 1 (Bloomington, IN, 1995). A more traditional (and now widely challenged) approach to assessing the importance of gender in modern literature is Sandra Gilbert and Susan Gubar (eds), *No Man's Land: The Place of the Woman Writer in the Twentieth Century* (New Haven, CT, 1988). Rita Felski, *The Gender of Modernity* (Cambridge, 1995) is the most ambitious recent attempt at a theoretical reassessment of the issue. A link between the ambivalences of gender and those of colonialism in Joyce is provided in Joseph Valente, *James Joyce: Negotiating Sexual and Colonial Difference* (Cambridge, 1995).

9. McDonald

Sigmund Freud, 'The "Uncanny" ', in *Art and Literature*, ed. Angela Richards and Andrew Dickson, The Pelican Freud Library, 14 (London, 1985), pp. 335–76, and 'Repression', in *On Metapsychology: The Theory of Psychoanalysis*, ed. Angela Richards and Andrew Dickson, The Pelican Freud Library, 11 (London, 1984), pp. 139–58, are the traditional psychoanalytic reference points of McDonald's essay. A reassessment of repression as productive can be found in Jacques Lacan, *Four Fundamental Concepts of Psychoanalysis*, trans. Alan Sheridan, ed. Jacques-Alain Miller (New York, 1978). Further studies that use a psychoanalytic approach to the repressed and its resurfacing in Joyce in a wider textual and ideological sense are Sheldon Brivic, *The Veil of Signs: Joyce, Lacan, and Perception* (Urbana, IL, 1991) and Susan Stanford Friedman (ed.), *Joyce: The Return of the Repressed* (Ithaca, NY, 1993).

10. Duffy

Fredric Jameson, *The Political Unconscious* (Ithaca, NY, 1981) and Cary Nelson and Lawrence Grossberg (eds), *Marxism and the Interpretation of Culture* (Urbana, IL, 1988) are examples of ideological readings of culture. Louis Althusser's influential essay 'Ideology and Ideological State Apparatuses', in *Lenin and Philosophy*, trans. Ben Brewster (New York, 1971), pp. 127–86, proposes a theoretical link between ideology and the establishment of subjectivity. A study that provides a background for an assessment of the characters in *Ulysses* as consumers is Thomas Richards, *The Commodity Culture of Victorian England: Advertising and Spectacle 1851–1914* (Stanford, CA, 1990). Benedict Anderson, *Imagined Communities: Reflections on the Origin and Spread of Nationalism* (London, 1983) is an influential recent study of the problematic foundations of national identity. Further postcolonial approaches to Joyce are David Lloyd, *Anomalous States: Irish Writing and the Post-Colonial*

Movement (Dublin, 1993) and Vincent J. Cheng, *Joyce, Race and Empire* (Cambridge, 1995).

Further Reading in Aspects of Theory

Modernism/Postmodernism

A useful comparative background of modernism is provided in Peter Nicholls, *Modernisms: A Literary Guide* (Basingstoke and London, 1995). Malcolm Bradbury and Joseph McFarlane (eds), *Modernism: 1890–1930* (London, 1976) and Michael Bell (ed.), *The Context of English Literature 1900–1930* (London, 1980) contain essays dealing with the structural issues and intellectual background of modernism. Astradur Eysteinsson, *The Concept of Modernism* (Ithaca and London, 1990) is perhaps the most convincing attempt at a definition of the term. Jean-François Lyotard, *The Postmodern Condition: A Report on Knowledge*, trans. Geoff Bennington and Brian Massumi (Minneapolis, 1984) remains the seminal philosophical outline of postmodernism. Ihab Hassan, *The Dismemberment of Orpheus: Towards a Postmodern Literature* (Madison, WI, 1982) and Linda Hutcheon's studies *A Poetics of Postmodernism: History, Theory, Fiction* (New York and London, 1988) and *The Politics of Postmodernism*, New Accents (London and New York, 1989) link theory and literature. Thomas Docherty (ed.), *Postmodernism: A Reader* (New York, 1993) provides an overview of positions. The conflict between the advocates of modernity and the defenders of postmodernity is presented in Ingeborg Hoesterey (ed.), *Zeitgeist in Babel: The Postmodernist Controversy* (Bloomington and Indianapolis, 1991).

Psychoanalysis

Collections of essays on psychoanalytic literary criticism are Maud Ellmann (ed.), *Psychoanalytic Literary Criticism*, Longman Critical Readers (London and New York, 1984); Sue Vice (ed.), *Psychoanalytic Criticism: A Reader* (Cambridge, 1996); and John Lechte (ed.), *Writing and Psychoanalysis: A Reader* (London and New York, 1996). An overview of positions is provided in Elizabeth Wright, *Psychoanalytic Criticism: Theory in Practice*, New Accents (London and New York, 1984).

Marxism

Fredric Jameson, *The Political Unconscious: Narrative as a Socially Symbolic Act* (Ithaca, NY, 1981) powerfully reopened the Marxist literary debate. John Frow, *Marxism and Literary History* (Oxford, 1986) is a useful introduction. Douglas Kellner, *Critical Theory, Marxism and Modernity* (Cambridge, 1989) attempts a critical assessment of the relation of Marxism and contemporary theory. Ajaz Ahmad, *In Theory: Classes, Nations, Literatures* (London, 1992) adds a postcolonial dimension. Michael Ryan, *Marxism and Deconstruction* (Baltimore, 1982) links marxism and poststructuralism. Recent overviews are Jeremy Hawthorn, *Cunning Passages: New Historicism, Cultural Materialism, and Marxism in the Contemporary Literary Debate* (London and New York, 1996) and, more generally, David Hawkes, *Ideology*, The New Critical Idiom (London, 1996).

Gender and Sexuality

Overviews of recent developments in feminist theory are provided by Linda Kauffmann (ed.), *Gender and Theory: Dialogues on Feminist Criticism* (Oxford, 1989); Linda Nicholson (ed.), *The Second Wave: A Reader in Feminist Theory* (New York and London, 1997); and Catherine Belsey and Jane Moore (eds), *The Feminist Reader: Essays in Gender and the Politics of Literary Criticism*, second edition (Basingstoke, 1997). Jean Pickering and Suzanne Kehde (eds), *Narratives of Nostalgia: Gender and Nationalism* (Basingstoke, 1977) combine gender debates with those on nationalism. Peter Brooks, *Body Works: Objects of Desire in Modern Narrative* (Cambridge, MA and London, 1993) and Joseph Allen Boone, *Libidinal Currents: Sexuality and the Shaping of Modernism* (Chicago and London, 1998) assess sexuality and desire in modern culture.

Postcolonial Theory

Among the most influential theoretical studies are Edward Said, *Culture and Imperialism* (London, 1993) and Homi K. Bhabha, *Nation and Narration* (New York, 1990). A useful collection of essays is Bill Ashcroft, Gareth Griffiths and Helen Tiffin (eds), *The Postcolonial Studies Reader* (London and New York, 1995). Overviews are provided in Bill Ashcroft, Gareth Griffith and Helen Tiffin, *The Empire Writes Back: Theory and Practice in Post-Colonial Literatures*, New Accents (London and New York, 1989) and Ania Loomba, *Colonialism/Postcolonialism*, The New Critical Idiom (London and New York, 1998).

Deconstruction and Poststructuralism

Harold Bloom et al., *Deconstruction and Criticism* (New York, 1979) and Christopher Norris, *Deconstruction: Theory and Practice*, New Accents (London, 1982) are two important introductions to deconstruction. Robert C. Holub's *Crossing Borders: Reception Theory, Poststructuralism, Deconstruction* (Madison, Wl, 1992) and Raman Selden (ed.), *The Cambridge History of Literary Criticism*, vol. 8, *From Formalism to Poststructuralism* (Cambridge, 1995) position deconstruction in the development of literary theory. Aspects of poststructuralism are outlined in Josue V. Harari (ed.), *Textual Strategies: Perspectives in Post-Structuralist Criticism* (London, 1980). An important introduction of this position into Anglo-American literary criticism is Robert Young (ed.), *Untying the Text: A Post-Structuralist Reader* (London, 1981). Antony Easthope, *British Poststructuralism since 1968* (London, 1988) attempts a historic genealogy of poststructuralist positions. Important critiques of poststructuralism are collected in Derek Attridge, Geoff Bennington and Robert Young (eds), *Post-Structuralism and the Question of History* (Cambridge, 1987).

Notes on Contributors

Enda Duffy is Associate Professor of English at the University of California, Santa Barbara. He is the author of *The Subaltern Ulysses* (1994), and co-editor (with Maurizia Boscagli) of a forthcoming collection on correspondences between Joyce and Walter Benjamin. He has just completed a book on speed and velocity in the modernist period.

Richard Lehan is Professor of English at the University of California Los Angeles. His last book is entitled *The City in Literature* (1998). He has recently completed another monograph on *Realism and Naturalism: Text and Context.*

Michael Bruce MacDonald was Assistant Professor of English at the South Dakota School of Mines and Technology. His PhD thesis (University of Oregon, 1991) focuses on 'James Joyce and the Aesthetics of Dissonance'.

Clara D. McLean received her PhD in English from the University of California Irvine in 2000. She is currently Assistant Professor of English at Chabot College in Hayward, CA. Her recent articles include 'Borders, Bridges and the Value of Humanities Outreach' (2000) and 'Lewis *The Monk* and the Matter of Reading' (1999).

Michael Murphy is Emeritus Professor of English at Brooklyn College, City University of New York. He has published an edition of Chaucer's *Canterbury Tales* and other studies on medieval literature as well as articles on Conrad, Beerbohm and Melville.

Mark Osteen is Professor of English and Director of Film Studies at Loyola College in Baltimore. He is the author of *The Economy of Ulysses: Making Both Ends Meet* (1995) and *American Magic and Dread: Don DeLillo's Dialogue with Culture* (2000). Most recently he has edited a collection of essays entitled *The Question of the Gift: Essays Across Disciplines* (2002).

Michael Stanier completed an M.Phil as a Rhodes Scholar at Oxford University, where he wrote a thesis on Angela Carter and Isabelle Allende as picaresque writers. He now works as a life coach, helping people around the world and from all walks of life to define and start living a completely creative, thrilling and fulfilling life.

Jeffrey A. Weinstock is Assistant Professor of English at Central Michigan University. He is the editor of *The Pedagogical Wallpaper: Teaching Charlotte Perkins Gilman's 'The Yellow Wallpaper'* (2003), *The Nothing That Is: The Blair Witch Project and Its Controversies* (forthcoming), and *Spectral America: Phantoms and the National Imagination* (forthcoming). He is currently at work on a book-length study of short supernatural fiction by nineteenth-century American women.

Adam Woodruff recently completed his PhD thesis on 'Walter Benjamin and Modernism' at the Centre for Critical and Cultural Theory, University of Wales, Cardiff. His essays on Joyce, Eliot, Benjamin and Breton have been published in a range of scholarly journals, and he is currently researching the diverse correspondences between modernism and critical theory.

Ewa Plonowska Ziarek is Professor of English and Gender Studies at the University of Notre Dame, where she teaches Modernism, Feminism, and Critical Theory. She is the author of *The Rhetoric of Failure: Deconstruction of Skepticism, Reinvention of Modernism* (1995), *An Ethics of Dissensus: Feminism, Postmodernity, and the Politics of Radical Democracy* (2001); an editor of *Gombrowicz's Grimaces: Modernism, Gender, Nationality* (1998); and co-editor of *Revolt and Affect: The Unstable Boundaries of Kristeva's Polis* (forthcoming) and *Intermedialities* (forthcoming). She has published numerous articles on Kristeva, Irigaray, Derrida, Foucault, Levinas, Fanon and Literary Modernism.

Index